ISLAMOPHOBIA AND RADICALISATION

TAHIR ABBAS

Islamophobia and Radicalisation

A Vicious Cycle

HURST & COMPANY, LONDON

First published in the United Kingdom in 2019 by
C. Hurst & Co. (Publishers) Ltd.,
41 Great Russell Street, London, WC1B 3PL

© Tahir Abbas, 2019

All rights reserved.

The right of Tahir Abbas to be identified as the author of this publication is asserted by him in accordance with the Copyright, Designs and Patents Act, 1988.

A Cataloguing-in-Publication data record for this book is available from the British Library.

ISBN: 9781787382015

www.hurstpublishers.com

Printed in India

*To the pioneers,
forever in your footsteps*

CONTENTS

Acknowledgements ix
Chronology xi
Preface: A Tryst with Destiny xv

1. Race and the Imagined Community — 1
2. The Racism of the Radical Right — 15
3. Muslim Origins and Destinations — 29
4. Framing Muslims — 45
5. Islamophobia as New Racism — 57
6. Islamism *Redux* — 71
7. Multicultural Radicalisms — 85
8. Far-Right Versus Islamist Extremism — 97
9. Plugged into the Rage — 107
10. Vanquishing False Idols — 119
11. Tomorrow Belongs to Those … — 133
12. The Postcolonial Subject's Discontent — 141

CONTENTS

13. Fear and Loathing at the End of History	153
14. In Conclusion	167
Epilogue: Rumi's Corner	177
Notes	181
Bibliography	211
Index	237

ACKNOWLEDGEMENTS

This book took nothing less than every fibre of my being. I began with the aspiration of intersecting two aspects of my work that have evolved separately over a two-decade period, namely my studies of Islamophobia and radicalisation. I wanted to traverse the parallels, to see, feel and recall, understanding their development over time, reflecting on the recent past.

I began writing this book during my time at New York University in late 2015. This opportunity furnished me with the necessary time and space to think and engage with the history, arts and culture of Manhattan while contemplating the issues I was investigating. Little was I to know that a certain well-known neighbour on my street would be elected president of the United States less than twelve months later. After returning to Istanbul in January 2016, where I was a professor of sociology, I continued to develop my thoughts during a period of growing political and ethnic conflict across the Middle East that had also begun to affect Turkey. However, when President Tayyip Erdoğan took measures to crush the foundation that supported my university, I hurried to the relative safety of London and the offices of the Royal United Services Institute (RUSI) in Whitehall, London. I arrived in the UK a few days after the Brexit vote of 23 June 2016. In the following year, as my work on countering violent extremism at RUSI went on in earnest, five terrorist attacks were carried out on UK soil. With Islamic

ACKNOWLEDGEMENTS

State's (ISIS) Caliphate collapsing in Iraq and Syria, copycat terrorists were causing havoc and misery in British society. I wrote the bulk of this book during the periods immediately after those heightened phases of alarm and disquiet caused by terrorism, a migration phenomenon that created considerable political discord across the Global North, and the folly of Brexit, which was generating unremitting tensions at home. I finished this book in The Hague, where I currently live, work and teach.

I would like to thank my colleagues in New York, Istanbul, London and The Hague for their listening ears and warm smiles as I ranted and raged at the wickedness around me. I thank the Institute of Security and Global Affairs of Leiden University for allowing me the opportunity to work with my ebullient colleagues here, for the space to think and write, and also to engage with incisive and determined students. Last but not least, I would like to thank Michael Dwyer for agreeing to take on this book project over a fine sushi luncheon one spring afternoon in Covent Garden, and Farhaana Arefin for her meticulous editorial work. Any errors that remain are of my own making.

CHRONOLOGY

1973–4   Arab Oil Crisis—neoliberalism takes over as the postwar welfare system faces pressures from states looking to the financial sector to shore up indigenous growth and domestic demand; Western powers take further steps to secure their interests in Middle East oil

1975   Fall of Saigon, at the hands of the North Vietnamese Army

1978–9   UK Winter of Discontent

1979   Soviet invasion of Afghanistan

The Siege of Mecca

Iran, last of the classical social revolutions moves to a theocracy

Zulfiqar Ali Bhutto hanged by General Zia-ul-Haq, who introduces Islamisation to Pakistan

Conservative Party wins power in the UK, Margaret Thatcher becomes prime minister

1980s   Reaganomics in the United States and Thatcherism in the UK introduces privatisation of public utilities and further deregulation of the banking sectors

CHRONOLOGY

1980–8	Iran–Iraq War, both sides armed by the West
1981	Presiden Anwar Sadat of Egypt assassinated by Islamic Jihad
1981	Inner-city riots in Handsworth, Toxteth and Brixton
1982	Falklands War victory over Argentina
1983	Second term for the Conservative Party
1984–5	UK miners' strike
1987	Black Monday, due to Hong Kong-led global stock market crash
1989	Salman Rushdie Affair erupts
	The Berlin Wall falls, precipitating the end of the Cold War
1991–5	Bosnian War
1992	Exchange Rate Mechanism debacle causes a run on the pound
1995	Srebrenica Massacre
1997	New Labour elected, applying 'The Third Way' doctrine
2001	'Northern Disturbances' in Burnley, Bradford and Oldham
	The events of 9/11, followed by the 'war on terror' and the invasion of Afghanistan
2003	Invasion of Iraq to eliminate 'weapons of mass destruction'
2004–5	'Home-grown' terrorist attacks in Madrid, Amsterdam and London
2008	Global financial crisis due to subprime mortgage collapse
	Barack Hussein Obama elected as forty-fourth US president, and first African American to take office

CHRONOLOGY

2010	UK Conservative–Liberal Democrat coalition introduces austerity in public spending
2011	Occupy movement in the West, Arab Spring in the MENA region
	Fall of Gaddafi government in Libya
2014	Emergence of the Islamic State as self-declared Caliphate in Iraq and Syria
2015	Germany accepts 1 million refugees
2016	Assassination of Jo Cox MP by Thomas Mair
	UK Brexit vote defined by hostility to immigration and the EU
	Election of Donald Trump as forty-fifth US president
	Islamist-inspired attacks in the United States and the EU grow as the Islamic State's Caliphate collapses
	Centre ground in politics hollowed out
	Far-left and far-right discourses in the ascendency
2017–*present*	A sustained rise in Islamophobia and far-right extremism
	Muslim groups and other minorities face heightened levels of racism and discrimination
	Rampant neoliberalism creates a backlash against globalisation, which is organised locally, but is misdirected at the centre of politics
	Growth of hyper-ethnic nationalism and white supremacism as forms of political mobilisation from both above *and* below in an age of psychopolitics across North America and Western Europe

PREFACE
A TRYST WITH DESTINY

Being and becoming are in a perennial state of transition and transformation. This is no less true in my own case, having been born in a city that designed the shackles and invented the steam engines that made the Atlantic slave trade a highly efficient but deadly instrument of power. I am the grandson of a British Indian merchant seaman who risked his life for the 'mother country' during the Second World War during the Battle of Singapore in 1942. I am the son of a man who drove an omnibus every day for forty years. This book is both a personal and intellectual journey of the mind, the soul, of my being and my becoming. It is also the story of the concepts of Islamophobia and radicalisation—two themes that have led to a reinforced focus on Muslims, both in Britain and elsewhere in the West.

Sometime in the mid-1700s, Allah Ditta and his two brothers migrated to an area in what was haughtily called British India. This group of three men established a village known as Ankar-Bachlakra, located in the expansive city of Dadyal, in what is now Azad Kashmir. Ankar is a cluster of ten villages, with Bachlakra situated at the centre of this constellation. Altogether, seventy or so other villages are spread across a plain on this mountainous terrain. The Ditta brothers were of

PREFACE

Bhatti Rajput descent. Their ancestors converted to Islam in the 1600s, during the time of the Mughals. Since the inception of the village some years later, these Bachlakrans gradually multiplied, establishing thirty-two households. Today, the village is all but empty—a ghost town, with mere flickers of a once-thriving community that had long-standing relations with the local geography and its people. Emigrating Bachlakrans were pioneers in the first waves of migration following the reconstruction of Britain in the late 1940s. Over time, subsequent Bachlakrans migrated west, as did many others from Dadyal, in the process becoming a transnational community. They established multi-generational diasporas, primarily in the city of Birmingham, with some Bachlakrans subsequently moving and starting a new life in New York City in the 1970s.[1]

Life in Kashmir is generally unforgiving. The norm is for sizzling summer months, heavy tail-end monsoon rains and biting frosty winters, followed by a brief but cool spring. In the past, Kashmiris maintained their existence in subsistence-level economies, and if the harvests failed, the villagers suffered immeasurably. When the crops became insufficient to meet Bachlakra's dietary and economic needs, and with no other economic opportunities, the early generations began searching for a better life. Perhaps they also wanted to see the world. In the 1930s, with India still under British colonial rule, word spread that the Bombay-based British Merchant Navy was recruiting workers to stoke the fires of its fleet. In the hope of a brighter future, a few of the men from Bachlakra made the long trek to Bombay seeking work on the ships. Demand from the recruiters was so great that they encouraged many more to join the band of committed labourers.[2] The British, however, also showed signs of racial prejudice. They believed that Indian men were somehow inferior, making them perfectly suited to work in poor conditions, in the face of red-hot coal-furnaces that powered the steam ships that carried the goods to service the empire. British seamen also exhibited signs of resistance towards South Asians on the steamships themselves.[3] Yet, ultimately, while the toil was harsh and difficult, it was eminently more secure than life as a humble farmer.

My paternal grandfather Zaman Ali and his close relative Ghulam Rasool were so keen to join the Merchant Navy that they hitchhiked their way from Kashmir to Bombay sometime in the early 1930s. It was a trek of over 1,100 miles. On the ships, away for many months at a time sailing on the high seas, they visited all the world's major ports. As the Second World War progressed, the British Merchant Navy was obliged to take an active part in supplying important equipment to service the war effort in affected areas. Unsurprisingly, these two brothers and many others from Bachlakra who worked as lascars found themselves caught up in the action. During the Battle of Singapore (1942), the Germans torpedoed their steam ship, and they jumped into the waters to save their lives. The Japanese fished both brothers, along with other Bachlakrans, out of the sea but then incarcerated a few in the infamous prisons of Burma, where they were forced into hard labour, building roads and railways until they were liberated once the war ended. After the war, most were back on the high seas, labouring on the SS *Empire Fowey*, which was managed as a troopship by the P&O from 1946.

The end of the Second World War precipitated the end of empire, and British India was destined for a new dawn—a tryst with destiny, no less.[4] But partition in 1947 saw the beginning of a different era. Many of the villages in and around the area of Ankara were Muslim, but there were also some that were Hindu and a few that were Sikh. It was the time of Hari Singh and of the Dogra *zamana* (era). Maharajah Hari Singh, ruler of Kashmir, dithered over which side to join after partition. Was it to be Pakistan or India? Around 80 per cent of the territory of Jammu and Kashmir was Muslim, but influenced by Nehru, of Pandit Kashmiri origin, and Sheikh Abdullah, a Kashmiri Muslim dubbed the 'Lion of Kashmir' and a staunch secularist, Hari Singh did not want Kashmir to join Pakistan. Sheikh Abdullah believed that feudalism would reign and did not consider Mohammed Ali Jinnah capable of alleviating it. Hari Singh wanted Kashmir to be independent from India and Pakistan, but with the 'K' in Pakistan representing Kashmir, Pakistan was incensed. Communal violence ensued. Although the elders of Bachlakra rarely spoke of the women and young girls on both sides who were captured and raped, official and personal accounts state that, throughout Kashmir, from the announcement of partition to the time when Hari Singh finally made his decision to join India less than two months later, killings and plunder were frequent occurrences.[5] Outnumbered, the Hindus around Bachlakra left for the

Indian side. Other Muslims emerged from the surrounding villages and took over Hindu- and Sikh-owned land as their own.

The idea that there was an indivisible unified Kashmir in the first instance, however, is a misnomer. The territory is divided now, as it was then, although both India and Pakistan have claimed it and fought each other over it three times. In 1947, Pakistan formally annexed a section to the east and north of the region, Jammu, known as Azad Kashmir. Neither Kashmiri nor Pakistani, Azad Kashmir has its own distinct identity but no international legal status. Well before partition, Azadis from Jammu started the movement that led to the struggle for unification with Pakistan. The level of violence and conflict was greater in the Azad Kashmir region (as a proportion of the population), but a forgotten history of its people endures, as historians and political scientists tend to focus on the numerically significant dislocation of the people of the Punjab. Partition occurred at the heart of a greater India torn in two, causing the flight of 10 million people and the loss of 1 million lives on both sides. It was the largest forced exodus of the twentieth century.[6]

After the Second World War, domestic demand began to increase in Britain. Indigenous workers did not want to work in the less desirable employment sectors and instead sought higher standards of living in other roles. While many returned to Kashmir as partition was looming, many other Bachlakrans came to Britain in 1945 to find employment in Birmingham's engineering and manufacturing sectors, often jumping ship at the ports in Dover and Liverpool, too. Others joining these pioneers of the late 1940s and 1950s formed a wave that continued for two decades, peaking in the early 1960s. In 1957, my father arrived in Birmingham at the age of seventeen. Two years later, his uncle Abbas Ali came to the UK, aged sixty-one, but his father Zaman Ali stayed behind. A decade older, Zaman Ali held the responsibility of being the village *lambardar*—a hereditary, state-appointed position in which he was responsible for collecting taxes and resolving any local land disputes. The now Birmingham-based Bachlakrans worked in the older parts of the city, living in multiple-occupancy dwellings, with up to ten to a house. Many worked night shifts and slept during the day while the day workers were out at work.[7] They hoped to save all their money to send 'back home' as remittances to their families, but, importantly, they also viewed their stay as temporary. Without doubt, majority British society shared this view.[8] Men from numerous other Azad Kashmiri villages also settled in towns and cities such as Birmingham, Bradford and Bolton, and they too worked in the industrial, manufacturing and engineering sectors of the economy. Many had links to the former British Empire through their time in the Indian Army or as merchant seamen. African Caribbeans, including those of the *Windrush* generation who came as British citizens from 1948 onwards, were largely forced to live in the poorer parts of West and South London to take up employment, mainly in the transport and health sectors.[9]

In the early 1960s, Pakistan set about building the largest dam in South Asia in the Mirpur area of Azad Kashmir. The Mangla Dam megaproject, however, led to immense dislocation and relocation. As the submergence of over 200 villages was necessary to build the dam, villagers received compensation for the loss of their land and property. Now with the money to buy an airline ticket to Britain, some of the younger men also began to join the others now establishing themselves as British Pakistanis all over the country in a chain migration process. The common academic and policy parlance was to refer to these groups as British Pakistanis, but they were a burgeoning Azad Kashmiri diaspora, largely because of the creation of the dam and due to the link to the Merchant Navy. Despite the historical linkage to empire, the visible presence of groups in parts of towns and cities generated alarm among British policymakers in general and among the white English working class in particular, which was beginning to exhibit a form of racism inherited from British colonialism and the civilising missionary zeal of days past.[10] In 1961, Abbas Ali had a tragic traffic accident that left him mortally wounded. He died on the way to hospital. He was one of the first British Pakistanis flown back to their family villages for burial, in his case in the ancestral burial grounds of Bachlakra. By 1962, legislation prevented primary economic migration, replacing it with a voucher system where additional workers entered the country only if existing workers sponsored them. This accelerated the process of chain migration. In 1963, my father made the decision to return to Azad Kashmir to marry my mother, who hails from a village to the west of Azadi territory—in the city of Jhelum.[11]

PREFACE

When British policymakers changed the legislation again in 1968, ending the voucher system, single Azad Kashmiri men were left with the choice of staying in Britain on their own or bringing over their remaining dependants. Many chose the latter option; however, doing so meant the inevitable concentration of populations in the same poorer parts of towns and cities, with increasing demand for housing, education and health in under-resourced areas. The policy was designed to halt immigration, but in practice it did the exact opposite. Nor did it abate the racial tensions between poor white groups and ethnic minorities. From the 1940s to the 1960s, young men continued to leave the village of Bachlakra, with spouses joining husbands who had migrated earlier. Presently, the graveyard that sits in one corner of the village contains numerous unmarked graves, including those of the elders. With a few exceptions, the dates of those who passed away end at around the early 2000s. Later British-born generations are now burying their loved ones in increasingly expansive cemeteries in the Midlands and the North.

At present, Birmingham-based grandparents are slowly disappearing, but some Bachlakran grandchildren continue to extend the chains of familial relations. The future of the village is of a thriving transnational community of Bhatti Rajput Bachlakrans, who are closely connected but far away from their origins, never to return on a permanent basis. The British Bachlakran diaspora is currently in its fourth generation. Around 5,000 people are now the direct descendants of the three brothers who began the journey over 300 years ago. As many as 4,000 or so live in Birmingham, the city of my birth, with a few hundred spread over various towns and cities in other parts of the Midlands, and around 100 in Bradford and the surrounding areas, and thirty or so in Brooklyn, New York.

On the fateful morning of Tuesday, 11 September 2001, I was working on my computer in my study, getting ready to shadow the visits of a researcher to various homes in Coventry. I had been employed to help carry out a large national survey funded by the Home Office in London, my employer at the time. In stepping downstairs from my study, a newsflash interrupted the general gamut of irreverent daytime television. Unfolding before my eyes was the ghastly aftermath of a terrible freak accident in New York City—or so I thought. Moments later, a second plane hit the second tower of the World Trade Center. Soon after, pictures emerged from Washington revealing the impact of another plane attack, this time striking the Pentagon.

Looking in amazement at these images, vivid but scrambled thoughts rushed through my mind: had someone declared war on the United States? How had a foreign entity been able to invade US airspace with such ease? Surely, no one in the world had the means, the logistical capability or the sheer gall to strike out at this colossus caught sleeping. At the time, the idea that some deranged so-called Muslims had carried out a suicide-attack on the 'Great Satan' seemed utterly implausible. If that were the case, Muslims across the globe would now be at the mercy of the angry response that would undoubtedly ensue. Other immediate questions also came to the fore. The 'why' question was easy to answer, as any number of countries across the world had gripes against the United States for all sorts of deep-rooted grievances affecting their peoples, nations and civilisations. Answers to the 'how' question, which focused on the mechanisms and processes, on the other hand, only became apparent in the clear light of day.[12]

Since the end of the Cold War, the Muslim world has faced its own internal challenges of democracy and development. The US and Western European countries no longer had a single enemy that could be defined in straightforward ideological terms, as had been the case with the former Soviet empire. During the 1990s, conflict in Algeria, Somalia, Sudan, Nigeria and Bosnia, together with Russia's military intervention in Chechnya and the internal struggles within Afghanistan and Pakistan, suggested there were deep-seated problems within these countries. The events of 9/11, with fifteen of the nineteen hijackers having Saudi origins, furthered the impression that something deeply problematic was going on in the Muslim world. As the 'policeman' of the world, the United States now had the necessary rationale to take action in defence of the rest of the 'civilised world'.[13]

Immediately after 9/11, British Prime Minister Tony Blair joined forces with President George W. Bush to assure the world of the need to react swiftly and expeditiously in seeking out the global threat, which was soon identified as Al-Qaeda. Osama bin Laden and his followers, operating out of the mountainous regions of northern Afghanistan, were the prime targets in an effort to protect the 'free world' from an imminent attack on Western targets. The renegade Saudi multi-millionaire with a grudge against his own country, presented as the chief architect of 9/11, was 'Wanted: Dead or Alive'. A war on terror led by a 'coalition of the willing' was almost immediately launched in Afghanistan, followed by Iraq two years later. These military interventions were part of a coordinated effort to 'root out the evildoers' and eliminate the threat that Al-Qaeda posed to the world. The coalition attacked Afghanistan because the Taliban would not give up Osama bin Laden. Two years later, the invasion of Iraq began because the country allegedly possessed 'weapons of mass destruction' (WMDs).[14] By November 2001, Britain was fully immersed in the war on terror, sending troops to Afghanistan as part of Operation Enduring Freedom. People watched the news for information and read reports from journalists embedded in the conflict, but the first casualty of war was the truth, as the maxim goes. In May 2011, US Navy Seals assassinated Osama bin Laden, having found him living in a compound in Abbottabad, Pakistan, less than a mile away from the Pakistan Military Academy. Questions around his killing still linger.

As the war in Afghanistan commenced largely unchallenged, the powers in Washington projected Saddam Hussain and Bin Laden as one, and claimed that Iraq had WMDs ready to strike Western targets with impunity. Tony Blair had to convince the UK Parliament of the need to maintain military efforts, now in Iraq, in the hope of finding and destroying these WMDs, which could 'strike British targets within 45 minutes'.[15] Today, there is little discussion about eliminating the Al-Qaeda threat. Nevertheless, the war in Afghanistan rages on, even though ISIS, formed out of the conflicts in Iraq and its neighbour Syria in the aftermath of the invasion of 2003, has come and gone as a territorial entity. The Afghans saw the British and the other forces as invaders, not liberators—just as they viewed the Soviets in the 1970s and 1980s and the British in the 1840s.

After a painful process of cajoling and manoeuvring MPs, Parliament voted for what many now see as an illegal war, and in 2003, Baghdad faced the 'shock and awe' of a potent military force. After the invasion, various US-led forces worked to 'modernise' Iraq using the country's own natural resources and physical infrastructure. The Iraqis paid for their own reconstruction with their own resources, while profits moved to corporations in the West. In late 2003, the Americans found Saddam Hussein hiding in a hole in his hometown of Tikrit; eventually put on 'trial', he was executed by hanging. The power base in Iraq, now inverted, without the ability to establish itself organically, destabilised the country and the entire region. The ensuing conflict led to the deaths of over half a million Iraqis and the displacement of many millions more. In 2007, after much public and private criticism, the UK government had little choice but to announce that it would begin removing British troops from Iraq. This whole episode caused immense damage both to Iraq and to the credibility of Britain as a global player. Britain had yet again aligned too closely with US foreign policy interests. The Arab Spring and the further destabilisation of Iraq and later Syria led to the emergence of the evil death cult, Islamic State.

In the summer of 2001, the UK experienced its worst inner-city race riots for over two decades. These so-called northern disturbances were the result of frustrations borne out by second- and third-generation British South Asian Muslims who were facing ongoing patterns of racism, discrimination and prejudice in localised settings.[16] The lack of education and employment stemmed from limited local investment rather than having anything to do with the community's lack of motivation or aspiration. The government response, however, was to focus on the idea of 'communities lacking cohesion' rather than on the specific resource needs of a region that had suffered from deindustrialisation and a lack of inward investment for the best part of the preceding three decades.[17] By the end of 2001, when Britain was at war, it became clear that matters would become worse for various racial and ethnic groups now viewed as religious and cultural groups, especially British Muslims. The 2003 Iraq invasion was making young Muslims in Britain at home angry and agitated. No one was listening to them, let alone the community leaders whom New Labour had wooed into conformity.[18] Problems were emerging in local communities, and there was a genuine sense that media reporting and misreporting on the wars in Iraq and Afghanistan was causing considerable angst.[19]

The disturbances demonstrated that young second- and third-generation British Muslims were bitter and resentful of the racism, intolerance, bigotry, exclusion and vilification they were facing in their local communities. Their fury exploded on the streets in five locations that summer: Bradford, Oldham, Leeds, Stoke and Burnley, with significant violence and physical destruction in parts of Bradford, Oldham and Burnley.[20] After local newspapers printed the photographs of the assailants, fathers and uncles turned in their young. These young men received up to five years' imprisonment for throwing stones at the police, even for first-time offenders, increasing the resentment felt by many local Muslim communities towards the policing services. In late 2001, David Blunkett, as the incumbent home secretary, established a commission to look at these problems. The solution, presented as 'communities lacking cohesion', overlooked the real issues and offered an opportunity for politicians retreating from multiculturalism to return to an assimilationist ideal that had originally been promulgated three decades earlier.[21] The dominant paradigm that subsequently emerged focused on 'values' at the expense of an emphasis on institutional racism, discrimination and the need to rebuild physical infrastructure. British Muslims in the North of England received a raw deal, and their plight remains unaddressed to this day.

As these domestic policies came into effect, and the war on Iraq unfolded, matters on the ground took a turn for the worse. Radicalisation of young Muslims in inner-city areas was becoming a growing concern.[22] There was huge intergenerational disconnect, as young Muslims realised that their elders were not listening to them. Imams were out of touch, the media was biased and the government was intent on war and pursuing its external interests, while the elites in the Muslim world turned a blind eye. Young British-born Muslims began seeking violent political solutions to their concerns. Some of these disillusioned, disenfranchised and isolated Muslims became the new radicals. As confirmed by the Madrid train bombings in March 2004 and the assassination of Theo van Gogh in November 2004, some second-generation Muslims were prepared to kill others or annihilate themselves in the pursuit of local and global political goals.[23]

The question was: would such acts happen in the UK? It was clear that some young Muslims were prepared to carry out martyrdom

PREFACE

missions, as was highlighted by the April 2003 Tel Aviv Mike's Place bombing by two second-generation British Muslims. Britain was careless, both about the consequences of its foreign policy in the Islamic world and its domestic policies towards Muslims at home. Britain was becoming insensitive to the impact of policies and actions on groups in society that had experienced decades of intolerance, bigotry, violence, discrimination and racism.

On the morning of 7 July 2005, I was at the International Sociological Association annual conference in Stockholm, speaking on Muslim youth radicalisation and Islamophobia. After the panel had ended, I was roaming the book stalls when a colleague began quizzing me: 'The terror attacks in London, they're such a tragedy, aren't they?' I replied in astonishment: 'Terror attacks? What terror attacks?' Aghast, I quickly learnt that, a few hours earlier, four second-generation Muslims from the northern towns, one as young as eighteen, had attacked London. I returned to my hotel room to see the images of the carnage on the news. Initial analysis and punditry pointed to the idea that young British-born Muslims had carried out the attacks, which, as both a Briton and a Muslim, deeply troubled me. In early July in Sweden, the sun does not set until the small hours of the morning. Trying to sleep, I was unable to remove the London scenes from my mind, desperately wishing the light from the sky would dim so the day would finally end.

What was going on? How could we explain it all? What were we going to do? These were some of the questions asked by television crews, journalists, news reporters and commentators as well as professionals and activists working in the field. Muslims and non-Muslims, colleagues in the academy, community groups and government departments were all in a state of disbelief. The immediate reaction was to condemn the events and to suggest that this was simply a terrible act, but a few days later outspoken people such as Lord Nazir Ahmed dared to say what was on many people's lips—that this was 'Blair's blowback'. Most, however, resisted the temptation to lambast government policy when fifty-two innocent people had died and over 700 had been injured, some of them maimed for life. It was a pivotal moment in the history of Muslims in Britain. Emotions were running high. All sensitivity to over-reacting or blaming all Muslims for these issues quickly evaporated in the rush to find immediate explanations.[24]

This was a societal concern, and these young men were a product of society. They had justified their acts via a narrow understanding of political Islamism, yet their actions were not due to Islam or Islamism. Instead, their frustrations grew from a historical set of issues that required careful unpacking and understanding. Too many, unfortunately, were quick to point the finger at Islam and Muslims. The UK government had no engagement with young Muslims directly or indirectly through the main umbrella group with which it had built closest relations, namely the Muslim Council of Britain (MCB, established in late 1997). At the same time, some Muslims were quick to put themselves forward as experts to help solve the problems. Much attention focused on de-radicalisation from within the faith—a convenient ruse for those establishing the 'Islamophobia industry' and the 'professional Muslims' who competed within the sector, sometimes at the behest of government, and at other times because of individual motivations. The process led to disenchantment and internal conflict, rudely exposed in the context of engagement with the media and the political process. Interestingly, it also revealed the nature of intergenerational disconnect that had stifled the development of the British Muslim community. No longer were young people prepared to sit back and let the elders take the lead. As much as the events of 7/7 were tragic, they also allowed the younger generations to come forward in great numbers. These Muslims were perceptive, articulate, professional, well organised and highly motivated, presenting a view of British Islam as integrative, developmental and forward-looking— emerging as a force in their own right as 'Generation M'—urbane, tech-savvy, cosmopolitan, upwardly mobile and entirely comfortable with their religious identity—a decade or so later.[25]

Organisational dynamics within communities, however, were still weak, and others were easily able to exploit community groups, as politicians and various media outlets formed an unholy alliance around these concerns. Muslims with grudges against other Muslims were quick to blame their rivals—Wahhabis, Deobandis and Jamaat-e-Islamis were all pilloried; the Brewlvis and the Tabligis were attacked by right-wing Islamists; secularist Muslims condemned other conservative Muslims. The Deobandi and the Jamaat-e-Islami groups were the most closely linked with the government through their associations with the MCB. In 2007, the government response was a gesture of around £140 million to spend on localised Muslim capacity-building projects over a three-year period to help communities rebuild from below. But this sprinkling of glitter only fuelled a self-serving Islam industry with professional Muslims vying for access to power and privilege (the policing, security and intelligence services received around £2 billion during the same period).

The events of 9/11 were shocking but also disconcerting, and it was clear that the US military-industrial complex would respond with all its might, pushing forward the goals of the New American Century. Today, NATO forces are still in Afghanistan. British forces were in Afghanistan longer than they were engaged in the Second World War. Iraq, and now Syria and Libya, are in a dire predicament due to the war on terror. Some Western European Muslims, beleaguered and angry, have been led to the mistaken notion that jihadi-terrorism can solve their grievances. For a British Muslim, the events of 7/7 were devastating, not because of a sense of divided loyalty—far from it—but because the confluence of British *and* Muslim was still an evolving project, with much still to establish. The issues that 7/7 revealed remain in play, and with no clear solutions, partly because policymakers continue to ignore the social challenges faced by individuals at the margins of communities at home while simultaneously pursuing an interventionist foreign policy throughout the Middle East.

As the war on terror raged on, the Western economic model came to the point of collapse. The consequences of the 2008 banking crisis were more severe than the recessions of the early 1980s and 1990s, the stock market crash of 1987, or even the dot-com bubble that burst in 2000. Likened to the Great Depression of the 1930s, also caused by a banking crisis, the effects of the downturn are still being felt. The British government's decision to impose austerity in public spending helped pave the way for the country's vote to leave the European Union in 2016. Britain changed for the worse. A culture of violence has taken over. Immersed in the psycho-political powers of social media that have come to define the age, vulnerable minorities and majorities are unable to come to terms with their objectification and subjugation at the hands of global corporate players more powerful and influential than at any other period in modern history.[26]

The future of British Muslims is precarious because dominant discourses wrongly force them to choose between being British or being Muslim—as if some deep incompatibility exists between the two. Defined in negative ways, British Muslims have been castigated by journalists, civil servants, political leaders and members of the wider public, fuelling Islamophobia, which in turn affects the process of radicalisation and reignites anti-Muslim sentiment, creating a vicious cycle. This book is an attempt to understand the thinking and practices that have led to the duality of Islamophobia and radicalisation. Aimed at making a difference to the debate and encouraging dialogue, a left-realist perspective defines my intellectual and political approach in looking ahead, which we can only do if we truly and honestly understand the past and the challenges it raises in the present.

1

RACE AND THE IMAGINED COMMUNITY

The topic of racism is never far from controversy. But to understand the detailed historical, ideological and political underpinnings of racism, it is necessary to start at the very beginning by exploring its links with capitalism, colonialism, modernity, industrialisation and postmodernity.[1] The antecedents to modern racism rest in the period that began with the advent of capitalism, and just as capitalism has managed to reinvent itself, so too has racism and racialisation, with the various types of racism—including institutional, economic, symbolic, situational and cultural—being products of the periods in which they emerged.[2] But what is interesting is how, today, historically racist tropes relating to ethnic and religious differences concentrate specifically on Islam and Muslims.

A significant problem with racism involves coming to terms with its definition. The term has been politicised to such an extent that analysts are often guilty of transforming a complex issue into a political project in its own right. In the 1970s, anti-racists simplified racism to 'prejudice + power = racism'.[3] In the late 1990s, after the Stephen Lawrence murder inquiry in England and the resulting Macpherson Report (1999), the concept of 'institutionalised racism' surfaced in policy development and academic research.[4]

Racism continues to be misunderstood because of the focus on structural determinants and cultural explanations, when in reality it is both nuanced and specific, yet simultaneously generalisable across a range of fields. As a starting point for understanding racism, it is important to differentiate between racism and simple prejudice, as both possess similar characteristics, but prejudices are not strictly racist in nature or outcome, while racism shifts beyond prejudice to actions and patterns of discrimination and disadvantage that are systematic. Individuals, groups and communities can experience these realities as a whole, with numerous concerns operating at multiple levels, including with regard to concepts such as 'ethnicity and ethnocentrism; nation, nationalism and xenophobia; hostility to "outsiders" and "strangers", or heterophobia'.[5] This chapter outlines a general theory of race and racism and its relationship to the notions of nation, nationhood and nationalism. It considers the historical and contemporary processes of radicalisation of minorities and the implications of these processes for Muslim minority groups, particularly in the post-Cold War era. The conflict among the most dispossessed groups in society has generated a 'self'–'other' binary where ethnicity and religiosity are the defining characteristics of these tensions.

The antecedents to modern-day racism hark back to a much earlier period of ancient history. The ancient Greeks used the term 'barbarian' when referring to those who did not know the Greek language. This was a political identity because no differences existed between Greek-speaking and non-Greek-speaking subjects, other than their loyalty to the polis and its laws. For Aristotle, Greeks occupied an advantageous position between the colder northern races, who were thought incapable of ruling, and the southern darker races, who supposedly had a proclivity for inventiveness and intelligence. In the classical Roman era, people of darker-skin backgrounds were at the periphery of the empire, but they were nevertheless able to gain status, wealth and power at the centre. Antiquity thus reveals race as one layer in a complex relationship between status, values, nation, citizenship and law. Enmity towards Jews began to grow under the Romans and eventually stretched beyond its borders when Christianity became the religion of the empire. In the medieval era and until the fall of the Caliphate of Córdoba in 1492, Jews faced persecution throughout

Europe, regularly being expelled from their countries of birth. They went from respected minority to a persecuted 'other' in Turkey.[6] During this time, intolerance towards Muslims was not due to race or physiology but rather antagonism towards a particular religion and its characteristics.[7]

The term known today as racism first originated in the 1930s in the context of Nazi prejudices towards Jews, and it also has similarities with the term anti-Semitism, which was common parlance by the 1870s. But while dominant features in majority society give rise to prejudice and discrimination based on religion and race, including skin colour, racism is also concerned with the values, attitudes and behaviours of the minority group in question. In this framing, minorities are viewed as reluctant to integrate or assimilate, thereby conserving their distinct ethnic and cultural norms, which are then projected as threats to the wider body politic.[8] For some, the problems are thought to exist within the communities themselves, caused by those who are accused of not wanting to take part in majority society. The narrative is that aspects of the values and behaviours of foreigners, immigrants or minorities are wholly contrary to the values of dominant society, including ideals such as liberalism and individualism, or even the majority religion of the society itself. In this regard, ethnic and racial conflict is an inevitable outcome of tribal identities that begin as localised entities but that then materialise as a result of domination and subordination within a political and social context.

———•———

The period in which race was allied with the discovery of foreign lands by the Europeans was also the time when the origins of racism were being firmly established. The year 1492 is noteworthy in this regard, as it denoted the expulsion of religious, racial and ethnic groups at the hands of a conquering force that regarded the former dominant group as a threat to their order, namely the expulsion of Jews and Muslims in Córdoba and Granada, combined with the exploration and exploitation of distant terrains and peoples far across the seas.[9] These lands were eventually subjugated during the colonial era, the legacy of which continues to exert an influence in the present day. Originally, the Conquistadors were ambiguous about the groups they encountered in what they originally thought was India. Spain believed that these non-believers could be civilised by being converted into good Christians. At the same time, the dominant view was that native Indians were lower human stock, akin to the apes. Rather than marking the onset of a civilising mission, this period was one in which ethnic communities were enslaved and subordinated.

By the sixteenth century, notions of race included ideas of family, nation, lineage and blood, reflecting the continuity of the Middle Ages. For the aristocracies, the antecedents to race signalled lineage and ancestry. The Age of Discovery, followed by the Age of Reason in the eighteenth century, also known as the Enlightenment, led many to consider rationality as the highest human quality, but it was tempered with emotions associated with pleasure and sensuality, combined with a critique of the dominant religious discourses of Christianity. Science, technology, wisdom and knowledge were sought as far as China. For many, the period was the height of intellectualism, sophistication and technological innovation.[10] The aim of taming nature to meet the demands and needs of humankind, however, conflicted with the wish to ascribe harmony between man and his natural environment, which placed 'others' into the category of the natural—as the human 'other'.

The classification of humankind based on cultural characteristics, temperaments and innate ability took further hold among writers and thinkers enamoured by a sense of European progress. Immanuel Kant and John Hume interconnected culture and physiology with intellectual ability, consigning 'savages' as the direct opposite of nobility. But their personal relations with people of darker skin were limited.[11] Black servants were fashionable in aristocratic households, displayed to others in their social strata, dressed in fine clothing and presented as objects of ownership and desire—projected as a reflection of their masters' sophistication. While many black people lived freely in England and Scotland during the time of Elizabeth I, the common perception of black people was largely negative, in particular the views concerning black male sexuality and the proportions of their genitalia. This was in opposition to concepts of beauty, with ideal standards established through Greek and Roman fine art, including Greek male figures with small sexual organs—any representation of the erect male penis was seen as vulgar.[12]

Further developments during this period, moreover, had an important impact on the racialisation of black people in British society. The slave trade, led by Britain, transported millions of people across the Atlantic to the Caribbean. It exchanged 'free labour' for sugar crops, which then returned to Britain in the very same ships, fuelled by an unremitting demand for sweetened foods and beverages, helping to establish the ports of Liverpool, Bristol and Glasgow, transforming these cities into thriving urban entities. The slave trade made a number of people incredibly wealthy, some of whom were able to instigate the industrial revolution. The 'free labour' of slaves in the Caribbean islands was transformed into a tradable good, with some of the slaves being exchanged for more slaves to be transported across the Atlantic in an endless cycle. The triangular slave trade, also known as the Middle Passage, made Britain one of the most successful empires in history, turning the country into one of the most influential economic, political, financial and military powers the world had ever known.[13] It also cemented the racialisation of people of darker skin to such an extent that this process embedded itself into society—in its institutions, in popular culture, in the reification of the financial sector of the economy—thereby establishing the enduring essence of modern racism. These historical developments in turn underscored deeply held generalisations about black men in particular.

The science of racism developed during the nineteenth century, when various pseudo-scientists began to view humankind as comprising distinct races of man. They believed that it was principally race that caused the nature of differences between men. They argued that genotypic and phenotypic variations between humankind affected cultural behaviours, norms and values, thus setting groups apart from each other. For the European scientific racists, these races formed a hierarchy of man, with white men at the top and black men at the bottom. Crucial to this model was the notion that these races were in conflict with each other, consequently fusing class with race. This idea had popular appeal, spreading widely across society as it seemingly justified unequal relations between people of different skin colours and legitimising the aspirations of the dominant classes. People of darker skin were farthest away from those of lighter skin, with various gradations found even among people ordinarily classified as white. Robert Knox identified categories that differentiated Scandinavian, Russian, French and English men, where class conflict was akin to ethnic conflict within finer gradations of differences between white and black as a whole.[14] In this milieu, relations between race and nation began to converge with ideas of citizenship, belonging and identity, promptly taking a foothold in the context of seemingly endless challenges facing European states as they wrestled with nationalism and competing interests abroad. In this construct, outsiders were not only different because of their alleged inferiority, they were also a threat to the nation itself.[15]

Scientific racism gradually evolved to incorporate eugenics, also known as social Darwinism, which took the ideas of Charles Darwin in a direction that differed radically from his original intentions. Darwin explained the nature of the existence of humans and animals as a question of evolution, where subtle differences between human races led to divergent paths, but there was no question of hierarchy or status distinction based on biological differences. As later thinkers such as Francis Galton looked to the future with unease, Herbert Spencer coined the fateful phrase 'survival of the fittest'. His vision was to eliminate the so-called backward races or the inferior classes as they 'bred faster' than the supposedly rightly guided middle or upper classes, who, according to his theory, were better placed to lead and rule by nature.[16] The IQ test, initially designed to exclude the so-called inferior stock or the supposedly less intelligent as part of school selection policies, continues to be used today despite its limited efficacy as a measure of capacity. In Britain, eugenics was widely supported by the Fabians, including Sidney and Beatrice Webb, the founders of the London School of Economics and Political Science, but also other notable figures such as George Bernard Shaw, H. G. Wells, Winston Churchill, Rudyard Kipling and Charles Dickens.[17]

Eugenics was popular across Europe and the United States from the 1880s to the 1930s, with eugenics societies established all over North America, Scandinavia and Western Europe. All promoted the selective breeding of the 'noble' (Aryan) race. The introduction of immigration controls was precisely designed to limit the allegedly unfit, the undesirable and the unwieldy from entering into society, thus preventing the emergence of further pressures on already stretched resources and opportunities.[18] These anxieties, combined with alarm that the dominant racial stock would seemingly be contaminated due to miscegenation, eventually led to the Nazi Holocaust that killed 6 million Jews, communists, leftists, homosexuals, Slavs and other groups deemed undesirable in the 'Final Solution' of the Third Reich.

In 1950, UNESCO issued a statement fundamentally debunking the idea of any scientific differences between the races that define differences in character, nature or the potential for intelligence among humankind as a whole.[19] Yet, by then, racism had embedded itself in all aspects of society, politics, the economy and culture. Even the reasoned scientific statements made by the most celebrated minds of the time were not going to eliminate racism on their own. The need for remedial social policy was therefore urgent.

If races do not exist and there are no differences between groups in societies across the world, why does racism persist? Why are there racialised differences in outcomes such as employment, education, the criminal justice system and health, all of which reflect systematic patterns of discrimination based on colour or ethnicity? Many nations have introduced and strengthened their anti-discrimination and anti-racism laws since the 1990s, but patterns of racial inequality continue to exist. The answer reflects the fact that much of the discrimination occurs because of the characteristics of culture and ethnicity ascribed to race and nation, including how anti-discrimination laws define ethnic groups. These realities are also contextual and situational. The persistence of racism raises the question of how racism has been able to reinvent itself as structural and cultural racism, involving distinct patterns of discrimination based on culture or religion, as demonstrated in current instances of Islamophobia, which is a distinct combination of anti-Muslim prejudice, discrimination and stereotyping.[20] The current malaise is due to internal challenges to the identity of the nation and the shift from traditional to post-traditional norms that have accompanied the move from colonialism to post-colonialism. The fundamental bedrock of post-war cultural racism is the idea that immigrant or minority groups do not wish to assimilate into an indivisible unitary whole known as 'majority society', completely ignoring the complex challenges of class, culture, gender, history and memory that afflict wider society. This form of racism reifies the 'us' and 'them' distinction, legitimising patterns of cultural racism as a reality of the 'immigrant other' who has refused to integrate into society. In doing so, it places such groups in a double bind. At one level, the historical paradigms of racism have systematically discriminated against the group in question, while, at another level, those belonging to these groups have simultaneously been cast as unfit humans. Much of the current controversy over anti-Muslim discrimination focuses precisely on these issues, which have in turn led to Islamophobia—the fear or dread of Islam and Muslims—becoming the dominant paradigm of racism today.

The multiplicity of identities that operate in different contexts and situations underscores the problem that it is possible to be racist and non-racist at the same time. That is, the racialisation of ethnic groups and their descriptions manifests on certain occasions, but in other instances, recognition and support of egalitarian and anti-racist developments have emerged in post-war societies. This ambivalence has created the conditions for patterns of cultural racism, the nature of which has altered depending on the challenges of different times. It can also introduce further dilemmas. In some instances, it leads to victimisation, and in others, scapegoating—as in the case of blaming British Muslim groups for all of society's current ills. Both ambivalence and contradiction occur as the reality of racism, between and within majority and minority groups, thus projecting and compounding the interpretation of events.

Over a period of two centuries, racism, prejudice, stereotypes, discrimination and institutional racism have seeped into the popular cultural narratives of everyday life. At the beginning of the nineteenth century, European men considered themselves purveyors of knowledge, power, authority and moral righteousness. Such narratives led to the subjugation of European women, as well as vast swathes of the world's population that remained under colonial rule. Racism lives on in cultural racism combined with embedded patterns of institutionalised racism.[21] In the current climate, numerous European countries, many of which helped to lay the foundation of racist dogma, scientific racism and patterns of discrimination towards different religious and ethnic minority groups, are undergoing further shifts to the political right, where localised far-right activities have taken centre stage, a process particularly evident in Germany, France and the UK.[22]

The challenges of racism endure when issues of race and nation combine with nationalism and regionalism. Groups that believe their societies are in decline as a result of immigration and the apparent challenges it poses to their culture are spearheading this 'new racism'. Far-right fringe parties have been able to thrive due to the inequality and structural disadvantages facing the working class. Such support therefore also reflects wider disaffection with politics and the economy, and ultimately combines with racism. Efforts to transcend racism are difficult given the 'combinations of biological determinism, desire for imagined cultural and biological purity, and myths about the immutable qualities of different cultures and ethnicities'.[23] With globalisation and multiple identities, elites are under greater pressure to hold on to the markers of nationhood that set their countries apart as uniquely distinct, inadvertently mobilising stereotypes and a form of racial thinking that seeks to maintain the status quo and the dominant paradigms found in prevailing social norms and values.

The processes needed to eradicate such tendencies are complex and multi-layered. The problems are multifaceted, and so too are the solutions, given the need to respond to ongoing challenges and opportunities that are both cultural and political in nature, and hence contested by all sides in a struggle for status, recognition and acceptance.

Racism has historical links with xenophobia and Orientalism, but it also has its own specific features. Racism is predominantly about power and differential types of access to power to wield it in a way that suits particular interests and aspirations. While much modern racism is rooted in the physical, discourse also affects the material, which has its own descriptions. This is determined in one way through the media, and in particular print and online news. Research continues to show that press barons and media moguls perpetuate stereotypes and prejudices relating to ethnic minority groups on a systematic basis in Western Europe and the United States.[24] The media has the power to define the state of affairs of interethnic conflict in societies. Media panics about muggers, rapists or criminality associated with black groups in the 1970s have now been superseded by notions of terrorism, grooming and Islamisation among South Asian Muslims in twenty-first-century Britain. Such a set of observations suggests that television news and news media outlets are susceptible to the institutionalisation of racism, whether of a structural or cultural nature. Journalists, writers and reporters unwittingly foster elite racism: 'Employing "race" as real, whether in news media or entertainment, is to participate in racialization: it is a reproduction of "race" thinking.'[25] The truth is often more complicated than is reported in the media, but such reports are nevertheless plausible for an audience psychologically primed to absorb sensationalism.[26]

While the media is guilty of creating and then reproducing bogeymen, political processes have also played an important role. After the terrorist attacks in Amsterdam, Madrid and London in the mid-2000s, politicians increasingly promoted the idea of assimilating minorities into a robust and indivisible national political entity based on a monocultural identity. Issues of extremism and radicalism were projected as wholly defined by the nature of ethnic and religious minorities and their 'alien values and norms', rather than how structural disadvantage and foreign policy alienate groups seeking to address grievances via political acts of violence against the state and its citizens, justified through the veneer of religion. In such instances, multiculturalism is often described as having somehow failed.[27] Rather than promoting common national identities that would allow ethnic differences to enhance a sense of national identity, the fault lines of integration and assimilation are designated as being these very same variations in culture. The castigating of Muslim differences accelerated during this period. Ever since 9/11, there has been a wide-ranging discourse that has stigmatised Islam and Muslims as a threat to a range of concerns that affect global society, in particular Western nations. Yet 9/11 took place at a time when Western nations had been targeting Muslim countries with an aggressive foreign policy, a process that began with the fall of the Berlin Wall in 1989 and the end of the Soviet era soon after. The Salman Rushdie Affair of 1989 highlighted the extent of intolerance, bigotry and illiberalism, not merely on the part of people speaking out against the publication of a novel they felt contravened the principles of their faith,[28] but political and media elites also perpetuated divisions, planting markers of separation firmly in the popular imagination and narrowing the focus of the debate to culture rather than structure. Such processes resulted in the essentialism of a vast global religion and its variations, promoting stereotypes based on age-old prejudices and reinforcing a sense of 'us' and 'them' through local, national and international narratives that were routinely exploited by political actors and media outlets.[29]

In analysing the origins, development, experience, reality and outcome of the concept of racism over the centuries, it is important to make a number of distinctions. Several issues come into play when considering how racism operates in practice—from the psychological, the historical, the structural, the temporal, to the imaginary. The idea of racism is closely related to the idea of blood, heritage and nation. Racism is allied to the denigration of the physical differences thought to exist in people of darker skin in the non-Western parts of the world, legitimising their colonisation and subjugation. Racism was institutionalised with the help of dubious scientific claims that sought to legitimise a notion of superiority, granting an entitlement to govern, administer over and 'enlighten' people of darker skin, with a primary role for Christianity in this supposedly civilising mission. As such, racism was at the heart of defining the Age of Enlightenment. The system of bonded free labour made Britain and other parts of Western Europe immensely rich, wealth that in turn prompted the industrial revolutions of all the European nations associated with slavery and trade. From this privileged vantage point, European societies turned towards securing their national interests, which led to internal divisions and social hierarchies, cementing notions of inferior and superior both within and without. Doing so created the conditions for racism to continue despite immigration in the case of Britain, first with Irish groups in the late 1850s, then to the post-war immigration of Caribbean and South Asian groups, whose progeny continue to face ethnic disadvantage, social exclusion, alienation and cultural racism.

Since the 1990s, much of the 'old racism' based entirely on colour has been replaced by a new form of racism centred on culture, and, more recently still, on religion, although in many instances it is the layers of these racisms that affect the most marginalised groups.

Racialisation and the need to fight against racism have undoubtedly created the opportunities for legislation and policy to reverse the inequalities of the past and to ensure the fairness necessary for a stable and diverse future of nations and their peoples. Racism is able to reinvent itself through dominant interests in the same way capitalism is able to reproduce itself. The future remains uncertain as inequalities rise, nation states define national identity in ever narrower terms, and the role of identities becomes increasingly multi-layered and multifaceted, demarcating the lines of conflict in ever more subtle ways, entrenching existing differences while further opening up others. Breaking the link between race and nation, consequently, requires further struggle. The notion of 'imagined communities', which entered into the lexicon of nationalism studies during the 1980s, provided an analytical framework for understanding the origins and destinations of modern nation states by using the lens of sociology and international relations to interpret the nature of ethnic and cultural conflict. In the twenty-first century, the digital age and the acceleration of globalisation heralds a new era of real *and* imagined communities. In this conceptualisation, nations rise and fall because they imagine themselves as possessing a certain racial, ethnic and linguistic nature. Thus, ethnic nationalisms are doomed to collapse and re-emerge because of historical materialism. Since the end of the Second World War, every national conflict has 'defined itself in nationalist terms'.[30] Nationalism maintains itself through globalisation, internationalisation and the challenges of ethnic diversity. Crucially, these nations are *un*real. They reflect the imagination of elites, who define the nature of the people contained within specified geographies or boundaries within a limited political and legal framework. Rarely do people know everyone in any one particular nation, which would clearly be a requisite condition for creating a sense of national identity based on all who are contained within it. Nationalism is invention.

The cultural roots of nationalism can be traced to religion and the dynastic realm. A central facet in religion is the continuity of language across vast geographical tracts that unite different communities with their own distinct ethnic heritage. The religion of Islam is an apposite example, but Christianity, Confucianism and Buddhism are also germane. In Islam, the concept of *ummah* translates into a notion of a 'global brotherhood', which has significant political, cultural and social underpinnings in everyday life, as well as in the imagination of Muslims across the world, past and present, although much has eroded due to the age of colonialism, imposed at the hands of the European powers. Many of these colonial projects challenged the dominant cultural order of traditional societies in the East. Power and politics, economic interests and the importance of the individual over the self altered the nature of exchange between different global communities, with the implications still being felt to this day. The emergence of Western modernity aligned with nationalist conceptualisations, where nations are social constructs, operates in similar ways to the cultural geographies Edward Said discussed when imagining the Orient.[31]

In parts of post-war Western Europe, the emergence of far-right nationalism reflects the extent to which imagined communities remain fundamental to the conceptualisation of the nation state. Immigrants and minorities are often used in an instrumental way to attain certain ends by those seeking to reshape essentialist and reductive national identities. As part of this process, elites often present issues that are due to the wider workings of society as having emanated from the conditions and realities created by immigrant or minority groups, with the problems afflicting society often attributed directly to minority communities themselves. Immigrants and minorities are seen as responsible for a range of issues such as terrorism, violence towards women and cultural relativism. In certain sections of the media, there is a consistent focus on the idea that these groups are over-reliant on welfare, restrict the employment opportunities available to native workers and drive wages down. Elites promulgate these claims in their efforts to reconfigure the dominant group consciousness.[32]

How the nation is imagined has clear political implications. In the postmodern era, the role of the internet is of great consequence in the transformation, mobilisation and the virtual or real configurations of nations and their imagining. As racist and nationalist ideas are now able to spread virtually, instigating changes beyond the capacity of elites in nations or states to control or manage them, the digital space is creating new imaginings for communities that were unimaginable until relatively recently. The interplay between the symbolic and the imaginary thus continues in the virtual world, with all the consequences this raises for race, racism and the imagined nation.

2

THE RACISM OF THE RADICAL RIGHT

Since the 1970s, the emergence of the radical right in Europe has been associated with the relative economic decline of the Global North.[1] Since the advent of Reaganomics in the United States and Thatcherism in the UK, with their primary focus on the financial sector and supply-side economics, working-class and ethnic minority groups have faced the brunt of deindustrialisation, the negative consequences of technological innovation and the internationalisation of capital and labour.[2] This is important in understanding the growth of the far right among formerly working-class groups that have been left behind—itself a misnomer, as it suggests these groups are responsible for their own fates—by structural economic transformations accompanied by the decline of welfare-redistributive politics. But the role of the radical right in society has a much longer history, much of which originates in the context of discussions around tribalism, heritage, nationalism and ethnic identity.

In the UK, the rise of National Action, Britain First and the English Defence League (EDL)—an offshoot of the British National Party (BNP), with its origins in the National Front, the Anti-Paki League[3] in the 1970s, and before that the British Union of Fascists in the 1930s—points to a deep-seated problem of nationalist racism. All of these groups emphasise the supposed purity of the nation and its peoples, and see their heritage as a racial community entirely set apart from other groups. Although these politicised groups tended to emerge in the twentieth century, it is quite clear that a modern notion of racial hierarchy first established itself through the European colonial project of the nineteenth century.[4] Scientific racism underpinned the view that colonialism was not simply about civilising backward peoples but that there was also a scientific basis for a hierarchy of humankind. The inexorable link between capitalism, racism and religion was formalised to a considerable degree through the systematic exploitation of people of darker skin across distant lands.[5]

Tribalism is a related concept. It refers to the processes through which groups identify as having a separate but unique identity. While the differences between tribalism and racism are not always clear, in various ways all individuals and groups are racialist at some level.[6] That is, people can identify the racial characteristics of others but without instrumentalising the modes of oppression associated with racism itself. Identification with the self is in direct opposition to the other, derided for being wholly different, but not to the extent that their elimination or absorption is considered necessary. Alternatively, the others identify themselves as not this lesser other, in part in an attempt to survive or thrive in a local context or at a much wider level. All these groups are racialist. Race defines the choices people make in terms of how they relate to other people. Racism demarcates how they treat these others, from selecting or deselecting marriage partners to a desire to exterminate an entire category of people. Both occur in the name of ideology, culture, nation-building and a sense of the exclusivity, or, more specifically, the exceptionality, of one group in relation to others.[7] But racialism is not mono-directional. In everyday life, any one particular ethnic group can regard the other as in some way different because of a notion of purity, natural intelligence, culture or moral fibre.

If it is possible to agree that racialism affects all, that is, categorising others who are seen as possessing regressive norms, values, traits, characteristics, personalities or behaviours, then how one group relates to the other is based on the power of the 'self' in competition with the 'other'. This dominance is realised instantaneously or it acts as a function of the long-term impact of a historical legacy associated with an earlier experience of local area tribalism that subsequently translated into empowering one group at the expense of the other. The central variation is the differential access to power that groups have over others that shapes the wider processes of racism in reality and how these relations are mobilised despite all humans being racialist to some extent, whether they acknowledge and accept it or not. Humans learn racialism through everyday socialisation processes, often when least realising it.[8] It is a socially learned process. To become anti-racist, racism must be unlearnt, with individuals needing to learn to be anti-racialist and anti-racist to understand how to prevent racism.

This chapter develops the problems associated with race and racism to focus on the particular dynamics of contemporary far-right practices, especially given the events surrounding Britain's decision to leave the EU in 2016 and its repercussions for questions of immigration, national identity and citizenship. The case study of the 2016 Brexit vote indicates a virulent atmosphere of hate, intolerance and bigotry in the context of rampant ethnic nationalism and nativism with significant implications for the most 'othered' of groups in Britain, namely Muslims and immigrant groups. To appreciate the extent of these challenges, it is necessary to return to history in order to determine what lies at the heart of the question.

Racism exists today in many different forms, but it primarily manifests via a dominant group oppressing a minority group through processes by which the dominant racial categories benefit from advancement, substantiation and even reformulation through social institutions.[9] When a dominant ethnic category is reified at the expense of all other ethnic groups, minorities inevitably face subjugation, marginalisation and disenfranchisement in a cyclical process that encompasses a symbiotic relationship between the dominant and dominated, the oppressor and oppressed, the powerful and powerless.

Many of the world's current ethnic conflicts need to be understood in the context of ethnic relations harking back to the colonial era, especially the ways in which scientific racism legitimised pre-existing forms of domination and subordination. By enslaving people of darker skin, described as 'free labour', a process of capital accumulation became the primary driver of wealth creation in the development of European economies and societies from the seventeenth century onwards.[10] Although it is also true that the Arabs engaged in slave trading and that the Romans and Greeks had slaves, these slaves were not selected because of the colour of their skin, and the slave trade did not amount to the wholesale annihilation of entire societies.[11] Thus, unlike earlier forms of racism, modern racism originated in the vast scale of the European imperial colonial experience, which in turn affected the workings of a number of different European institutions, entering into the mechanisms of Western societies through the exoticisation of groups not only presented as different but, more importantly, as inferior. The Atlantic slave trade, for instance, divided people on the basis of skin colour, creating a hierarchy of race that served the interests of the rich and powerful. The abolitionists of the nineteenth century, both in the newly forming United States and in the UK, did manage to mitigate and eventually eliminate the slave trade in meaningful ways,[12] but racism nevertheless found ways to re-establish itself after the end of slavery. In the period that followed, racism was reformulated to continue the process of exploiting the resources of people in distant lands and establishing the power structures of Western European economies that became authoritarian, competitive and self-serving in their approaches towards these people from different parts the world, enhanced further as the European powers fought each other for lucrative trade and capital accumulation.[13]

At the height of the colonial project of the early nineteenth century, the nature of racism underwent a change in which it was increasingly based on anti-immigration sentiment among indigenous Europeans who were beginning to receive ethnic minorities fleeing persecution, particularly Jews[14] and those coming to the 'mother country' as elites from the sending regions in an effort to engage with commerce, enterprise and education in medical schools and law faculties. In the UK, this new form of racism started with hostility towards Irish groups[15] but attention then shifted to Jews who were experiencing persecution in Europe, particularly at the end of the nineteenth century. Somewhat paradoxically, capitalism would have been unable to develop at the pace it maintained during this period and after the Second World War without immigration, as all the formerly colonial Western European economies needed migrant labour.[16] Immigrant workers were invited to work in the industries and economic sectors in which native populations were reluctant to be employed.[17] Racism was at the heart of this project. These temporary migrant workers came to factories in places like the UK, France and Germany to take the undesirable jobs, but once their employment was over, it was not only anticipated but hoped that they would return to their home countries. Employers prevented workers from different minority backgrounds from coming together to formalise collective resistance strategies against systematic processes of racism in the workplace.[18]

Racism mutated further in the context of anti-Semitism, which is a direct form of racism that nevertheless differs from other forms of racism by being based on opposition to people of both a particular religion and race, namely Judaism.[19] Jews experienced persecution throughout Europe for hundreds of years, having been expelled from England in 1290 under the rule of Edward I and cast out from the Iberian Peninsula in 1492 when Isabella and Ferdinand acted together to recapture Portugal and Spain from the Muslims. The Ottomans were instrumental in saving many of these Jews and bringing them to Constantinople and parts of Anatolia as architects, traders and scientists to support the empire. At the turn of the twentieth century, out of a total population of 15 million people across the territories of Anatolia and Constantinople, over 1 million were Jews, Christians and adherents of other minority religions.[20]

In late nineteenth-century Britain, racial anti-Semitism was important in maintaining the workings of capitalism.[21] For the working classes, anti-Semitism was a means to attack the mechanics of capitalism by focusing on Jewish groups as a specific problem. It led to a relationship between anti-Semitism and fascism, the latter emerging in response to the interests of the middle classes and petty bourgeoisie. In Germany, as anti-Semitism grew, the exclusion of Jews in society gained wide-ranging support. The Nazis combined this sentiment with a racial purity thesis that appealed to the popular imagination. Jewish groups in Germany were the target of a range of different attacks on many different fronts, from the cultural and the economic to the ideological and political.[22] Such was the groundswell of anti-Semitism in Western Europe during the Second World War that the Nazis were able to seize virtually all the Jews in the Netherlands with little or no resistance from the native Dutch.[23]

The tragic murder of Jo Cox MP, in 2016 brought to the surface acute fears over radical right extremism in Britain. This act was no aberration. Reports continue to suggest that far-right extremism is regarded as a major concern by Western European security agencies. However, when far-right extremism occurs, it is often underreported or misreported, and when a discussion does ensue, the dominant argument tends to be that the violence was carried out by loners or the mentally ill.[24] No direct associations are usually made with far-right groups, encouraging the view that these actions are a policing issue, not a matter for counterterrorism policy. But when it comes to young Muslims involved in acts of violent extremism, on the other hand, far greater linkages are often made with jihadism, Islamic radicalism or even ISIS and other similar groups, adding to already heightened tensions. There is a clear reporting bias when such crimes are covered in certain sections of the mainstream media. 'Islamic extremism' is often given far more weight in news reports, while far-right radicalism is often treated less prominently. In the murder of Cox, for instance, while evidence emerged relatively quickly that the assailant had direct associations with far-right groups, as well as having a chequered history with far-right activism, commentators were slow to reveal the full details of the story.

Both far-right and Islamic terrorist acts can usually be traced to two highly polarised causes facing various challenges near the bottom of society—both are 'left-behind' groups, yet they are also diametrically opposed to each other: one is racialised and alienated, the other is marginalised and disaffected, but both have emerged in the context of neoliberalism and economic restructuring in post-industrial societies. Each group vehemently holds on to a sense of identity in relation to others who are understood as a potential risk due to these 'others' taking away or diluting the purity of the group's identity. Such representations are ideological, selective and political. The very idea of being a Briton, after all, is to be among a nation of immigrants, but for some of these groups, the idea of being English is related to having Anglo-Saxon blood. Race is the signifier here, but a perpetually imagined race that is cultivated within the sphere of ethnic nationalism.[25]

Muslims who came to Britain at the end of the Second World War found themselves subordinated and subjugated by the workings of industrial capitalism.[26] In the structural adjustments arising from the transformation into a post-industrial society, many Muslim communities faced the prospect of residential concentration in the inner-city areas of the places in which they first migrated. In locations such as Birmingham, parts of the North and areas of Greater London, diverse groups lived cheek by jowl with indigenous Britons in relatively peaceful harmony. As the pace of deindustrialisation accelerated, the extent of 'white flight' grew due to fears of specific ethnic minority groups. These fears were of a political origin then, and it remains the case today. In various parts of these same inner-city areas, while groups who desired and were able to leave departed, the poorest and most excluded white Britons are locked alongside the third and fourth generations of Muslim minority groups who have remained trapped in the same areas due to racism, structural disadvantage and social immobility.[27] These processes have excluded groups in an intense competition for the least in society. During these transformations, Islam and Muslims have replaced race and ethnicity as the main signifier of difference in the politics of difference for these groups.

The state's attempts to respond to these challenges have inadvertently fuelled conflict at the bottom of society. As elites became ever more powerful and wealthy relative to the rest of society, a notion of Britishness is promoted as exclusive and inward-looking. The working classes continue to be loyal to the workings of classed British society, in particular the monarchy.[28] In an effort to sustain their existence, some working-class groups have enhanced their identity formations through an allusion to a purer Englishness. While elite groups with no interest in groups at the bottom of society routinely denigrate these others as a blot or a burden on the state, right-wing politicians constantly focus on immigration as a way to protect British society from 'alien others' whose apparent objectives are to dilute the identity of the host society. Vehemently internalised by majority groups suffering downward social mobility pressures, this idea has led such groups to project their anxiety on to others. Such sentiments generate alarm and eventually hate towards their nearest neighbours, namely Muslim minority groups in inner-city areas.

In the case of Muslim groups, since the end of the Cold War, Western foreign policy has increasingly focused on the Middle East, while in Western European societies Muslim minorities are increasingly seen in religious rather than ethnic or cultural terms, enhancing the undesirable negative exposure, which is in some cases hostile and violent. Political elites have often used local tensions for political gain, both nationally and internationally.[29] The tendency of some young Muslim men to exhibit hyper-masculine behaviours—i.e. exaggerated stereotypical male qualities, such as an emphasis on strength, sexuality and/or aggression—and then engage in acts of violent extremism has led to automatic associations being made with a global phenomenon, further legitimising invasive foreign policies and regressive domestic policies concerning integration. With securitisation of multiculturalism as the main discourse, Muslim minorities have increasingly come under the spotlight, receiving ever greater attention from vast swathes of society who now generalise Islam and Muslims as a whole, hence the accusation of widespread Islamophobia. As the levels of frustration among some young Muslim men reach the point of no return, many have sought to vent their anger at the global level, rendering the local realities of their area invisible. These Muslim men do not fight for their local communities but for an imagined global project. The vacuum at the local level is then filled by the machinations of right-wing politics, fomented locally but maintained nationally.

Governments throughout the world have failed to introduce policies that bring about equality and fairness to limit the deleterious consequences of neoliberalism. A loss of the imagination of the nation in a global climate of inequality and competition has ensued, where national elites hold on to an invented notion of the nation and its peoples. Social justice and equality are no longer presented as key aspects of policy, with rather vacuous notions such as 'values' taking their place, despite them having no purpose in bringing communities together in reality. Groups at the bottom of society are pushed further down by the machinations of elites, creating intense levels of competition and conflict in local communities that are occasionally leading to violence and terrorism. Acts of terrorism carried out by extremist Islamists and the radical right are the result of the biopolitics of the state, but the two groups are in opposition to each other due to their narrow definitions of identity.[30] These realities emerge in various spatial formations, reflecting the search for self-actualisation due to their disempowered status with little or no alternative route out of disadvantage and disruption.

Helen Joanne Cox (née Leadbeater) was born into a working-class family in Batley in 1974. Her sharp intelligence assured entry into a grammar school, later winning a place to read social and political sciences at Pembroke College, University of Cambridge. Upon graduation from Cambridge, she became a political advisor to Glenys Kinnock, wife of Neil Kinnock, leader of the Labour Party from 1983 to 1992. After a brief spell advising Kinnock, who was a member of the European Parliament, Cox worked for a number of charities before formally entering politics on a Labour ticket in the 2015 General Election to represent the constituency of Batley and Spen. An active campaigner for the rights of refugees, particularly Syrians fleeing the conflict in the region, she drew much-needed attention to the plight facing individuals and groups fleeing persecution. She routinely urged the British government to show empathy and openness. Cox lived on a barge on the Thames with her husband and her two young children.[31]

Cox was deeply committed to humanitarian causes and worked passionately to support people suffering due to displacement, inequality and problematic domestic and foreign policies. Outspoken, passionate and committed, she had fortitude in a hostile environment, especially in 2015 when the Syrian refugee crisis was at its peak, and remained an active supporter of the European Union. Yet in 2015, these two issues, the support of refugees and the EU question, were politically toxic. Her championing of these issues ultimately led Thomas Mair to target Cox, shooting her with a sawn-off rifle before stabbing her repeatedly. He walked away but returned to shoot her twice in the face while exclaiming 'Britain First!' This heinous and distressing political murder was carried out in the middle of the afternoon on a street outside the public library where she held her constituency surgery. The event led to three days of mourning and the suspension of the Brexit campaign.[32]

Thomas Mair was born in 1963 in Kilmarnock in Scotland. The son of working-class parents, he had a history of obsessive-compulsive disorders. In his quest for meaning, he became increasingly drawn to radical right-wing and white supremacist material online. Many media outlets described Mair as a recluse. However, part of the problem of the discourse around far-right extremism, as mentioned previously, is that perpetrators are habitually presented as loners or isolated individuals who operate on their own to carry out acts of violent extremism. Rarely discussed is the wider social, political and cultural context in which these ideas are able to foment, nor the associations such individuals have with others holding similar sentiments. Real-world off-line connections are not scrutinised, nor are the wider social movements that psychologically and politically motivate these men to carry out acts of violence against others. Certainly, it is nowhere near comparable to the focus on radical Islamists.

A deeply divisive Brexit campaign acted as the backdrop to this horrific murder.[33] During the campaign, both those wishing to leave and those seeking to remain within the European Union were guilty of exaggerating their respective claims, but it is now clear that the leave campaign in particular went to unprecedented lengths to fabricate the costs of remaining within the EU and concealing the potential damage of leaving. A particularly toxic environment was created where any semblance of balanced argument disappeared as senior politicians promoted the lies that evoked the emotions that created the political reaction. The murder of Jo Cox MP happened only a few days after Nigel Farage stood before a now infamous poster carrying the slogan 'Breaking Point'.[34] Those promoting immigration had their loyalty, integrity and Britishness called into question, negatively affecting Britons promoting multiculturalism, tolerance and respect for differences as a means to enrich society as a whole. Thus, two simultaneous denials took place. One was the question of whether Mair was simply a lone actor, who developed his hateful far-right ideology in a vacuum, without resources or organisation, while the other was a denial that the Brexit campaign had generated the febrile atmosphere that motivated Mair to kill Cox in cold blood. These interrelated and mutually supportive themes had serious implications for a discussion of how to accept differences in society, and for the nature of government and politics as a whole.

Ideology plays a crucial role in racism. There is clear evidence that Mair was inspired by David Copeland, who mounted three terrorist attacks, including the fatal bombing in April 1999 of the Admiral Duncan, a Soho pub popular with the gay community. He bought books on explosives and right-wing ideology two weeks before the pub bombing. Mair also kept press cuttings on the Anders Breivik case.[35] The common link between these different perpetrators is a specific ideology that promotes anti-Muslim sentiment, but it also opposes Marxism, feminism, same-gender relationships and multiculturalism. Sentencing Mair to life in prison, High Court Judge Mr Justice Wilkie said: 'There is no doubt that this murder was done for the purpose of advancing a political, racial and ideological cause, namely that of violent white supremacist and exclusive nationalism most associated with Nazism and its modern forms.' Leading up to the murder of Jo Cox MP, the febrile, volatile and combative context of the Brexit vote campaign heightened the conditions that ultimately outraged killer Thomas Mair.[36] The rise of the far-right counter-jihad movement is indicative of a general trend of authoritarianism, populism and extremism in politics. It signals a particularly divisive politics driven by the ruthless self-interest and ideology of the problematic forces of the darker echelons of the internet, propelled by the interests of shadowy financial figures, with the only choice for progress presented as the status quo.

The year 2016 heralded a new dawn in political spin and in many cases sheer lies, marking the Brexit campaign as one of the most conflict-ridden and damaging in recent British political history. The leave campaign ultimately won, but the result split the country down the middle. Not to be outdone, Donald Trump delivered an equally unexpected victory in the US presidential elections a few months later, supported by Cambridge Analytica, the dexterous tech company able to tap into and generate online sentiment to alter political outlooks and behaviours. Defying his detractors, Trump overcame all odds to become the forty-fifth president of the United States. Inaugurated in January 2017, the Trump era has spawned unprecedented ways and means of carrying out and communicating politics, using Twitter as his own personal digital communications tool to share his convoluted whims to a vast audience[37] while deriding the democratic process and calling critical reporting 'fake news'.

Trump represents the failures of the symptom rather than the cause of the current malaise facing Western liberal democracies. In the hands of political leaders, truth has always been susceptible to manipulation, especially when the need arises to disassemble opposition or break down opponents—as classically pronounced in Machiavelli's *The Prince*. Truth has often been a casualty of the age of globalisation, as national boundaries and identities have less meaning and significance to elites whose wealth is often spread throughout the globe. Societal differences are now presented as risks to the self. In the absence of an alternative voice able to cut through the rhetoric of the political classes, this post-truth politics is increasingly permeating those parts of society 'left behind' by the economic and social changes which result from a hollowing out of the centre. It does so against a backdrop of increasingly radical right-wing populism, much of which is grounded on anti-Muslim and anti-immigration sentiment, as well as economic protectionism and the casualisation of the indigenous labour market. In this post-truth world, extremist right-wing voices are increasingly gaining legitimacy, raising the prospect of radicalisation and violence on all sides.[38]

With the political mood in the UK becoming desensitised to anti-immigration arguments as well as anti-European and anti-Islam discourses, it is within these spaces that some feel compelled to transform their political and ideological beliefs into violent extremism. The resurgence of the radical right is not merely a threat to security, however, as the radical right promotes an ethnonational identity and an associated politics of memory that is both myopic and inward-looking. As the idea of 'Englishness' surpasses that of Britishness, it is presented as a distinct ethnic category whereas the latter is a cultural legacy with legal status. This is creating huge obstacles to the promotion of social cohesion and tolerance in society. Radical right extremist ideology and extremist violence are tantamount to terrorism; however, the reality is that efforts to fight extremism have not yet taken into full consideration the threat from far-right groups. Cox's murder exposed the risks from radical right violent extremism as real and urgent. An online and off-line community of right-wing ideologues has created an 'echo chamber' of sinister views with global reach. However, when it comes to far-right extremism, the tendency is to underplay the role of ideology, when ideology is ultimately central to its beliefs and action.

The far right has been gaining momentum ever since the murder of Jo Cox MP. Wave after wave of attacks on European and North American soil have helped to create a deep sense of fear. Populism is also taking greater hold in Turkey and India. Governments in Poland and Hungary, meanwhile, are using anti-immigrant and anti-Muslim rhetoric as a powerful sedative for societies coming to terms with their Middle European existence. The Dutch, French and the UK elections in 2017 confirmed the view that left-leaning thinking still holds some sway, especially among the young, but growing right-wing populism is afflicting an older population and those suffering the localised implications of neoliberal globalisation. These worries are important in light of the ongoing difficulties facing Western European economies struggling to emerge from the recession stemming from the 2008 global financial meltdown. It is within this feverish context that political divisions breed and extremisms flourish, adapting racism from a real-world experience into a virtual space and then back on to the streets.

3

MUSLIM ORIGINS AND DESTINATIONS

Since the end of the Cold War and 9/11, the number of studies on Islam and Muslim minorities in the West has grown exponentially. However, while there has been a special interest in Muslim groups, Muslim diasporas *de facto* exhibit all of the same characteristics found among communities migrating elsewhere across the world. Migration policy and practice, cultural adaptation and adoption, intergenerational continuity and change, and identity politics and political integration affect Muslim groups just as they do other groups on the move. For Muslim minority communities, however, religiosity is also a consideration, given the complexity of secular and liberal Western democracies in which many find themselves. The postcolonial milieu, where, in many instances, the once-colonised migrated to their former 'motherland', is another noteworthy dynamic, especially given how racism, discrimination and ethnic disadvantage afflict groups seeking to achieve parity with the majority populations of their new host societies. An ongoing dynamic, echoing xenophobia and Orientalism, is the added concern of Islamophobia. These diasporas also raise to the fore ongoing cultural, social, economic and political linkages between the sending regions and the new home, referred to as transnationalism.

This chapter examines the lives of British Muslims in the post-war period, focusing on patterns of migration, settlement and adaptation in the context of changing social and economic conditions. Having discussed the nature of race and racism in Britain in recent periods, and having delineated the implications of the increasing presence of radical right violence in society, the book then turns to ethnic nationalism, which is taking Britain in profoundly opposing directions. The prospect of leaving the EU has raised concerns over national identity and 'others', something felt acutely in relation to the 'Muslim question', which this chapter sets out to explain in terms of the internal dynamics of 'Muslimness' in a space increasingly seen as 'Englishness', once celebrated as a mode of 'Britishness' that included diverse minorities as part of an inclusive, enriching collective. The framing of British Muslims as the group most antithetical to the idea of 'Britishness' has in turn created divisions, sowed discord and challenged the idea of nationhood for all.

In the Middle Ages, the lands and peoples beyond Constantinople remained wholly unfamiliar to the vast majority of Europeans. To many, these groups were 'barbarians', 'uncivilised' and 'sinister'. Among European elites, however, there was a tolerance and respect for Muslim lands and Islamic civilisations. In particular, the Elizabethans had constructive relations with the Ottomans, to the extent that the Ottomans helped to thwart the Spanish Armada in its efforts to convert England back to loyalty to the papacy. Among writers, commentators and those evoking the popular imagination, the seeds of demonisation grew during this time and over subsequent years. Two extremes materialised at once. One viewed Muslims in positive ways, while the other regarded Muslims with disdain. The first helped to develop a robust intellectual interest in Islam, while the second cultivated a deep trepidation of the 'other'.[1]

Muslims have been in Europe for as long as Islam has existed. The presence of Muslims in what is present-day Spain lasted for over 750 years, until 1492, when the Reconquista expelled Muslims and Jews from the Iberian Peninsula. Modern Europe emerged as a response to the decline of Islam and the power Europe gained through mercantilism. As the Ottomans grew in influence and authority, Muslims entered the Balkans and the Caucasus.[2] Pushed back by the expanding European powers, thriving on nationalism, commerce and the geneses of industrialisation, Muslim communities became distinct entities at the borders of Europe—but invisible to the outside. Assimilated into the body politic of European society, simmering ethnic tensions rose to the surface at the end of the twentieth century, for example in former Yugoslavia, foreshadowing war between ethno-religious groups during the 1990s. Despite opposition to British and French colonialism, certain opportunities for interconnectedness did arise between the populations of the Muslim world and their European rulers. These exchanges were characterised by economic exploitation, but also by forms of cultural interaction and engagement that occasionally resulted in the cross-fertilisation of progressive post-Enlightenment thinking and practice.

Colonialism, scientific racism and eugenics were critical in the establishment of Western perspectives on the Muslim world in that they ultimately proceeded to xenophobia and Orientalism, remnants of which are observable as Islamophobia today. The racialisation of ethnic groups was fostered by wider society through popular culture and literature, reified through the class structures of host societies that stimulated immigration from once-colonised lands at the end of the Second World War. These Muslim groups, among others, took up employment in industrial sectors deemed undesirable by indigenous populations seeking higher standards of living during the post-war reconstruction process. A striking feature of the immigration of Muslim groups, once under the yoke of colonialism, was that they spread wide and far—not only to their 'mother countries'. In Britain, the first Muslim incomers were Yemenis who worked on the British merchant ships and later inhabited port cities such as South Shields and Cardiff. From there, they relocated to the urban centres of Britain in search of better employment prospects. Muslims associated with the British also migrated to the United States during the early part of the twentieth century.[3] In these phases of extensive migration from Eastern and Central Europe to parts of the United States, Bengali Muslims arrived and settled in New York in the 1920s and 1930s, some of whom ran boarding houses and lived in Harlem and the Lower East Side. A community of Muslims from the Ottoman territories settled in Lower Manhattan from the 1880s to the 1940s, in the area known as Little Syria. Somali Muslims came to New York on Italian merchant ships as early as the 1900s. They also settled in Harlem. These Muslims were also among the first to establish *halal* restaurants and mosques in the United States.

The period immediately after the Second World War led to mass Muslim migration to Europe, the United States and Australia. Driven by the economic needs of various nations undergoing rapid transformation, the emergence of groups from Muslim nations led to patterns of economic, political and cultural subjugation that have remained resilient in the intervening years. One such community in Europe is the Turks. The Ottomans made huge advances into Europe during the seventeenth and eighteenth centuries, especially in Hungary, the Balkans and Greece. However, the Ottoman Empire began to decay during the late nineteenth century. After the Second World War, Turks entered into Europe as migrant labour, in particular to Germany and Denmark, where opportunities arose in the vehicle manufacturing sectors. Many of the Turks who migrated came from the lesser-developed regions of Anatolia. These workers possessed little formal education or skills before arrival, resulting in marginalisation due to the lack of opportunities to up-skill once the motor-industrial sector of the economy began to decline in the 1970s. This was a pattern repeated for Pakistanis working in the heavy engineering sectors in the UK and Denmark. Moroccans and Algerians faced similar problems in the major industrial cities of France.

Much of the growth of the Muslim population in the United States came about after the country became more open to immigration in 1965, when highly qualified immigrant Muslim groups from various parts of the Muslim world came to North America to seek higher returns from their human capital. This migration of Muslims to North America differs when compared with those who came to Western Europe in the periods immediately after the end of the Second World War. American Muslims, particularly those that came after 1965, were highly educated, integrated and at the same time loyal to a republic that built its identity on the idea that hard work leads to prosperity.

Over time, Muslim groups established themselves through attempts at integration, attempting to achieve economic and social mobility plus political and cultural assimilation. The demands placed on various states concerning particular Muslim religious needs and wants created tension among the majority,[4] which reflected the prevailing attitudes among certain sections of society, inducing social conflict near the bottom where these groups were concentrated. Many decades later, these Muslim groups continue to occupy lower socioeconomic positions. In the case of Britain and France, issues stemming from the legacy of colonialism endure in defining the locale of social relations between Muslim minority and non-Muslim majority groups during all phases of immigration and integration, although this did not apply to Turks in Germany.[5] Despite these developments, racial and ethnic exclusion is persistent and systematic for many Muslim minorities across Western Europe.[6] The end of economic migration during the 1970s resulted in a process of family reunification as the primary means of moving from Muslim lands into Western Europe. This episode in history also witnessed the Arab Oil Crisis of 1973–4 and the emergence of confrontations such as the Iranian Revolution and the Soviet invasion of Afghanistan.[7] In more recent periods, another layer in this newfound emergence of Islam in Europe relates to how Muslims arrived as refugees and asylum-seekers, in particular during the disintegration of former Yugoslavia in the 1990s. This has continued since the war on terror, the Iraq war and in the aftermath of the Arab Spring and the collapse of ISIS as a territorial entity, which has displaced countless Muslims due to oppression, political unrest and violence.

Deindustrialisation, globalisation and neoliberalism have gone hand in hand since the 2000s. A notable shift to the political right has also taken place across a whole host of Western European nations during the same period. Along with Britain, France and Germany, nations such as the United States and Australia are struggling with the question of how to deal with their own so-called 'Muslim problem'.[8] Caused by their geographical concentration in poorer parts of towns and cities, the visibility of Muslim groups adds to apprehensions framed by elites promoting the idea that Muslims are unable to assimilate, combined with a focus on the security threat they supposedly pose. Discussions of Muslims living 'parallel lives' have also abounded during this time,[9] resulting in polarisations between the words of political elites and the realities facing Muslim communities in towns and cities.[10] Despite these discourses, a 'myth of return' is no more: Muslims in Western Europe and in North America are a part of the fabric of their new societies, which they now regard as their homes. They are engaging with the political process and continuing to advance their positions in education and employment within diverse urban centres.[11] The vast majority of Muslims maintain open-minded religious and cultural norms and values. Muslims in Western Europe are becoming increasingly confident despite the political and cultural challenges they face.[12]

The post-war migration of Muslim communities into the centres of Western European societies has led to the emergence of questions relating to community, identity, integration and equality. The prevailing political discourse, however, routinely rejects the question of the potential assimilability of Muslims in Europe. In recent years, political actors and commentators have raised distinct challenges in response to various acts of terrorism carried out by European-born Muslims of South Asian, Middle Eastern or North African descent. The young men implicated in these attacks have presented their acts of violence as being carried out in the name of Islam, despite the palpable but often underreported outcries by Muslims elsewhere. The solutions identified by states converge on pressing the need for deeper loyalty to a set of dominant cultural values, which are usually left largely undefined. Simultaneously, Muslims are subject to widespread surveillance. The 'clash of civilisations' thesis, first expounded in the early 1990s but still widely propagated today, dominates this rhetoric. It has convinced many on the political and radical right that their apprehensions have materialised with regard to the seemingly unavoidable clash between Islam and the West, with the origins of the conflict inherent only in Islam, not the West.

In seeking to understand the experience of Muslim minorities in the West, the nature of intergenerational change and continuity is an important area of research. First-generation immigrants brought with them a unique set of norms and values from the sending regions. These cultural attributes persisted in the new home for various reasons to do with group formation and wider issues of racism and discrimination. For the second generations, however, the previous norms and values of their parents can lead to disagreements, as many of the societies from which British Muslims originated are conservative and pious. They also have collectivist tendencies, where beliefs around the greater good far outweigh individual needs and wants. Through centuries of the post-religious experience, combined with secular and liberal approaches to social and political life, an emphasis on individuality has triumphed in Western Europe and North America. Second-generation Muslims are in the unenviable position of having to find a path between the new and the old, the past and the present.

In some instances, young Muslims adhere to identifiable religious identity markers as a way of expressing resistance to the racialisation and discrimination encountered by the group as a whole. In doing so, they are also attempting to diverge from their parents' values and beliefs. In this environment, young Muslims aspire to a 'purer' notion of Islam as a way of minimising the deleterious cultural impact resulting from Muslims being demonised by members of society who single them out as distinct. Gender also becomes important when young men and women frame their identities as both European and Muslim in different ways, challenging men to re-affirm their masculinity and women to reconsider notions of femininity. Innermost in this internal transformation is the reorganisation and reconfiguration of the role of Islam, a process ultimately being led by young people. Not only do mosques act as places of worship; they also host conferences and events that bring together other communities, thus addressing diverse issues and concerns that affect young Muslims and their relations with others in wider society.[13] Although this reflects a process of integration, rather than a retreat into religion, far too many presume the latter.

According to migration theory, over time minority communities adopt secular norms and values as they integrate into their host societies. Yet the presence of Muslims in Western Europe suggests a convergence around religious identity. In the UK, Germany, the Netherlands and Sweden, second-generation Muslims have maintained their religious norms and values despite the differences in the respective migration histories and integration policies in these countries.[14] While some identities are borne out of resistance and social change, the long-term outlook is for convergence around secular social identities.[15] Others argue that when Islam is least accommodated, Islamism among the younger generations is absorbed by society.[16] This might be true for Turks in Germany, but it also reflects attempts to integrate German Turkish Muslims into the national imagined community. It may well also reveal the emergence of greater equality and opportunity in education and employment terms rather than opposition to majority ethno-national formations as a response to ethnic disadvantage. All of these instances indicate the important role of policy. Critical discussions about integration are important, but wider philosophical and policy-orientated deliberations around incorporating differences have also emerged as aspects of the debate on Muslims in the West. Perils arise, however, in concentrating on Muslim groups solely through a religious lens, as patterns of pre-migration history, economic integration and acculturation are also relevant. A critical element relates to adjustments made in majority society to accommodate differences while Muslim minorities immerse themselves in various social milieus. It becomes a question of adoption of versus adaptation to society as a whole and concerning the communities in question,[17] thereby generating philosophical and political questions and thus introducing the idea of multiculturalism.

Multiculturalism is a contested term that has had different meanings in different spaces and at different times. At a conceptual level, it is a philosophical question relating to the acceptance of difference, where toleration is seen as a marker of its success. As a policy, it attempts to manage differences in society, alleviating racism but also encouraging participation and engagement to build a national consensus based on respect and interdependence. It is not surprising, therefore, to discover that the term has become politicised, with the way it is understood being subject to responses to events as much as objective realities. Whereas the political left focuses on equality and opportunity, for many of those on the right, individualism and the 'rejection of Western universalism' trump wider collective notions.[18] Unease over concentrations of Muslims in specific residential populations renders groups more visible in the urban sphere, thus leading to the emergence of polarisation and alarm in broader society, exacerbating suspicions and widening social divisions. As an alternative to 'retreat' at the hands of those who wish to promote social cohesion or integration at the expense of valuing individual and group differences, multiculturalism enhances diversity rather than subduing it. Multiculturalism is a liberal rather than illiberal position. It protects against discrimination while promoting diversity and unity at the same time.[19]

Although these are all important considerations when exploring the accommodation of Islamic practices in the Global North, the vital component of gender is missing. In the immediate post-war era, as Muslim groups were invited to take up employment in unpopular sectors of Western European economies, a particular strand of thought emerged whereby Muslim men were seen as effeminate, having eviscerated their masculinity and their religious identity in the sphere and domain of industrial societies. Today, the intense gaze on Muslim men as aggressive and extremist partly reflects the reconfiguration of their identities with hyper-masculine features. To a significant degree, this reconfiguration has been driven by aggression, frustration and anger borne out of downward pressures on social mobility. The lack of opportunity or equality, as well as the utterances of political elites supporting the global war on terror, has undermined Muslim men's sense of themselves. As such, these Muslim masculinities are not separate from wider discussions of ethnicity, identity and nationhood.[20] The persistent focus on Muslim women's bodies through an emphasis on the hijab is a related construct. Women too are at the intersection between race, gender and religion. Their invisibility becomes visibility in societies that regard their difference as threatening. By adopting the Muslim garb, however, the positions of Muslim women move from subject to object,[21] but given the right circumstances, this space has the potential to advance both Islam and feminism.[22] And given the impact of various emotive developments implicating young Muslims since 9/11, the emergence of these gender differences allows for a nuanced perspective on Islam itself.[23]

Numerous variations exist within Muslim communities themselves. Muslims do not comprise a single, monolithic, ethnic or religious category, nor are there always synergies within and between different subcategories of Islam. However, the prevailing narrative nevertheless focuses on Muslims having been invariably 'radicalised' outside of their traditional modes of Islam. Across Western Europe and the United

States, most Muslims hail from diverse backgrounds. This can be seen in the Sufi *tariqas* (orders). After the events of the first war of independence in 1857 (or the 'Indian Mutiny'), this South Asian Sufi Islam shifted in diverse directions. One route promoted technological, rational thinking and scientific endeavour in the pursuit of Islamic goals. The other reverted to a narrow quest for psychological and political objectives with the distinct aim of determining an Islamic perspective on all aspects of modern life. One response was spiritual and otherworldly; the other was political and ideological, aiming to accomplish transformation in the here and now. The existence of both trends, resulting from the migration and religious transmission process, in places such as the inner-city areas of Birmingham, have provided an opportunity to maintain the diaspora over time, with all the divisions that exist in the sending countries and the ways in which they manifest themselves in the new home.[24]

Due to the divergence between the Barelwi and Deobandi orders, which was first seen in India in the late nineteenth century, a larger quarrel exists between these Sufi sects and the Salafis—the collective term for an ultraorthodox variety of Sunni Islam, promoted and supported by a political ideology with funding originating from the Gulf States. As a result of competition and infighting among the Sufi orders, literalist interpretations have exploited fissures between the two groups, offering black-and-white answers that young Muslims sometimes seek. But another viewpoint is that young Muslims can reconnect with their spiritual heritage over time, as adherence to literalism reflects a rejection of wider society, rather than its acceptance (although most of the rejections are formed due to the realities of local social conditions). A return to the spiritual and ascetic amplifies the space to contribute to society, while maintaining a strong religious identity that is not in opposition to it.[25] Sufism is not antithetical to modernism (nor is non-violent pro-integration Salafism). The supra-local nature of Sufism has always allowed it to spread globally.[26] In the United States, Sufism also has the advantage of countering the damaging associations between Islam and extremism, which have entered into the wider national public psyche through a dominant discourse that routinely frames Islam in disparaging terms.[27]

When thinking about the positions of Muslim minorities in Western Europe and across the Global North, many refer to their anxieties over the question of citizenship. Critics argue that Muslims are demanding rights from the state that are beyond their abilities to reciprocate in kind. Detractors add that these claims are disingenuous for the rest of society, encouraging competition between groups. The conflation between individualism versus collectivist ideals throws the multiculturalism question into sharp relief, both as a political philosophy and as a policy approach. Where there is mounting criticism against growing differences in society, it encourages nations to withdraw into narrow definitions of ethno-nationalism, reinforcing a sense of 'them' and 'us'. All these concerns raise further unease about the law, including where questions relating to 'parallel lives' extend to the idea of an alternative legal system that Muslim communities supposedly operate through 'sharia councils'. Presented as counter to the interests of wider society, in reality these committees, which are run on a voluntary basis, seek to resolve Muslim legal issues by directing individuals to civil law, for example on matters of marriage, divorce and property.[28] Despite these realities, identifiable practices within Muslim communities, driven by culture and tradition rather than religion, such as forced marriages, violence against women or 'honour crimes', have received a particular emphasis within the legal systems of Western Europe, aiming to protect otherwise vulnerable groups.[29]

A continued interest in the 'Muslim other' delegitimises petitions for recognition and acceptance, for example in education, the desire for *halal* food or protection under the law. The reality is that there ought to be a coming together at a midpoint between the majority and the minority to support egalitarian multiculturalism.[30] However, this has been hampered by the fear that societies have become too diverse, making social cohesion impossible, with the onus on Muslim minorities to assimilate at all costs. One of the problems with this is the presence of an imagined multiculturalism, which is quite different from the reality of life facing different ethnic and religious minority communities in the urban areas of older towns and cities across Western Europe. This illusory multiculturalism is romanticised and idealised. It also has the undesirable consequence of reinforcing stereotypes and generalisations by alluding to assertions that Muslims are 'self-ghettoising'—which is a wholly problematic understanding of urban disadvantage and poverty.[31] These arguments claim that Muslims are not only a threat to the social cohesion of the nation but that a securitisation agenda needs to be upheld in order to counter it, thus further demonising and excluding Muslims and ultimately perpetuating the status quo and legitimising existing modes of domination and subordination. The problems are heightened by the actions of policymakers who placate voters by justifying actions such as the restriction of refugees escaping the war in Syria or escalating air strikes in response to acts of terrorism in France at the end of 2015.

The persistence of popular and political anxieties surrounding Muslim groups in Western European societies raises many different questions for scholars working in this area. 'The Muslim' is both an experience and an analytical concept. Since 9/11, Muslims have often been viewed in virulent terms. How scholars use the categories are as fundamental as how they come to be established. This is important in the present context of heightened alarmism and the increased potential for subjectivity.[32] This issue is imperative given the profile of Muslim minorities in the public sphere—as a lived experience but also as an analytical perspective. States tend to define what they regard as the ideal Muslim, that is, Muslims who belong to groups that are loyal and undivided, and whose allegiance is directly to the state. Muslim groups, however, occasionally adhere to an outward manifestation of their identity, projected both locally and globally, which has the potential to create and recreate the Muslim experience through an Islamic theology realised through citizenship. Consequently, both opportunities and threats materialise, although myriad differences within and between groups exist.[33]

Former industrial workers who migrated to the urban centres have become increasingly visible in the public sphere due to their demands for recognition, as well as the growing numbers of Muslim religious facilities such as mosques and Islamic centres. Without rejecting the norms and values of wider society, Muslims tend to distinguish between legitimate expressions of citizenship.[34] New waves of migration to urban centres, where existing ethnic minorities are concentrated, further conflate these concepts. The new publics carry with them different conceptions of community and identity as additional layers to existing social conflicts. The diversity found within these new peripheries has led to the emergence of new analytical perspectives challenging the prevailing methods of social science on Muslim communities in Europe.[35] With attempts made by Muslim groups to enter the political sphere through active participation, room for manipulation can also surface—how Muslims are perceived but also instrumentalised has far-reaching implications. The dominant political narratives tend to describe Muslims in generally unfavourable terms; however, Muslim voters are crucial for political parties vying for electoral gain in key constituencies.[36] Panic over the participation of Muslims in politics has been projected through the claim that Muslims have stronger adherence to their faith based on a global system. What is often overlooked are the multiple differences within groups, and the decentralised nature of Islam itself.[37] Muslim political participation and economic integration in the United States are inexorably interrelated. Upwardly mobile Muslims are more politically engaged in majority politics than those from lower socioeconomic positions. Such findings are consistent across all groups in US society, which suggests that economic interests coincide with political expectations, which is hardly surprising given the character of late capitalism in the United States.[38]

It is important to distinguish between the political participation and the representation of Muslim minorities in Western societies. In this regard, the balance has skewed away from simply supporting majority parties to a position where Muslim votes can sway the outcomes of local elections, operate as political actors within the main parties and develop political movements that have close associations with established political thinking. Muslim voices are organising themselves in politics, creating political parties through alliances with left-leaning, or, for example, anti-war coalitions. This was especially the case with RESPECT—the Unity Coalition in Britain established in the wake of the 2003 invasion of Iraq before disbanding in 2016.[39] While the party was able to mobilise Muslim and non-Muslim votes as a response to Britain's foreign policy and the war on terror in Iraq, internal Muslim community issues prevented broader penetration among voters. The concept of *biraderi*—loosely defined as patrilineal clan kinship networks—is of great consequence among South Asian Muslim communities concentrated in Britain. In the past, the promise of political influence, originally by the Labour Party but then also by the other main political parties, lured community leaders into compliance. Muslim voters, however, were resistant to change, which had consequences for the RESPECT party in electoral terms, which brought to the fore internal divisions within South Asian Muslim communities that reflected promises made in the past and their hopes for the future.

Politics is the arena in which decisions between competing alternatives transpire, but the media nevertheless continues to play a pivotal role. Politics and media are odd bedfellows, sometimes working in close harmony, at others working against each other. The concentration of political power at the centre at the expense of the periphery, aided by the power of a few business elites with vast holdings across a range of media sectors, from press to television to film to the online world, has generated new anxieties. Numerous considerations have emerged for those who speak in the media on matters affecting a community that is already under intense scrutiny. Actors materialise from a small pool of homogeneous voices whose utterances legitimise the status quo. In the process, the media perpetually emphasises Muslims as the 'other'.[40]

Certain sections of the media have been swift to associate Muslims with dissent and implicate them in a clash of civilisations. By concentrating on international relations, media reporting tends to divert public interest away from domestic issues. The Palestine–Israel conflict, for instance, is rarely discussed when referring to the interests and grievances of global political Muslims, and the same applies to the realities facing different Muslim nations undergoing transformations due to social, political and economic events and realities. Underdevelopment, corruption, post-colonialism and cronyism are all associated with Islam and Muslims. This approach neutralises attempts to underscore the ongoing impacts of globalisation and neoliberalism, permitting the media to continue to concentrate on fundamentalism and extremism as the principal drivers of hostilities. By blocking out utterances rooted in dedicated objective social research, the opinions of those with vested interests in promoting the idea of Muslims as terrorists sustain the pursuits of a media wishing to keep audiences in a state of perpetual fear.[41] This in turn serves to help political elites in the pursuit of their global interests, for example after the events of 9/11 and following Western interventions in Syria in 2015.

An ongoing illustration is the question of the hijab, which frames Muslim women as suppressed by Muslim men and the Islamic faith. It has led to a public focus on the impossibility of integrating Muslims into secular liberal democracies. The hijab has been a particularly prevalent issue in France, a country that banned the *niqab* (face veil) in the 2000s. These actions convey more about France than its Muslims; in particular, how the policy characterises an entire Muslim community as unable to adhere to the norms and values of *liberté*, *égalité* and *fraternité*. Yet such a focus is inconsistent with the vast majority of French Muslim women who do not wear any kind of headscarf.[42] Disapproving representations of Islam and Muslims, therefore, reproduce the power relations between Muslims and non-Muslims, objectifying an entire community of communities. Through tokenism, selectivity and the inherent bias attuned to maintaining the status quo, the formulation of curiosity in relation to Muslims is through the frame of anxiety, dissonance and difference, affecting Muslim and non-Muslim relations in significant ways. The issue of how the media creates and enhances Islamophobia is explored in further detail in the following chapter.

4

FRAMING MUSLIMS

The concept of Islamophobia has received a considerable amount of attention from academics and policymakers. Some vehemently dispute its very existence, arguing that it masks genuine challenges within Muslim communities, while others maintain that it is as old as Islam itself, such that there has been fear of the religion since it first emerged and as part of the process of its spread first across the Middle East and then the rest of the known world.[1] The Runnymede Trust made its first attempt to define the concept of Islamophobia in 1997.[2] Since then, Islamophobia has gained both notoriety and acceptance.

In the 1990s, as the Bosnian War raged on, with various parts of the Muslim world in flames in localised disputes, parties in Algeria and the Sudan began to adopt Islamist ideas.[3] As the Western world moved beyond the Cold War, the Islamic world was presented as a major threat, propounded by thinkers such as Bernard Lewis, Francis Fukuyama and Samuel Huntington, all variously sponsoring the idea of a clash of civilisations, albeit in slightly different ways.[4] But while Islamophobia captures a moment in time, reflecting on the related concept of anti-Semitism, there are problems with the term itself.[5] First, for too many, the notion evokes the idea of some 'irrational' fear of Islam—but observable, realisable, measurable and evidential processes and outcomes define this fear or dread of Islam, not mere conjecture. Second, the extension here is that the term is presented as a descriptive concept, used to recognise a general fear of the religion rather than it being an analytical or theoretical category in its own right. Third, while omitting the analytical and focusing on the illustrative, the term characterises a whole host of general experiences but reduces them to a descriptive concept without advancing their relationship to historical encounters or contemporary politics. The reality of Islamophobia has local and global effects that have implications for society and politics, and there has accordingly been a widespread debate over definitions, categorisations and discussions on the nature of the idea of Islamophobia.[6] Yet what is important is the ways in which Islamophobia affects the lives of people and its implications for how we think about the reality of the Muslim experience in the West.[7]

Islamophobia has many manifestations. It is partly based on hostility to immigration. Other elements include misunderstanding Muslims as monolithic and monocultural—including the idea of Islam as culturally, intellectually and emotionally opposed to the European 'self'.[8] The view that Muslims are not simply a threat to multiculturalism but also a danger to the security of the nation has served to reinforce many aspects of Islamophobia.[9] This perspective largely emerged in response to the terrorism carried out during the 2000s in various parts of Western Europe, including the Netherlands, Spain, the UK, Germany and France, and since the rise and fall of ISIS as a territorial entity in the period between 2014 and 2019. Another element of Islamophobia is that it reflects a particular situation related to the politics of empire, especially in the context of US foreign policy. Islamophobia in the United States is an increasingly recognisable phenomenon, creating alarm within certain quarters, particularly within the academy but also among wider society as a whole. Islamophobia is the clearest manifestation of anti-Muslim racism realised in the US social fabric since 9/11.[10] While enmity between Muslims and the 'other' based on present manifestations of politics exists historically, there have also been positive relations between the Muslim world and other civilisations. However, memories are selective and emotions easily swayed.

The ideological nature of anti-Muslim discourse in the British media has resulted from the power of dominant media capital, held in ever fewer hands, which often seeks to castigate British Muslims by presenting an explicitly negative view of Islam. This has been especially noticeable since the Iranian Revolution of 1979 and the end of the Cold War that effectively came with the fall of the Berlin Wall in 1989. The media plays a central role in providing people in society with a portrayal of encounters and events that happen beyond our immediate social experience. As such, it has a powerful role in including or excluding social content, and where content 'doesn't happen, it is made, it is a socially manufactured product'.[11] The media is responsible for the creation of 'folk devils' and 'moral panics'. Groups in marginal economic and social positions become targets for stereotyping, with their actions placed outside explicitly defined boundaries[12]—'news media in general and the press in particular are crucially involved in the reproduction of elite racism'.[13] Newspapers and television as well as individual journalists are dependent on other elite groups who define the dominant view, especially as minority journalists are poorly represented within the media as a whole.

Islamophobia is a well-established fear in European history. Since the genesis of Islam in the seventh century, awareness of Muslims in Europe has been fraught with negative perceptions, trepidation and apprehension. Throughout the history of Western European contact with Muslims, established powers have often framed Islam and Muslims in the worst possible light. In part, this was to prevent conversions to Islam, but it was also to propel the inhabitants of Europe to resist Muslim forces at their borders. The central characteristic of this period, as is also found in the current climate, is the representation of the 'other' in a negative light in order to aggrandise established powers and legitimise existing systems of domination and subordination. The negative representation of Islam and Muslims can thus be seen as a variant of pre-existing historical discourses, with perceptions and conceptions of Islam in Britain and in the West formed over centuries of contact. While there have been periods of learning and understanding by the West, ignorance, conflict and demonisation are the norms today.[14] Acceptance of the most outrageous myths has become normalised, with Muslims branded as barbaric, unenlightened and closed-minded. Terrorists or intolerant religious zealots are the other prevailing themes. As much as Islamophobia in modern times relies on history to fill the substance of its stereotypes, the fear of Muslims has its own contemporary idiosyncratic features, which connect it to the recent histories of colonialism, immigration, xenophobia and racism.

In Britain, the immigration and settlement of Muslims, and their seemingly alien culture, is often regarded as having diluting British culture in much of the current media framing. This media focus comes at a time when economic and social differences in British society are at an all-time high. In order to prevent the dilution of their own identities, Muslims have sought to maintain their own faith and culture. Yet the more this occurs, the less society perceives Muslims to be part of it. In many ways, the collapse of communism in the Soviet Union and Eastern Europe has left an ideological vacuum that the spectre of Islam has filled.[15] In *Orientalism*, his seminal work on the Western construction of the Oriental and Islamic other, Said claimed that 'knowledge gives power, more power requires more knowledge, and so on in an increasingly profitable dialectic of information and control'.[16] Orientalism was thus a means of 'cultural domination' by which the Orient and Orientals could be contained and misrepresented, constructed through a power relationship in which the West is unconditionally dominant. The Orient is a Western construct made for Western purposes, but it also reveals a fear of a confrontation between East and West, 'even when the Orient has uniformly been considered an inferior part of the world, it has always been endowed both with greater size and with a greater potential for power (usually destructive) than the West'.[17] Furthermore, 'Oriental culture', trapped in a state of eternal stagnation, is viewed as primitive and backward—left on its own, the 'East' would degenerate into despotism and corruption. The main traits of the Orientalist stereotype are the irrationality, violence, cruelty and barbarism of the East, which has come to symbolise 'terror, devastation, the demonic, hordes of hated barbarians'.[18] Images of 'bearded Mullahs', 'violent extremists' holding guns and a focus on the political instability of Muslim societies and their treatment of women are 'echoes of the medieval polemic'.[19]

Muslim commentators often start from the premise that the media deliberately demonises them, criticising the media for simplifications and generalisations. This charge of media bias is a serious issue. Coverage of extremist groups and Islamic terrorism has increased since the 2000s, as a result of which Islamic words have entered into universal journalistic vocabulary but with new meanings that are generally aggressive and extremist. Apocalyptic headlines across many sectors of the media use such words as 'violent extremist' and 'radicalisation' without nuance. This creates the impression of an organised and coherent army of bloodthirsty agents mounting a universal conspiracy against British norms and values. Such a perspective castigates all Islamic movements as originating from the same root and as being equally hostile to the West. Cultural differences, previously unknown or communicated second-hand by travellers or scholars, are projected on to screens in homes and on mobile devices, leading to perceptions of an 'alien culture' and the threat of a cultural and religious invasion. Raising defensive barriers has become the norm in an effort to maintain a coherent identity.[20]

Negative representations of Islam and British Muslims in social and mainstream media today are not a new phenomenon but are a variant of pre-existing discourses and narratives.[21] From the collapse of the Byzantine Empire through to the crusades and the colonial period up to the present day, specific images of Islam and Muslims have served to frame and cement a 'common-sense' view of Islam.[22] 'The Rushdie Affair' that began in 1988 with the publication of Salman Rushdie's novel *The Satanic Verses* and the 'book burning in Bradford' in the following year, together with the now infamous fatwa declared by the late Ayatollah Khomeini, continues to have important implications for discussions of religion, culture, identity, faith and the nature of diverse societies. The Rushdie Affair encouraged the view that British Muslims are committed to extreme ways to express their discomfort. The lampooning of British Muslims during this episode was especially prevalent in newspapers.[23] It was based on a 'perceived threat to a particular ideological structure, a cultural hierarchy organised by an essential Englishness, which defined British identity'.[24] Such is the legacy of this episode in British history that the questions it raised on how to deal with the challenges of diversity, inter-faith dialogue, tolerance and co-existence remain as important as ever.

Islamophobia coheres with its medieval, imperial, colonial and post-1945 equivalents through to the modern day. But Muslims across the globe are ill prepared to defend themselves from this 'onslaught'. Innovations in communication technology have developed rapidly, making it easier to reinforce popular stereotypes of the Muslim while continuing to highlight areas of conflict and confusion. A newfound contempt for Islam and Muslims has come to define this offensive across the globe. Certain sections of the media are effectively reacting to demands from readers, with local and global events being used in such a way as to shape further negative content. In doing so, parts of the media use approving language when referring to white English groups while directly or indirectly implying that Muslims are responsible for their own problems, rarely, if ever, highlighting real and observable patterns of racial and ethnic disadvantage. The right-leaning press seeks to portray incidences of 'black crime' and 'Islamic political militancy' rather than the economic, social and educational disadvantage experienced by the vast majority of British Muslims. Such reports rarely discuss the historical context of ethnic relations in Britain, still less the legacy of exploitation or colonial and imperial rule over India, Africa and the Caribbean.[25] In this simplistic narrative, Muslims are portrayed as reluctant to integrate into British society, as a threat to an essential Englishness, and thus antithetical to the principles of an Anglo-Christian Britain.

A range of events took place in the 2000s that help to provide a number of insights into the negative framing of Muslims, a process further enabled by developments in various media communication technologies, particularly social media. The media has played an important role in manufacturing Islamophobia—as an aspect of elite racism in particular—and in subsequently magnifying it on a global scale.[26] In September 2005, the satirical Danish magazine *Jyllands-Posten* published twelve cartoons depicting the Prophet Muhammad. The aim was to highlight how artists were self-censoring in order to avoid negative reactions from Muslims. This became a self-fulfilling prophecy when the reactions to the cartoons affirmed the premise the magazine was trying to illustrate. The event became a global controversy that had significant implications for Muslim and non-Muslim relations. At the time, the Iraq War was in full flow and a whole host of cases relating to torture, abuse of prisoners and extraordinary rendition were creating alarm across different sectors of society.[27] The controversy over the publication of the twelve cartoons depicting Prophet Muhammad in 2005, and then again in 2006, affirmed the deep-seated malaise at the heart of Muslim and non-Muslim relations in Western Europe.

The Danish magazine that published the cartoons, as well as the other European presses that subsequently republished them, sought to justify doing so on the grounds that it was a form of commentary on the apparent self-censorship that had seemingly gripped reporting on sensitive issues on Muslims in Western European contexts. The aim was to engage in meaningful debate through satire,[28] in much the same way as political cartoons have been used in Western newspapers for over a hundred years and, more recently, in Muslim newspapers, too. Using humour constructively is of course a valid way to depict politically sensitive issues of the day. However, what was distinctive about these twelve cartoons was that they sought to caricature the Prophet in stereotypically negative terms by referring to violence and other reactionary modes of being.[29]

Of the twelve cartoons, most were simply unamusing, but one or two did capture attention and provided a humorous outlook on a sensitive topic without physically denigrating the Prophet. Not all of the cartoons featured the Prophet. Debate, discussion and endless media chatter focused on the idea that two processes were in play. One suggested that freedom of expression should not be denied to artists, writers and journalists wishing to cover sensitive issues in order to raise awareness—if an audience does not wish to engage with the topic, they are free to ignore it. This is similar to the notion that if someone feels a book might offend, then they can avoid reading it, an issue that had already been raised in the aftermath of *The Satanic Verses* over a decade and a half earlier. It is well known that many who demonstrated or engaged in the 'book burnings in Bradford' may not have read the book, or were directed largely by local Islamic leaders compelled to react based on religious zeal.[30] The other main argument put forward by critics of the cartoonists and indeed of the *Satanic Verses* is the idea that while freedom of expression is an important right, should there not be a limit placed on this to curb the freedom to offend?[31]

Any notion of freedom of expression cannot be realised without some degree of associated responsibility. For some, this is what the Danes, followed by five other European newspapers, had failed to appreciate. Satire is acceptable, but representation of the Prophet, positive or negative, is not permissible in Sunni Islam. *Jyllands-Posten* surely knew this when it first published the cartoons in September 2005, having first received a backlash from eleven Muslim European ambassadors.[32] What, then, drove a whole host of other Western European publications to do the same? Clearly, they sought a reaction and one that seemingly confirmed the underlying message in publishing the cartoons in the first place: that Islam and Muslims are reactionary, bigoted and violent. This in turn became the reality when young men, disillusioned and disaffected, took to the streets in aggressive protests, confirming the original premise. Intransigent mullahs, clerics and faith leaders encouraged their devotees to rise up, especially in Egypt and Syria.[33] Any Muslim action that was confrontational, to any degree, was picked up by the media and used as evidence to support the increasingly negative views held on Islam and Muslims.

In an atmosphere of mistrust, misrepresentation and misinformation, the initial publication and the subsequent republication of the cartoons demonstrated an unfortunate lack of judgement, perhaps even a deliberate attempt to provoke already disenfranchised, isolated and disempowered groups. At the time, Western Europe was still reeling from the effects of the Madrid bombings and the murder of Theo van Gogh in March and November 2004. Seen in this context, the editorial decision to publish the cartoons was tantamount to indirectly inciting religious hatred. The newspapers fanned the flames that were spreading across Europe.[34] But the subsequent reaction by (some misinformed) Muslims was misplaced and narrow-minded, as they fell for the trap set for them. None of the actions led to any meaningful dialogue. Instead, the episode provided radical right groups with further ammunition while polarising debate among wavering liberals and leftists.

The publication of the *Satanic Verses* had profound implications for the ways in which the positions and experiences of Muslim minorities in Britain and in the West would be seen for the foreseeable future, and the events stemming from the 2005/6 publication of the cartoons ensured that this legacy would continue to endure. The Rushdie book led to a new focus on the Muslim presence in Britain; however, it did so in a fundamentally negative and reductive way. As much as there was and is huge diversity among the Muslims of the West, the dominant media and political discourse invariably characterises this group in essentialist and homogenised terms. With ongoing global conflicts involving Muslim nations and peoples, and with the events of 9/11 in the United States and 7/7 in Britain, much has continued to remain the same. Those who regard religion as a negative force while endorsing a secular, liberal and democratic outlook have sometimes defined themselves in opposition to 'Muslimness', which in reality is the experience of minority groups vying for recognition, acceptability, equality and fairness. The war on terror is presented as a choice between a Muslim East and a Christian West, adding to the realisation of a globalised dynamic that affects people directly due to the forces of liberalised broadcasting markets and the internet.

An 'us' versus 'them' approach has consequently come to prevail in the media, which has served to accentuate and exacerbate underlying social and cultural divisions. The media does not neutrally report or present a fair view of the world but shapes popular sentiment, increasingly through social media. Accordingly, the portrayal of Islam in overtly negative terms has resulted in a change in attitude and behaviour for all. Virtuous news rarely spreads, while damaging reports spread exceptionally fast. A concentration on difference is increasingly replacing an emphasis on sameness. As Western nations develop a profoundly critical relationship with religions, an Islamophobic discourse is taking hold, with Muslims falling for a ploy established by neoliberal and neoconservative European elites.[35]

In early 2006, I was in Indonesia delivering lectures and attending meetings organised by the British Council as part of an effort to improve the image of British Islam. I saw first-hand the demonstrations objecting to the publication of the Danish cartoons. These rallies were peaceful, well organised and focused on the idea of there being limits to freedom of expression. In 2012, I was again in Indonesia, this time spending a month or so in the city of Jakarta at the Graduate School of the State Islamic University, when another major controversy came to the fore, and I was able to witness yet another set of demonstrations. On this occasion, the controversy stemmed from anti-Islamic YouTube film, *The Innocence of Muslims*, which was first broadcast on 11 September 2012.[36] Local television news reported on mass rallies, demonstrations and violent behaviour from a number of Muslim communities all over the world. Indonesian television reported violence in Pakistan, suggesting that the whole country was on fire in response to the film. Rioting, looting and destruction were the scenes depicted. Media platforms in the UK looked towards moderates and asked why Muslim leaders did not speak up to prevent the violence at times like this.

As Western media questioned the middle ground for lacking intent, all the while focusing on the violent fringes, media in the East did much the same. The basic premise was that the 'moderates'— i.e. most Muslims—are silent, which is far from accurate because those who have the power simply choose not to listen. Few hear the voices of calm and reason when many different agendas define the extremism debate. Fear is a means of social control, in which 'news' is increasingly used to keep audiences gripped in a state of anxiety while they await further 'news updates', supposedly to calm their anxieties.[37] So-called extremist Muslims comprise a tiny minority, yet the issue of 'Muslim extremism' is nevertheless presented as one of the major threats to Western society.[38] Have Western nations reached the limits of toleration?[39] Communities react to the impediments they face as they reach a tipping point, at which juncture nation states respond with further illiberalism and intolerance, whether it is towards the working classes, minorities or disgruntled ethno-religious groups. This applies in the West as well as to the East. Globalisation has eroded the territories once held by nation states, now replaced by fractured identities, tribalism and localism. In such settings, the interests of the dominant few have taken hold, perpetuating the cycle. This problem is further compounded as Western economies struggle to compete globally while maintaining social cohesion at a national level. In the East, similar processes are at play in Muslim-majority nation states that mimic systems of domination and authority originally devised by the West.

In the UK, at around the same time as the *Innocence of Muslims* demonstrations were being held across the world, many British Muslims spoke out against a Channel 4 documentary on the early formation of Islam made by Tom Holland, as well as a BBC sitcom entitled *Citizen Khan*. The former was criticised because of its lack of academic independence and omission of early Islamic sources, whereas the latter was seen by some as perpetuating a stereotype of Pakistanis with roots in antiquated 1970s British television humour.[40] Channel 4, the producers and broadcasters of the Holland programme, pulled a private screening due to security fears, creating the impression that Muslims were seeking to restrict freedom of speech, while the opposition of many to *Citizen Khan* was viewed in some quarters as evidence that Pakistani Muslims lacked a sense of humour. Both examples evoked and sustained the crude subtext that Muslims are intolerant, bigoted and reactionary. The human need for the construction of the 'other' as a way of self-identification and self-assurance is a universal one,[41] yet it ultimately foments racism, prejudice, hatred, and, in the most extreme of cases, violence. Repressed desires and frustrations, whether conscious or unconscious, are projected on to the 'other' as scapegoats. The depictions of Muslims as evil, irrational, barbaric and lecherous are a way to deny the presence of these impulses in the 'self' in Western society. In contrast, Muslims emphasise the secularism of the West, its immorality, materialism and delinquency as a way of denying that they too might have such 'evil' desires. It is thus important to understand the nature of Islamophobia in the media; however, doing so would be incomplete without a thorough grounding of the idea of Islamophobia as racism itself. This follows in the next chapter.

5

ISLAMOPHOBIA AS NEW RACISM

Racism has long been present in Britain, and it has persisted in the post-war period, shifting from an explicitly racialist discourse to include a focus on culture and the religious practices of ethnic minorities. Unlike the racism directed at black people, which is primarily based on the colour of their skin, anti-Muslim racism is based on perceived cultural relativism and the presumption of potential radicalisation on the part of conservative Muslim groups. Elite actors have sought to construct a conflict narrative between far-right and 'Muslim extremist' groups, using the oppositional positions taken by mutually competing groups to reinforce reductive discourses on the threat of extremism and the apparent failures of multiculturalism. Islamophobia and Occidentophobia sustain a national and international hegemon that objectifies working-class and 'underclass' groups in order to reinforce existing local and global ethnic and class relations. In reality, both positions reflect the struggles of economic marginalisation, cultural exclusion, political alienation and social anomie specific to each group.[1]

The previous chapter's examination of the media's role in manufacturing, sustaining and reinforcing Islamophobia suggested that the problems are deeply entrenched in a range of institutions. The focus in this chapter is on the ways in which Islamophobia can also be seen as a form of structural racism, where the anti-Muslim dynamic reveals itself not merely in terms of misrecognition and misrepresentation but in the physical manifestation of outcomes that have deleterious consequences for groups in society already facing the weight of 'othering'. The growth of the radical right is a consequence of Islamophobia, but it also has the implication of recreating Islamophobia, as the radical right does not merely reinforce an existing political discourse; it also generates anti-Muslim sentiment among groups seeking violent, vengeful retribution against Muslims. The cultural and the structural interactions of Islamophobia feed into different radicalisations of the radical right as well as Islamist extremist groups. An elite discourse depicts social conflict at the bottom of society as mirrored misrepresentations of each other, omitting their shared characteristics. Such is the nature of racial and class formations in Britain today.

In thinking through the issues on British Islam and Muslims in Britain, one of the first topics that caught my attention occurred in the 1980s. Known as the Honeyford Affair, the controversy centred on the utterances of a disgruntled head teacher, Roy Honeyford, who criticised multiculturalism and its effect on British education in terms that were described as borderline racist. But was Honeyford racist or correct in calling out the need for Muslim integration through and in education?[2] Alternatively, should an anti-racist multicultural education cater for differences, providing opportunities to celebrate those differences as part of a collective national psyche? The controversy erupted during a period when there was a growing disparity between the home lives of Muslim children and practices within schools in parts of Bradford where the outrage surfaced.[3] However, the incident was not a peculiar local anxiety, as swathes of the British Muslim community, especially Muslims in the Midlands and in the North, were suffering the deleterious consequences of deindustrialisation and automation. Their lives were moving in the opposite direction from that of wider society. With Thatcherism came financial deregulation and the liberalisation of markets through global trade and financial exchange. Moving farther apart became the dominant paradigm during this period, but it was also indicative of something deeply problematic. To some extent, the episode can be seen as the beginning of an attack on political correctness and on the race equality or race relations sector. It was only a matter of time until the dismantling of these systems, originally established to keep racist, sexist and homophobic individuals and institutions in check.[4]

In 1999, seven UK-born Pakistani Muslims, implicated in the kidnapping of foreign tourists and a plot to bomb the British embassy and a nightclub in Sanaa, the capital of Yemen, served around five years each in a prison in Yemen. Soon after, the events of 9/11 took place. The world today continues to live with the implications of this event and the ensuing war on terror. The present urgency is over Islamophobia, which has increased dramatically since these events and is based on the widespread perception that the problem of violent extremism is a problem within Islam itself. This was reflected in the British response to 7/7, when four British-born Muslims hailing from Bradford were implicated in the London suicide bombings of three tube stations and a bus. In the aftermath of the incident, Prime Minister Tony Blair announced that the 'rules of the game' were to change,[5] and the 'Prevent' policy subsequently became the main means for engagement, community-development and countering violent extremism in UK counterterrorism policy.

Prevent is the community-facing dynamic of the UK government's counter-extremism strategy. Despite being in existence since 2006, there is only limited public knowledge of its effectiveness. For many, Prevent conflates legitimate political resistance among young British Muslims with the likelihood of violent extremism, thereby providing credence to critics who argue that the policy is a form of social engineering.[6] Beginning with the Blair era, the policy approach has focused on ideology as the root cause of extremism. Since 2015, Prevent has been a statutory duty affecting numerous public sector institutions, including education and the health services. But academia, civil society and government are unable to come to terms with their disagreements over its precise aims and application.[7] Since the war on terror and 7/7, questions of terrorism, radicalism and the sociocultural realities of British Muslims are usually spoken about in the same breath, now heightened due to a number of issues occurring in more recent years, including the rise and now decline of ISIS, the Syrian refugee crises, the predicaments facing the Eurozone after the global collapse of

2008 and the rising levels of populism that have resulted in outcomes such as Brexit and the election of Donald Trump in 2016. Though this populism is opposed to difference, immigrants and anything regarded as 'other', it is also specifically anti-Islam. This opposition to Islam and Muslims is not individualised, but is instead opposed to the collective concept of Islam itself.

Counterterrorism, conceived as an overarching framework, seeks to create a set of policies and interventions that deal with terrorism through active counter-narratives, as well as operational matters of security, policing and intelligence. Counter-extremism, on the other hand, is the notion of building community resilience and capability to defend and counteract problematic ideas that are viewed as posing a threat to national security. When a young person wears a hijab or adopts different attitudes towards certain norms and values, it is usually deemed as acceptable, but when they decide to withdraw altogether from their peer groups, it suggests that something far more complex is going on. Prevent should come into its own as an assessment tool, separating conservative social behaviour from actions that reflect a problematic outcome. But the reality is that most cases referred to the Channel safeguarding programme within Prevent are of merely frustrated young people who need direction and a cause in life. No policy is perfect, and it is no surprise that professionals working within the framework of supporting the delivery of Prevent in their local areas regard it as imperfect, in need of revision, restructuring and rebranding. The lack of public engagement on Prevent until 2019, however, has created mistrust, leading to disengagement on the part of the public with respect to the state.

Since the 1990s, the discourse surrounding integration has shifted in a new direction. Multiculturalism has been discarded yet without being fully tested or applied, while integration now means assimilation— much as it did in the 1950s and 1960s, or indeed until the 'liberal hour' (i.e. the late 1960s). Muslim groups are only visible through the lens of religion, but instead of supporting Muslim groups to achieve better integration through social mobility and equality of opportunity, the focus is on Islam as the unit of change—an entire religion, not its people. Where does all this leave Muslim minorities, of which there are more than 30 million in Western Europe and around 3 million in

Britain? Where does it place the role and position of Islam in the public sphere? Since the Rushdie Affair and the fall of the Berlin Wall, both of which occurred almost simultaneously, the desire had been to see differences as bounded by culture, ethnicity and even heritage, but not by religion, or specifically Islam. But Islam is now viewed as an alien monolith. Coupled with the socioeconomic inequalities facing all in society, alienated, marginalised and voiceless groups, both white and Muslim, are battling against each other, often for the least in society.[8]

When 9/11 happened shortly after the race-related riots in the North of England, the official government response sought to build community cohesion—and wholly abandon all concerns relating to ethnic equality.[9] Difference, of a kind, was tolerated, but ensuring that different individuals achieve equality of opportunity and equality of outcome was virtually eliminated from any social policy discourse. The language of containing Muslim identity politics—even voices that seek to resist domestic and foreign policy failures—had become the norm. By its very nature, the Prevent policy, depicted as an enabling force, is in effect a disabler of all other debates concerning Muslims in Britain. Prevent focuses on Muslims only through the reshaping of the Islamic presence in society, but such an approach is intrinsically flawed—and disingenuous—as it misunderstands Islam by homogenising, essentialising and reducing it to an immutable other. The collective shapes Islam, not the individual; however, attempts made by the state to engineer it for the population as a whole have resulted only in present-day political elites focusing on the few at the expense of the many. This has also led to a narrow understanding of Islam in the popular imagination due to an incessant focus on its supposed association with conflict and violence. Although there are a few prominent Muslim figures who do bridge the gaps between media, politics and society, they generally do so at the behest of the state. These opportunities are held in the hands of older men who are often out of touch with the needs and wants of the world today, and especially with the aspirations of the Muslim youth and millennials who are comfortable with diversity but uncomfortable with authoritarianism.

In effect, there are two competing forces that need to be considered here. One element of society is seeking to reduce Islam into a restricted space, while those who garner credit for their apparent authority over it stifle those who are trying to expand Islam from within the faith, creating malaise, discord and stagnation. The West's struggle with its post-Cold War future signals an opportunity but also risks. In reality, British Muslims are not fully in control of managing the idea of British Islam, as these challenges are beyond the ability of British Muslims to define it on their own, for now. The disturbing rise of populism plays on Islamophobia, but more worryingly, its reach has also extended into popular culture and mainstream politics. The anger and frustration felt by a significant and growing body of Muslims in the inner-city areas is likely to continue, and this is where most of the challenges will remain.

Various acts of terrorism throughout Western Europe since 2010 have led to a renewed focus on Islamophobia and its associated concerns. This mutually reinforcing discourse has perpetuated Islamic extremism as a reality of the religious norms and values associated with Muslim minorities in Western Europe. Outlier Muslim groups hold specific anti-Western attitudes that have caused them to disengage from wider society, further deepening their associations with a problematic religio-cultural identity that serves to set them apart from the mainstream. The forces of English elitism and classism are perpetuating a perennial conflict between different sectors of the working class and the 'underclass' of British society. The ideological concerns that affect white working-class youth and British-born Muslim minorities relate to issues of national and local identity, social opportunity and mobility, economic marginalisation, political disenfranchisement and cultural alienation. In effect, both groups experience the same kinds of issues, generated by an elite discourse that is internalised by the groups in question, which in turn regard their relative counterparts within the same oppositional framework, further legitimising existing modes of domination and subordination.[10]

Many question the efficacy of racism as a concept, with some claiming that the term itself has largely disappeared from the popular vernacular when seeking to understand differences in society. Rather than race, there is currently a greater focus on notions such as British values. Race has largely disappeared from the agenda, not by accident but by design. Anti-racism had its heyday in the late 1970s; by the 1980s, multiculturalism was the principal buzzword when discussing ethnicity and race and the policies that should be implemented in response. But while multiculturalism has raised awareness of difference, in practice it does not target racism, structural discrimination or ethnic inequality. After 9/11 and 7/7, multiculturalism has been reduced to a security agenda that isolates Muslims and immigrant groups. The conundrum today is that Muslims are treated as a racial group, where anti-Islam hatred enhances the defining characteristic of racism. Racism is not the same as racialism, which is the idea that all humans are tribalistic. A strong undercurrent in the current climate indicates it is acceptable to be anti-racist, but there are Muslim-specific issues that worry 'us' about their 'values', resulting in blindness to the deeper factors of structural discrimination and the inevitable focus on culture, or multiculture, as a means to fight racism, which is almost impossible because racism or indeed equality is not about culture. This Islamophobia as a newfound anti-Muslim structural racism has become the dominant hegemon that divides 'us' and 'them'—it is an implicit misrecognition of Muslim minorities in Western Europe.[11] This Islamophobia drives far-right social, community and political activism right across Western Europe. From the EDL, Britain First and National Action in Britain, to the National Front in France, to the Party for Freedom in the Netherlands, to the Northern League in Italy, to the Pax Europa Citizen's Movement in Germany, far-right groups have entered the popular imagination both locally and nationally.[12] Anti-Semitism is a related concept as an ideology of hate that permeates society.[13] Thus, the racialisation of Muslims through the political manufacture of Muslims as monsters goes beyond 'managing Muslim extremists' to the more general signifier of 'Muslim as extremist'.[14]

The EDL was formed in 2009. Its founding members, originally from the town of Luton, had witnessed a demonstration by angry young Muslims against the return of British soldiers. Local white English groups felt that the city was being penetrated by radical Islamism. The EDL promotes Islamophobia by claiming that the 'Islamification' of Britain and Europe is growing to such an extent that the only solution is the repression of Islam and Muslims—a thesis commonly propagated by many other far-right groups across Western Europe. In part, the EDL emerged out of the failure of the BNP, which effectively disintegrated due to internal struggles for power.[15] The leader of the EDL shortly after its foundation, Tommy Robinson, courted publicity for his organisation until August 2013 when he stepped down from the position due to mounting concerns about his criminal record as well as internal discord within the organisation itself. In January 2014, Robinson and a number of close associates were imprisoned for mortgage fraud. Today, Robinson continues to be involved with various groups that are regularly criticised for inciting hatred,[16] including being actively championed by UKIP in late 2018, thereby associating an anti-EU movement with wider projections of hate towards Islam and Muslims founded on cultural Islamophobia.

Attention is often devoted to the ways in which Muslim minority groups have used the lens of religion and culture to mobilise society, but these groups ultimately operate within the political landscape, where new political representations emerge alongside limited opportunities for integration. But it is impossible to eliminate the role of the state in the reproduction of elite racism. Racism is not the preserve of far-right groups. Nations imagine their identities. The construction of the nation is based on the selective memories of the origins of nations.[17] Ever since the economic downturn that began in 2008, there has been a growing tendency among certain sections of the media to project Britain's supposedly glorious past, a narrative in which Britain is presented as facing a defining moment from within and without, much of which also led to the Brexit vote in 2016.[18] The crisis of capitalism has led to illiberal policies on the part of seemingly liberal plural democracies.[19] Seen against this backdrop, the racism British Muslims and other ethnic minorities experience can be understood as part of a dominant worldview that intersects capitalism with racism: 'Islamophobia, like other racisms, can be colour-coded: it can be biological (normally associated with skin colour). But it can also be cultural (not necessarily associated with skin colour), or it can be a mixture of both.'[20] The resurgence of Orientalism combined with the current approach to Islamophobia has fused with imperialism and US foreign policy in the Middle East. Islam and Muslims, cast in reductionist and essentialist terms, evoke a sense of imminent danger from a seemingly primitive body of people and their ways. This framing has grown since 9/11, and it remains an ongoing phenomenon in the domestic and foreign politics of the United States.[21]

In the midst of the material challenges facing young men in British society today, concerns have emerged over hyper-masculine behaviours, both among those on the far right and by some British Muslim men. As such, 'jihadis' and the far right are similar in this regard, where differences in religion and culture of 'the other' are problematised and subsequently politicised. This process focuses on questions of identity, exploited through elite discourse—and at the bottom of society for former working-class groups and the offspring of immigrant groups. Hyper-masculinity encourages the need for young people to prove themselves—to seek recognition—to become somebody. An elite media and political discourse creates and sustains these oppositional perspectives between two sets of groups in society that are effectively suffering from the same sets of social, economic and political problems, thus fuelling Islamophobia and exploiting the social cleavages facing young men. At the heart of the issue is the need for elites to maintain their position while othering others. In reality, there tends to be a far more positive negotiation between seemingly conflictual norms and values, and it is precisely a sense of positive Britishness, European-ness or American-ness that encourages young Muslims to speak out and critically engage with a discourse that focuses on their apparent inability to be assimilated into broader society.[22] While most Muslims associate to some degree with a particular faith identity, the vast majority are in favour of integration, and foreign policy is a marginal issue in their daily lives.[23] A positive approach to improving ethnic and cultural relations with majority groups has become a distinct focus for Muslim minority communities in the North of England in particular—a body of people subject to negative attention given the race riots of 2001 and the ongoing problems of deindustrialisation and economic marginalisation facing the region.[24]

Although the subject of Islamophobia has attracted a great deal of interest, the concept itself has suffered from a lack of classification and categorisation. For some, Islamophobia is a step between an outcome and a process, where the latter includes history as well as contemporary politics, and the former relates to patterns of social life measured as distinct issues of racial, cultural and religious discrimination. There is also an analytical and ideological gap between conceptualisation, perception and realisation.[25] For others, the ambiguity of the concept is its strength, as Islamophobia takes many different shapes and forms depending on context. They have different local and global manifestations located within specific intellectual, political, cultural and social ontologies.[26] Other scholars have come to focus on Islamophobia's relationship with existing patterns of xenophobia, Orientalism and imperialism that affect liberal plural democracies and constructions of multiculturalism found within them.[27] The challenge of tackling Islamophobia, despite the problems involved in classifying it as a concept, is not one that Muslims can undertake on their own. Muslim groups must work with other religious minority groups facing comparable levels of discrimination, intimidation, violence, exclusion and racialisation, helping to reduce the likelihood of counter-competing narratives and wasting resources and political opportunities.[28] Today's Europe is experiencing a sense of disconnection from this historic construction of a continental identity because of associations made with extremism and violence regarding Islam and Muslims. The irony, however, is that the presence of Muslim minorities in Europe is helping to redefine Europe, recreating European-ness, and thereby reconfiguring notions of national identities.[29]

———•———

In June 2017, Grenfell Tower in North Kensington, West London, went up in flames, killing over seventy people in the process. Many of the victims were Black Muslims who were not on the radar of immigration or welfare services. Shortly after this tragic event, Darren Osborne deliberately drove into worshippers who were leaving late evening prayers on a balmy June night. Arguably, Osborne would not have been radicalised to carry out this act if Muslims did not encounter demonisation in the media on a daily basis. In his own words, he had no motivation other than wanting to 'kill all Muslims'. As a result of his actions, he was convicted of the murder of Makram Ali and the attempted murder of several others. Directed towards specific ethnic, religious or racial minority or majority groups, the murderous intent of terrorists derives from hate. Otherwise, any 'mentally ill', 'unemployed loner' or a 'drifter' with a history of domestic violence or abuse towards others could seemingly carry out these acts of violence. In under-exposing the objective explanations behind the political or ideological motivations underlying such attacks, this narrative suggests there is a far greater demographic capable of such acts. But the description of Islamism, portrayed as thriving among radicalised Muslims who use it to legitimise violence, avoids all nuance. In the case of far-right extremists, not only is there limited recognition of the wide-ranging problem of far-right extremism and terrorism, over-emphasising the 'loner' angle is a useful distraction from implicating the wider negative structural and cultural forces at play. Meanwhile, Islamophobia has become normalised in society to such an extent that even to evoke it is to suggest that those who seek to challenge it, in particular Muslims, are being disingenuous, at best, or downright treacherous, at worst.[30]

In reporting on responses to attacks, the media often intimates that Islamist extremists are purely ideological, while English or other white ethnic majority individuals have social and psychological problems. This suggests a general degree of acceptance on the part of society that their violence towards Muslims is somehow legitimate—i.e. because of something that Muslims espouse or adhere to, such as their faith, or because they are somehow responsible, as an entire faith community, for the actions of a limited few. Orientalism, scientific racism and now racialisation based on ethnic, cultural and religious categories suggest institutionalised Islamophobia, wholesale, widespread, menacing and omnipotent. Islamophobia takes attention away from structural racism, which further institutionalises Islamophobia. A deeper understanding of Muslim differences in society would reorient the counterterrorism/countering violent extremism space, while Muslims outside of this realm are not only rendered homogenous but, crucially, invisible.[31] This homogeneity is not open-ended, diverse or layered with class, racial, sectarian and cultural characteristics but is instead based on a more sinister representation of Muslims as threats to the social fabric itself. Engagement with Muslims is restricted to a focus on problems seemingly emanating from a Muslim cosmos. Relegating anti-Muslim hatred to the realm of counterterrorism further absolves the state from having responsibility towards Muslims in society.

Islamophobia is the normalisation of the anti-Muslim hatred that has grown exponentially since the onset of the war on terror. During this period, intolerance, bigotry and the development of alt-right, far-right, radical left and other religious extremist groups have found succour in the vacuum of the dominant discourses. These cumulative extremisms at the margins of society serve to incubate the discourses of intolerance and hate that allow these subgroups and their ideas to foment. Radicalisation and Islamophobia intimately tie with each other. Fanned by the internet, which acts as an echo chamber, there are similar fires burning in the United States and across Europe, breaking down existing weak community relations that are exacerbated by various media and political discourses that emphasise the inability of Muslim minorities to be assimilated into a host society. The number of Muslims in the West, especially in parts of Western Europe, will continue to rise relative to the indigenous population because of relatively higher birth rates. The visible residential concentrations of Muslims in parts of towns and cities creates consternation among commentators who argue that the problem of Islamisation is real, which has the effect of making majority groups even more fearful of the differences of others. That majority populations repeatedly overemphasise the numbers of Muslim minorities in their countries is no accident.[32]

The events surrounding the Grenfell Tower tragedy reaffirmed the state's neoliberal, majoritarian nationalist, anti-immigration, anti-European and anti-Muslim narrative, one defined by years of neglect, allowing shoddy practices to linger, paying little or no attention to criticism of policy from other sectors of society. The programme of austerity implemented by the Conservative Party since 2010 has led to a period of instability, populism and uncertainty, in which the state has no clear idea of where to take the nation, with British Muslims relegated to a lowly position, becoming convenient scapegoats for all of society's ills.[33]

Since 9/11, not only has an Islamophobia industry emerged but also a (de)radicalisation industry orchestrated by various government agencies in an attempt to placate domestic and foreign policy critics and to focus on group differences as the cause of extremism. As part of this process, many have come forward with various initiatives to support the government in identifying the underlying causes and solutions to Islamic political radicalism.[34] These initiatives have helped to sustain the view that the problem of violent extremism rests within the religion and culture of specific groups rather than the wider workings of society,[35] taking attention away from structural disadvantage and discrimination, which are arguably more significant in driving young Muslim men in declining urban areas to forms of Islamic extremism.[36] It is possible to see these periods in the social and political history of the Global North as determining a natural rate of racism as applied to Muslims through Islamophobia and radicalisation. External to the British Muslim communities there are specific instances of anti-Muslim rhetoric that have permeated public and private institutions, political systems and a general rhetoric about an 'us' and 'them' sustained by an elite racial discourse. This narrative has sought to securitise integration and diversity as well as institutionalise the securitisation of education, the charity sector and other civil society organisations. British Muslims generally receive a poor education while experiencing high unemployment, poor health and limited housing as realisations of structural disadvantage and discrimination. Muslim communities also suffer from limited political participation and representation. These issues have grown to become more problematic since the war on terror, which has led to a structural dynamic that polices, regulates and incarcerates young Muslims who are suffering the consequences of deindustrialisation and the internationalisation of capital in much the same way as the 'left-behind' working-class groups who are also seeking urgent direction, recognition and opportunity. The causes of Islamophobia and radicalisation are related to social mobility, anomie, political disenfranchisement, a national identity crisis and neoliberal globalisation, with the effects seen in rising levels of anger, fear, loathing, intimidation and violence. This Islamophobia is therefore political, cultural and economic. It has the effect of further radicalising both Islamist and far-right groups, where the counter-competing ideological perspectives take shape at the bottom of society among groups who are competing for the least in society. The challenge is that both Islamophobia and radicalisation need to be taken seriously as a problem for society as a whole. Until then, with ongoing geopolitical concerns in the Muslim world, widening social divisions because of neoliberal globalisation and the faltering of national identities, the challenges will continue to outweigh the opportunities. The following chapter explores the global dimensions of Islamism in order to arrive at a better understanding of the wider nature of critical responses to the crises caused by neoliberal globalisation and the international political economy of supranational elites.

6

ISLAMISM *REDUX*

There are a number of explanations for the patterns of global Islamic political radicalism. Yet, thus far, little attention has been paid to the interconnected geopolitical dynamics underpinning global societies in an economic and sociological context, specifically within the Middle East and North Africa (MENA) region, including the impact of the emergence and collapse of ISIS as a territorial entity. To a certain extent, this lack of attention on the social and political problems of the countries comprising the MENA region reflects the vested interests of the Western powers that benefit from Gulf oil and various military, security and defence opportunities,[1] leaving certain Gulf States free to promote a destructive form of Islam, arguably in opposition to the Shia Islam propagated by Iran, which has its own absolutist objectives.[2] Gulf State elites have limited interest in encouraging wider society to ask critical questions, instead preferring to curb any dissent.[3] This chapter explores the nature of Islamism in detail. It analyses the nature of the global dynamic that influences the local identity formations that produce violence. The chapter also discusses how different types of Islamism have been used in an instrumental way in the pursuit of certain ends by global political actors, as not all forms of Islamism are problematic for certain societies. Some forms of Islamism provide viable opportunities to improve citizenship and engagement among otherwise critical Muslims beleaguered by geopolitical and national tensions. In this regard, Islamism needs to be read as a progressive, pro-integration and pro-secular approach to engagement and participation in society that employs core Islamic beliefs to pursue active citizenship but without violating the laws of respect, freedom and tolerance for all.

———

The Middle East as a whole suffers from considerable levels of inequality, much of which can be attributed to the colonial legacy and the inability of independent regimes to deliver on their promises of providing development and democracy.[4] Western political, economic and military policy decisions based on short-term interests have further exacerbated this dynamic. The result has been to generate resentment on the part of the most affected local communities, combined with disdain and disconnection on the part of elites in the Middle East and across the world. When analysed against this context, Islamic political radicalism can be seen as originating from three distinct sources. One is the emergence of contemporary Wahhabism, fuelled by an ideology backed by significant levels of funding, which influences vast swathes of the Middle East as well as Muslims in the diaspora. The second strand originates from the emergence of the Muslim Brotherhood, the ideology of which has had the greatest impact in Egypt and neighbouring countries. The third concerns Jamaat-e-Islami groups that have spread from South Asia to South East Asia. All three forms of Sunni Islamism share many of their concerns and ambitions, although they are invariably separated by particular political and ideological differences.[5]

There are currently over 30 million Muslims in Western Europe and around 3.5 million in the United States, populations resulting from the migration of Muslim groups in the post-war period before settling and trying to adapt to society, all the while making valuable contributions as active citizens participating in institutions.[6] But in neoliberal societies, large numbers of Muslims continue to face the brunt of exclusion and enmity from different sections of society.[7] Western European political elites, especially those on the right of the political spectrum, are able to place the blame for all society's woes at the door of these most 'othered' of others.[8] Because of these processes and the lure of distant but ideologically determined enabling influences, a few beleaguered young Muslims have consciously chosen to take part in conflicts in the Middle East.[9] This process largely began with the 1979 Soviet invasion of Afghanistan and has continued in the current period, culminating in the role of foreign fighters in the rise and fall of ISIS. Certain aspects of regressive Islamism project a black-and-white worldview, subsequently absorbed by young Muslims at the margins of society and heightened by a culture of hyper-masculine violence.[10] Recruiters from inside or outside communities are not always involved, despite this being a theory regularly propounded in the early stages of thinking through questions of Islamist radicalisation. Rather, the mechanisms emerge virtually, and because of the push factors that emerge in inner-city and urban lived-experience issues, where a projection of a global identity emerges through contemporary politics affecting the local.[11]

The reasons why a few thousand European-born Muslims went to join the ranks of ISIS can be traced to a number of different pull factors that led them to radical ideas, and eventually, a belief that terrorism can be justified.[12] ISIS foreign fighters consisted of Saudis, Tunisians, Libyans and even Turks, but a significant number of West European Muslims also migrated to Iraq and Syria to join these cadres of foreign fighters from across the Muslim world. For those born in Western Europe, the push factors include failed integration policies, where the 'left behind' consist of young ethnic minorities facing a form of exclusion that their white counterparts may also face, but which is compounded by racism and discrimination because of their religion, ethnicity and skin colour.[13] It is clearly disingenuous to blame these outcomes on Islam, and doing so invariably perpetuates much of the status quo, in the process affirming the legacies of xenophobia, racism and Orientalism. It also acts to silence criticism from Muslims by perpetuating the notion that a faith-specific route leads troubled individuals with deeply held conservative Islamic views to violent extremism.

In clear and simple terms, radicalisation within the region comes into existence because the West pursues access to and control over Middle Eastern oil and gas while marginalising Muslim minorities at home. The radicalising forces unleashed within pluralistic Muslim societies in the Middle East have projected their resistance against the

West as they are otherwise immobilised due to little or no democracy in the societies in which they find themselves. In the West, racism and class structure have served to suppress Muslim minorities—where excluded, racialised and radicalised young Muslim men accept the black–white/right–wrong rhetoric because their own Western European societies give the appearance of having rejected them, leading them to take part in conflicts in war-torn countries such as Afghanistan, Bosnia, Yemen, Palestine, Iraq and now Syria. As Western bombs drop on these parts of the world, and as the West sells other armaments to the Gulf Arabs as they shore up their inventories, the more this whole cycle will continue to perpetuate itself. There is only so much that Muslim communities in Western Europe and in the Middle East can do on the ground if elites are solely interested in reproducing the status quo, maintaining the culture of violence that characterises the current period. Critical engagement with the Gulf, while eliminating racism and structural disadvantage at home, clearly offers the potential for an important way forward, but such issues are rarely seen as interrelated.

ISIS drew advantage from fissures in societies stemming from social and political divisions combined with economic and individual insecurity, problems that can arguably be attributed, at least in part, to the effects of late capitalism and the digital age.[14] In this sense, the anxiety that Muslims in the West and the Middle East experience at the national level becomes internalised at the individual level, causing dissonance and disaffection. Young men who face extreme alienation and exclusion are easily seduced by seemingly totalising solutions.[15] In reconceptualising how people see their opportunities in life, where hope and opportunity replace fear and discord, the likes of ISIS are able to capitalise on the malaise, breaking down the anxiety for all groups in society, but especially among the young.[16] While global human populations are highly connected digitally, physical and material divisions have grown in societies. Technologies that allow humans to be better connected with each other have also created profound cleavages that capitalise on enduring social, political and individual conflicts.[17]

Conflicts today occur for three reasons. First, geopolitical factors shape the overriding context, where the pursuit of maximum profits results in huge costs for those facing the downward pressures of social inequality. Second, sectarianism reflects an internal quagmire afflicting groups within failing Middle Eastern nation states. Third, a spiritual versus material struggle exists among Western European and Middle Eastern Muslims wrestling with what they regard as a godly world without God. All these tensions engender class, ideological and political battles, where inequality and social conflict, together with competition over ever scarcer resources, have become the norm. The ideals of diversity or the notion of a mosaic society are commendable, but, in reality, these terms mean little without equality or fraternity. As soon as one group or tribe regards itself as beyond or superior to the other, disputes inevitably loom large. This reality is as old as history; it is hardwired into human existence, since groups and tribes have always faced challenges from others, affirming the self and eliminating the other unless they are absorbed or assimilated. The need to exist in a precarious environment has created a predisposition to survive while simultaneously being in competition with the other. It is these seeds of existence that will ultimately provide the basis of human destruction.

The year 2016 was the worst year for the displacement of Syrians into Turkey and then into the EU.[18] Leaders in Turkey and the EU played politics with the idea of closing borders, either trying to retain the refugees in Turkey or working towards an unlikely political solution in Syria. However, there was considerable apprehension over what would actually happen when the conflict in Syria came to an end. If history is a reliable guide to the present, after major disturbances in the Middle East, the power vacuum left at the top and the sheer destruction and disarray that has occurred throughout society will inevitably leave a void that will need to be filled. Neighbouring powers, as well as the major Western actors, invariably place their chosen people in positions of authority as affected nations need reconstruction, initiating economic as well as political opportunities for these external actors.[19] In reality, destabilisation for the people and disenfranchisement from the political process will produce further anger, frustration and waves of resistance. The governing powers have responded by repressing this dissent. In a global age of resistance, where defiance in the Muslim world is revealed not through socialism or ethnic nationalism but through Islamic radicalism, what prevents ISIS from morphing into something much worse? The reality is that the conflict in Syria was a case of smoke and mirrors.[20] The so-called rebels were militarised Sunni groups supported and funded by the United States and Saudi Arabia through Turkey. The Russians continued to support Assad, as they had done since the beginning of the war, which is why the UN and the EU were reluctant to intervene. Meanwhile, Turkey continued to bomb the Kurds in Syria (the PYD) because they are close to the Turkish border and have powerful alliances with the PKK, but the Turks were also shelling Kurds in the PKK in Turkey. Turkey has consequently found itself in a complicated position, especially as it originally wanted Assad to resolve matters peacefully by stepping down and then holding elections, which would have resulted in a Sunni leadership, helping Erdoğan in his quest for a friendly Sunni neighbour and his neo-Ottoman imaginings.[21] The US policy was to fund the so-called rebels, train them and prepare them, but these insurgents were isolated as they faced attacks from Russia on one side and Assad on the other. Armed and logistically supported in late 2013, these 'rebels' ultimately transformed into what became the Islamic State.

From the period immediately after the end of the Cold War, the events of the first Gulf War in 1991, Bosnia during the mid-1990s, to Iraq in 2003 and the Arab Spring in 2011, there have been similar patterns of destabilisation, reconstruction and modernisation followed by intervention. All the while, the West has faced its own struggles as it confronts the prospect of increasing economic and financial challenges from the East, leading to an intense focus on the Middle East, combined with the re-emergence of tensions with Russia. Within the internal power structures of the MENA region, dominant elites have tended to focus on internal conflicts, not external issues, as they benefit from opportunities outside of their countries while suppressing any internal dissatisfaction. Domestically, the education sectors, criminal justice systems, the lack of economic opportunity and the focus on security and intelligence serve to maintain the discord, preventing internal change and development, and sustaining the people in subjugated and subordinated positions. The conflicts in the Middle East today are to do with the loss of a local identity and the ability of nation states to facilitate social mobility, equality and fairness for the 'left behind', whose reaction is to agitate against the geopolitical paradigms that pull nation state elites towards global bipolar paradigms driven by neoliberalism.

Inequalities are widening across the world.[22] In this context, there can be little peace when there is no effective opposition against individualism, competition, cronyism and selfishness. Simultaneously, the Arabs, the Iranians and the Turks have been in conflict for much of recent history. In the post-war period, with the Middle East becoming a series of once-colonised fragmented nation states in the wake of the Ottoman Empire's collapse, internal weaknesses and external interests have come to exist in a symbiotic relationship. The Gulf States, Iran and Turkey have become susceptible to proxy wars and internal challenges militarised by external interests, which have in turn exposed the manoeuvring of local elites by Western interests, resulting in a lack of investment in societies and the need to suppress social aspirations through misdirected or, conversely, neutralised religiosity. A choice between stability, security and democracy has emerged, but in which anti-globalisation sentiment is encapsulated by questions of sectarianism or religio-cultural identity politics.

Political Islam has all but run out of ideas.[23] One can argue that ISIS, as the latest incarnation of political Islam, had no future for the politicisation or the instrumentalisation of Islam in societies that also possess authoritarian tendencies. In the West, elements of political Islam co-exist with secular, liberal and other types of conservative Islamism. In these spaces, Muslims are diverse groups, with their different migration histories and narratives. Successful integration, in part, reflects the ability of inclusive governments willing to listen and accept opposing voices within societies while simultaneously remaining open to diversity for all. The main threats Muslim minorities encounter stem from the instrumentalisation of Islam by outsiders, limiting resistance against dominant ideas—in the East and the West. A specific type of culture generated by the war on terror has created significant problems for Western Muslim minority communities that already faced numerous concerns relating to alienation and stigmatisation. Because governments generally approach Muslim communities only through the lens of countering extremism, liberal Muslim voices open to the idea of cultural and political integration, even if they generally agree with government, have tended to be excluded. Governments only bestow Muslim groups with credibility if they support the dominant counter-narratives produced by officious counter-extremism policy thinking.[24]

Violence is a by-product of other illnesses in society.[25] While violent tendencies are not new, the violence that is the reality of the world today has many different local and global features—and with all the resultant impacts it has for communities, societies and nations the world over. This type of violence rarely occurs on its own, whether in the context of violence towards women, children, minorities or any group or idea seen as alien or opposite to the self. Much of the violence relating to the notion of violent extremism has emerged in the context of societies experiencing an acute democratic deficit,[26] where the voiceless and 'left behind' see an opportunity to hit back at the 'cosmopolitan elite', responding to populist notions put forward by charismatic elites that play on fears of diversity, immigration or terrorism.[27] The root causes of violent extremism are political and ideological, with ideology coming to the fore as passions for political change go on to result in radicalisation—from extremism to political violence and terrorism, although these processes are contested concepts in the literature.[28] Those who become radical Islamists are confused over their local and global identities and fearful of their future in post-industrial societies. They are unable to see their worlds beyond the immediate survival or growth of their group. The reality of political violence is that it occurs within a political space, formulated by elites at the centre, who work in the interests of dominant influences, whether corporate or geopolitical in origin. Huge regional divisions in Britain, ever widening as neoliberal economics strengthens the core at the expense of the periphery, occur alongside political disillusionment and cultural dislocation. The multi-layered nature of various exclusions stems from both individual and universal notions of identity.

The nature of Islamic violent extremism is also changing because of the internet—first, by bringing people together under various political and ideological banners, then in enabling operations and terrorist acts that create havoc and sow discord. During its peak, ISIS encouraged its followers, especially those in the West, to stay in their countries of birth rather than migrating to its 'Caliphate', urging those inspired by their ideologies to carry out attacks on local populations. ISIS was able to recruit online by focusing on Islamophobia and the idea that the West will never accept Islam, including in relation to Muslim women choosing to act out their 'Muslimness' through their modern and postmodern Islamic feminisms.[29] ISIS also focused on the notion that it was the duty of 'good Muslims' to help a major humanitarian cause created by war mediated by Western interests. Emotionally and intellectually weakening the pliable enables an Islamist strain of thought to take over. Terrorists have never been averse to technology. Vulnerable minds absorbed ISIS videos without criticism due to their slick and captivating production qualities.[30]

The reality of terrorism is that it does not work, as the terror of the act is quickly displaced by the power of governments to hit back hard, further fuelling the rhetoric of would-be terrorists. The cycles of political, economic and cultural exclusion intensify due to the rhetoric of political elites, especially when it affects the narratives of the radicalisers and the would-be radicalised violent extremists. The war on terror and the associated culture that has emerged in its wake have rarely helped to fight violent extremism. At some level, unfortunately, it has sustained it by feeding into the narratives of radical Islamist groups, confirming the idea that Islam is the main target in the West, when, arguably, the focus should be on would-be radicalised individuals as would-be terrorists and criminals. Military efforts in Iraq, Syria and Libya have been disastrous, not only destabilising entire regions but also causing the loss of human life and the destruction of world heritage. The conflict in Syria has displaced around 5 million people and resulted in the loss of around half a million lives[31] while creating the greatest flow of refugees since the Second World War. The debate within Western hosting countries has centred on concerns over the question of how to respond to the crisis, while also generating resentment or indifference on the part of prominent political figures and media elites.

—•—

Salafism, as a generalisation of Wahhabi Islamism, emerged in the late nineteenth century. The current dominant strain of Salafism is an anti-globalisation movement driven by the writings of a range of Islamic political ideologues, but principally Ibn Taymiyyah, Abd al-Wahhab, Maulana Maududi and Sayyid Qutb, affecting Egypt, Afghanistan, Iraq, Pakistan and Bangladesh in particular and vast swathes of the Muslim world in general. Salafism is a global cosmopolitan jihadi movement with a radical *takfirist* perspective best understood within a theological framework; however, it is important to note that Islamism itself is a political phenomenon rather than a religious outlook per se, something overlooked by many observers. In thinking through the types of Islamism that characterise the landscape, the following postulates a broad system of classification, including those on the areligious side of the spectrum of opinion and practice. This classification suggests that there are many different ways of working through Islamism other than merely associating it with acts of violent extremism.

1. *Anti-Islamism* is defined by the political and cultural ambition of removing religious identities from every aspect of the lives of Muslims as citizens of the state. The counter-extremism sector of the de-radicalisation industry takes this approach in dealing with what it regards as extremism as a foreground to eventual political violence and terrorism.
2. *Cultural Islamism* is a form of Islamism that upholds Muslim identities and practices that do not in any way interfere or prevent social, political and economic integration. To some extent, it can be seen as anti-Islamism in that it seeks to reaffirm a Muslim cultural experience without seeping into anti-integration practices. The vast majority of most Muslims in the West seek to apply their faith principles in practice in this matter, comfortable with the clear separation between religious interpretations and the need for civic participation and engagement.
3. *Radical Islamism* refers to the need to uphold and apply a literal reading of Islam in the context of a response to a global worldview as well as the realities of local area lived experiences. It is a variant of cultural Islamism because it chooses to draw firmer lines between what is deemed proper or otherwise, and what is desirable or not, narrowly defining acceptable or unacceptable practices. But it is also radical as it accepts no alternatives to its

own utopian vision. Muslim minorities pushed down by social immobility are likely to favour such approaches as they provide comfort and meaning when discomfort and insignificance shape the realities of their lived experience, and where cultural Islamism does not sufficiently cohere with their identity politics.

4. *Violent Islamism* is the reality of the forces of exclusion that combine with the power of ideology as interpreted by fringe Muslim groups who regard Islamism as the need to bear arms and exact a militarist solution to grievances affecting the Muslim world, including killing other Muslims in its name, also known as *takfirism*. It goes to greater lengths than radical Islamism as it seeks to present an explicitly Islamised solution, based on a literal reading of limited Quranic texts, inspired by ideologues, where murder, including of innocent people, is seen as legitimate, and where the reward is in the hereafter, absolving the sins of this world in the process.

Governments have introduced increasingly stringent pieces of counterterrorism and de-radicalisation legislation in the hope of thwarting future attacks in Western Europe. While this is necessary to maintain the safe and secure conditions that liberal democratic societies need to operate, it also carries certain risks. As such, legislation often places the entire onus on Muslims as 'suspect communities',[32] thus undermining the very freedoms West European societies have struggled so hard to preserve. Policymakers are currently placing great emphasis on providing the UK government with greater access to personal digital data; however, the risk here is that the UK will end up with additional information on its citizens but with no greater intelligence. Meanwhile, civil liberties, human rights and freedom of expression are increasingly under attack. These developments are reactionary, not pre-emptive.[33]

At the heart of the global problem of violent Islamism is the impact of capital and wealth creation in the hands of the few based on the neoclassical economic theory of the free market, which has become the single paradigm in which the whole world has found itself, including the Middle East. This process of capital formation affects the nature and output of the media, and the aspects of Orientalism and Occidentalism that help to propel propaganda. It supports modes of geopolitical competition, enhancing internal divisions by maintaining the frameworks in which elites seek to realise their geopolitical aspirations in the interests of the very few at the expense of the many. It is also realised through aspects of the knowledge and information economy, and the reproduction of technological outputs, which maintain the strengths of elites, both in the East and in the West.

Western European political elites lay the responsibility for integration upon Muslim minorities who are routinely asked to fend for themselves to achieve parity with 'our values'. This represents precisely what is wrong with the current approach to integration. Despite the immense challenges that Muslim groups face because of racism, discrimination, alienation and marginalisation, research confirms that they have and continue to make considerable efforts to integrate. They obey the laws of the land, take part in the politics of the nation and behave as upright citizens. Intermittently, however, a small number of Muslims have sought to challenge the prevailing system, traversing a route from educational and employment underachievement into criminality, extremism and radicalisation. Conversely, directly and indirectly, governments have encouraged majority groups to vent their frustrations towards immigrant and minority groups—usually meaning Muslim communities and refugees in the current climate. In response, Muslim communities have often been forced to turn towards a conservative form of Islam that offers groups a safe space, protecting them from the deleterious consequences of anti-Muslim rhetoric, but also reinforcing an inward-looking vision of the world, one that shields them from the problems affecting wider society, such as alcoholism, teenage pregnancy and violence towards women. As conservative Muslim groups begin to embrace their religious identities in observable ways, the unfortunate consequence is that it reaffirms the prevailing notion that Muslims are somehow refusing to adjust to the Western way of life and may even threaten the very existence of liberalism in secular Western nations. The following chapter explores the nature of the radicalisation process of Muslim minority groups, with a focus on how limitations to policy based on short-term thinking combined with populism reinforce the realities of exclusion, direct and indirect racism and neoliberal globalisation. Muslim groups require empowerment, opportunity and equality. It is a two-way process, but elite groups hold all the power and resources, and they show little interest in distributing them among the many.

7

MULTICULTURAL RADICALISMS

In the current debate over Islam and Islamophobia, Muslim youth identities have attracted a considerable amount of attention, with anxiety over the nature of extremism, radicalism, inter-culturalism and its implications for ethnonational multiculturalism. While significant attention has been paid to group characteristics, wider social issues affecting young Muslims in Britain today have received far less discussion. The issue of Islamophobia in Britain has gained notoriety in recent periods, generating a wide-ranging debate in the media and among political and community actors. As part of this debate, much has been said about the *niqab*—the face veil—which is seen by some as the antithesis to a post-Enlightenment age where individual choice, liberty and freedom are given primacy, and with questions of nationhood, citizenship and identity at the fore.[1] Other important issues include the impact of far-right groups that have sought to create negative associations between Muslims and their apparent lack of desire to integrate into wider society. In reality, the centres of towns and cities in which Muslim communities are observable are often cut off from their wider settings due to patterns of structural disadvantage combined with cultural relativism.

This chapter explores how the debate on multiculturalism has securitised the issue of integration, problematising the 'Muslimness' of Muslims in questions of political violence and extremism. This dynamic combines a set of cultural, political, theological and sociological debates around identity and belonging, as well as issues of immigration, integration, intelligence, counterterrorism, policymaking and securitisation, in the process further 'othering' an already beleaguered body of people.[2] Given the current reductions to public spending in most West European economies, the ongoing impact of the war on terror, and limited community, cultural and intellectual development, the challenges facing Muslim minorities are likely to endure for the foreseeable future. While the Middle East is currently facing its own internal trials and tribulations, and the wider Muslim world often lags behind the West when it comes to technological advances, divisions are likely to increase and tensions grow as the global continues to intersect with the local in shaping and playing out identity politics.

Many demographic studies of Muslims in Western Europe highlight Muslim engagement in limited spheres of social life, and the nature of political and cultural organisations as, for example, when seeking to establish mosques, when securing provision of *halal* food in prisons, schools and hospitals, and when lobbying for state-funded Islamic schools.[3] The building of mosques is reflective of a public expression of Muslim life.[4] Muslim beliefs and practices are characteristic of local contexts in the sending regions of the subcontinent reproduced by the newcomers to Britain as accommodations within multi-ethnic states.[5] These ongoing developments are useful in explaining how Muslim groups have sought to contain and reproduce practices associated with their faith in multicultural societies, and at specific times in their settlement and community development.[6]

Islamic revivalisms contrast with these efforts, as they seek to assert a particular identity and form of recognition, using characteristically 'Islamic' language or slogans in the face of injustices targeted at Muslim identity and culture. Islamic revivalisms are emancipatory social movements, manifested in urban Islamic culture, and as political protests, with the language of Islam used as the dominant mode of expression. They are defined by the conscious recognition of an identity that stretches into new political imaginaries that emphasise the primacy of grievances, including barriers to social mobility, lack of political and legal freedoms, economic despair and the Palestine–Israel issue, for example. The underlying assumption that socioeconomic and political crises generate these grievances is, however, not entirely accurate.[7] Numerous factors are important in understanding these issues, the foremost being the idea that Islam is under threat or at risk of being corrupted.[8] Issues such as the intrusion of the state into everyday life, legislation perceived as specifically targeting Muslims and ever-tightening immigration controls cause Muslim communities to feel they are under specific threat. In this way, Islamic revivalisms reflect the fears of many Muslims who feel that their religion and identity are under threat.

The Rushdie Affair was an example of Islam 'in danger'. As much as liberal values were perceived to be under attack by the intelligentsia due to their resistance to the idea of banning the book as well as concerns over freedom of speech, British Muslims were also nervous about the threat to Islam stemming from the loss of belief from within. In reality, Islamist movements develop politico-cultural transnational responses to contemporary problems facing Muslim communities largely because the state is unable to meet the economic expectations or cultural aspirations of Muslim groups, providing the context for Islamic revivalisms to develop.[9] Muslims in the West contending with negative representations in the media and popular culture are involved in an interaction between 'assignments', which are imposed by others in society, and 'assertion', which is a claim to authority through ethnicity made by the groups themselves.[10]

Globalisation, therefore, has implications for the ways in which people perceive and develop their identity. However, significant constraints are involved in the formation of an identity because of the powerful homogenising forces of individualism associated with globalisation. Globalisation, transnationalism and diasporic Muslim communities offer the potential to negotiate and form a newfound identity. But globalisation also has implications for the state, which in turn raises significant problems for ethnic minority groups within particular borders bound by policies that do not always meet their aspirations when it comes to integration. At the same time, migration is an essential part of globalisation, which renders it increasingly difficult for states to control the flows of populations, settlements and cultural exchange.[11] Multiculturalism therefore entails an essentialist understanding of culture as a 'container model'.[12] The historical continuation of this approach in contemporary multicultural societies has a role in (re)producing Islamic revivalisms due to the exclusivist notions of culture and identity defined and promoted by the monoculturalising effects of government policy. This has proven problematic for states that perceive, engage with and subsequently feel compelled to 'manage' the 'differences' that various ethnic and religious minority communities possess and seemingly wish to retain.

Britain offers ethnic and religious minorities a negotiated space; however, what is noticeable in the British context is the view that minority groups must adapt to a predetermined sense of belonging. The 'idea of England' and subsequent ethnocentric norms have helped to reinforce this approach and, in the process, produce chauvinist and racist outcomes. Individual cultures are homogenised and expected to assimilate into a wider mode of multicultural citizenship within an existing national cultural framework, eventually creating a monoculture. Cultures are in reality open and porous formations that interact with mainstream life at a variety of levels, requiring a degree of sensitivity to these differences.[13] Muslim groups, with transnational allegiances to their cultures and countries of origin, as well as to the concept of *ummah*, pose a problem for some multicultural societies. Global Islamic revivalist movements represented in events such as 9/11 and the resistance to occupation in places such as Iraq and Palestine have led to the objectification of popular assumptions and discourses that view Muslims as 'terrorists' or 'fundamentalists'. This stigmatising process has forced communities into retreat, prolonging the cycle of racism and revivalism. In certain instances, successful Muslim integration has led to a further growth in Islamophobia.

The lived experience of British Muslims is a complex phenomenon. Low social class positions coupled with religious and cultural isolation mean that many young Muslims feel they are unable to exert wider social influence. Where intergenerational tensions arise over tradition and faith, some young Muslims have sought to return to a literal interpretation of Islam as a means of self-empowerment in the face of regressive cultural practices. Some of these developments have encouraged young Muslim minds to explore Islam further, but their parents are not always able to provide the knowledge or wisdom that they are looking for, as they frequently lack the linguistic, intellectual and cultural skills to communicate with their children.[14] Muslim parents themselves sometimes adopt a new approach to Islam later in their own lives, occasionally in progressive Islamic terms.[15] But mosques, for the most part, provide only a limited learning environment, where Islamic instruction takes place at a basic level or within a specific linguistic and cultural framework. Consequently, the young seek alternative knowledge, whether via the internet, underground reading groups or religious study circles.[16] This information is occasionally laden with a radical message promoting intolerance, antipathy and the disregard of all things Western, particularly in the context of the resistance politics of the oppressed and disempowered. The theological nature of these messages stems from outside of traditional Islamic sources. Much of this thinking appeals to a small number of young Muslims (mostly men, though not entirely) who see it as a form of liberation—from the traditions, norms and values of their own communities and from states that subjugate Muslims. It should, however, be emphasised that reading websites or joining study circles is clearly not, in and of itself, a sinister activity. With increasing efforts to de-radicalise young Muslims through closer working relations between communities, organisations and government departments, some Muslims may feel the need to explore religious questions out of necessity.

The rise of identity politics is often used to explain the turn to radical political Islam among subsections of the British Muslim population, as well as the ways in which the British multicultural experience has facilitated a concentration on individual and group norms, values, lifestyle choices and cultural identities, thus detracting from an emphasis on structural inequalities at a time when such a focus is perhaps most urgent in the history of British race relations. In 1999, the publication of the Macpherson Report into the murder of Stephen Lawrence highlighted the problem of institutionalised racism, then seen as endemic in the Metropolitan Police Service.[17] The Macpherson Report led to an enhancement of the Race Relations (Amendment) Act (2000), which put a statutory duty on nearly 50,000 public sector organisations to measure and take actions to reduce race inequality, which remains a persistent feature of the social and political lives of black and South Asian minorities in Britain.[18]

The race riots of 2001 and the subsequent 'community cohesion' reports less than two months later led to a focus on identities, communities and behaviours rather than inequality, placing the onus of responsibility on Muslims to become better citizens engaged in an evolving multicultural society, and taking it away from the state in delivering active social policy interventions.[19] In the summer of 2001, second- and third-generation young South Asian Muslim men fought with local police and fascist groups on the streets of Burnley, Oldham and Bradford, as well as Stoke and Leeds, albeit to a lesser extent. Not only did these young men receive heavy sentences for first-time offences but they were also vilified in the press. At war in Afghanistan by November 2001, Britain and the 'coalition of the willing' had now begun to engage in a 'war on terror'. Although some individual British Muslims had become radicalised in the early 1990s, because of the problems in Bosnia–Herzegovina,[20] the war on terror caused British Muslims to feel even more ostracised. Some of these aimless young Muslims, using the internet and other media communication technologies, turned to radicalisation.[21]

The complete lack of appreciation of the needs within Muslim minority communities in inner-city areas experiencing deepening economic marginalisation and widening social inequality on the part of policymakers has further compounded this situation. Public attention tends to focus on culture rather than structural inequalities, with debates centring on dress, language or identity, for example—transforming cultural pluralism (or multiculturalism) into monoculturalism (or cultural imperialism). The other facet of this debate is the attention that has been placed on women, where Muslim women are seen as having a limited ability to exercise the freedoms enjoyed by other women in British society, thus requiring some form of policy intervention. The evidence on Western female emancipation continues to suggest a need for greater equality of opportunity and equality of outcome, although there have been significant gains since 2000, especially in education.[22] However, many Muslim women argue that wearing the hijab is a source of freedom and empowerment before Allah. Some young Muslim women are increasingly taking matters into their own hands as a direct response to the wider Islamic identity struggles in the diaspora,[23] whereby young Muslim women appropriate religiously inspired garb as a means of reacting to what they view as an onslaught against their faith, constituting a form of defiance in the face of the hostile discourses they encounter in wider society.[24] At the same time, a detailed discussion is necessary, as within Islam a debate has arisen on what this means for integration into non-Muslim societies over time, and how the veil or headscarf is a sensitive political topic, particularly in places such as France, which asserts that certain differences in the public sphere, such as the *niqab*, are intolerable.[25]

Europe and Islam share many aspects of their history, in which violence and conflict has characterised the interaction but also an immense appreciation of the 'other'. Over the centuries, Muslims were colonised, and when the 'masters' left, the once-colonised arrived in the 'mother country' to struggle for better living standards. Islamophobia intensified during these periods of contact and demonisation, and because of this experience, its features are remarkably resistant to change, particularly given the role that narrow readings of British social and economic history continue to play in the country's national identity. With global events in Muslim lands dominating the geopolitical landscape since the end of the Cold War, an Islamophobic discourse now permeates society at every level. Think tanks that have a role in influencing policy such as the Henry Jackson Society, Policy Exchange and Quilliam have all determined that Islamism is a wide-ranging problem but have failed to identify the nuances it involves. Meanwhile, Muslim umbrella organisations are competing with each other for authenticity and a seat at the table of the same power that feeds its thinking from the inkwells of right-wing think tanks and media-savvy politicos they seek to challenge. As to intellectual impact, policy development and the resultant action of these endeavours, little has emerged save from extensive community engagement and hurried policy responses fine-tuned to appeal to a middle ground that is shifting to the right.[26] Islamophobia is simultaneously individual, communitarian, organisational and societal, and it is local and global in its reach—it will not yield unless there is greater structural reform in society.[27]

Many British commentators and social thinkers have criticised the notion of multiculturalism and its role in Islamic radicalism. However, in doing so, they usually overlook the experience of other countries, such as France, which has an assimilationist notion of integration, and the Netherlands, which aspires to cultural pluralism, both of which have experienced attacks from 'home-grown' radical Islamists. The problem has more to do with the intersection of the local and global in how disaffected Muslims determine their relations with others, which are also connected to the perceptions and realities of alienation among local and global Muslims.[28] Muslim minorities brought various forms of Islamism with them as part of the migration process, especially Muslims from South Asia. These forms of Islamism, which were often established as a reaction to the colonial experience, have served to limit critical Muslim thinking. Regressive and reactionary tendencies in the face of hostility from and subjugation by the 'other' have hindered the progressive development of alternative ideas. As the British Raj attempted to regulate Islam, it led to further resistance among the Muslims of South Asia, some of whom felt acutely marginalised as part of the 'divide-and-rule' policy of their British overlords. When they came to Britain in the post-war period, many Muslims retained this antipathy, which in many cases became even stronger in the context of their experience of life in the inner cities.

Multiculturalism evolved as part of a post-war dynamic relating to the settlement and incorporation of various ethnic minority groups in British society. During the course of its development, multiculturalism sought to provide a way to recognise differences and a means through which these differences would find expression in the public and private spheres, from accommodation of the religious rights of worship in the public space to acceptance of such needs as *halal* food and Islamic marriage contracts in civil law. To some extent, multiculturalism allowed various expressions of Islamism to remain underexposed until the emergence of various crises, beginning with the Rushdie Affair of the late 1980s. But the West's ineffective integration policies and aggressive foreign policies led some Muslim groups to believe that

Western societies are waging a 'war on Islam', a feeling compounded by a lack of confidence and self-esteem among some Muslims.

Most British Muslims are physically concentrated in inner-city areas, where their needs are generally neglected by the state until something dramatic happens, such as the race riots of the early 2000s. In 2001, Muslims in Britain needed a 'Scarman Report', not a 'Cantle Report'. The former, which resulted from the inquiry into the Brixton race riots of 1981, suggested an important link between racism, discrimination, structural disadvantage and poor policing–community relations, the latter stressed the need for changes to culture and values in response to the northern riots of 2001, in the process significantly underemphasising the importance of structural inequalities.[29] This is precisely where the multiculturalism model in Britain is least effective. In celebrating differences and being culturally sensitive to minority interests, the notion of a universal national identity has not been sufficiently determined to permit the different ethno-cultural characteristics of British ethnic minorities and majorities to form strategic alliances against structural and cultural racism. At a policy level, notions of cultural identity politics have superseded those relating to the need to eliminate deep-seated socioeconomic inequalities for all.

There are extensive Islamic teachings on equality and social justice, comprehensively developed over the millennia, but Muslims and non-Muslims alike do not always understand them. With the UK government empowering and incorporating what is regarded as a 'moderate' class of Muslims, there have been some gains in how the process has positively engaged with confident and articulate young people, in particular Muslim women, despite the institutionalisation of the existing anti-terrorist and securitisation agenda. At the community level, differentiated by ethnicity, culture, social class, region and sect, a number of Muslim faith-based civil society and community organisations are working with government, and these projects are delivering valuable outcomes. As structural preconditions emerge to permit equal opportunities and outcomes, Muslims may well begin to further value their presence in society, becoming engaged citizens in the context of an ever-evolving national politico-cultural framework. Popular discourse, however, tends to converge on culturally essentialist notions of 'the Muslim', manifesting a 'blame-the-victim' pathology that is subsequently inculcated and then reproduced. In such a hostile local, national and international climate, radical Islamists can easily target susceptible young Muslims. In the context of a UK foreign policy that has occasionally supported forms of radical Islam when it has been in its interest to do so, the way in which British Muslims perceive and experience reality are important to consider when determining the space between multiculturalism and radical Islamism.

—•—

A speech by David Cameron, the then British prime minister, on anti-terrorism, security and multiculturalism on 5 February 2011 in Munich caused considerable consternation. At an event designed to discuss terrorism and security issues, his first public statement on the question of radical Islamism and its dangers for secular liberal nations claimed that the problem can be traced to radical Islamism and that Britain would no longer tolerate the intolerable—that is, apparently divisive communitarian ethno-political interests. Categorising the range of Islamisms as varieties of Islam ignored everything involved in the making of contemporary Islamism, which is a political and ideological project formed in response to historical colonialism, cultural exclusion and social disadvantage. In many cases, the government policy on preventing extremism, which is based on this interpretation, has in fact made matters worse, as it has alienated an entire community.[30] These government voices also have close connections to the intelligence and security sectors.[31] It is clearly the case that religion does not cause terrorism,[32] but treating Muslim groups as 'suspect communities' is not conducive to effective dialogue.[33]

At the time of this writing in early 2019, various Western European governments are continuing to engage with Muslims at a legal, social and cultural level on issues of 'extremism', with attempts to strengthen anti-terrorism legislation at home while fighting Muslim 'insurgents' abroad. Meanwhile, with the perpetuation of harmful media and political discourses vilifying, stigmatising and homogenising Muslims and Islam, some young Muslims continue to remain vulnerable to radicalisation. In the absence of greater efforts to tackle the structural issues and politico-ideological problems involved in 'being Muslim', the potential threat of violent Islamic political radicalism is unlikely to disappear, as national and international issues compound local area efforts, leaving many Muslims feeling further alienated and disempowered. The status quo cannot continue if society aspires to create a stable and prosperous multicultural future, confident of intercultural and interfaith relations as globalisation continues apace and individual freedoms are further eroded in the face of rampant capitalism and restrictions of basic freedoms since 9/11. This observation, however, does not cohere with current UK government thinking or the beliefs of centre-right think tanks, commentators and political actors in general. Populist voices claim that multiculturalism is inherently flawed owing to the cultural differences between Muslims and British society at large. Accordingly, the idea of multiculturalism, 'a philosopher's tool' in imagining the 'good society', has been subject to extensive criticism from both the left and the right of the political spectrum. Yet, in reality, a lack of integration should be attributed to economics and questions of social and political empowerment, rather than identity, culture or religion alone.[34] The debates on migration, integration, multiculturalism and radicalism are at the centre of much public concern. While radicalisation feeds off Islamophobia and vice versa, Islamophobia thrives on the negative connotations associated with Muslim communities. Radicalisation is similarly generated by reactions to the ineffectiveness of attempts to integrate, which reflects the inadequacies of equality policies at home and foreign policy abroad. At the local level, the situation is becoming worse due to the actions of far-right groups that focus on issues of immigration, perceptions of Muslim cultural relativism and geopolitical concerns relating to terrorism. There is consequently a symbiotic relationship between Islamophobia and radicalisation in the discussion of Islamism and multiculturalism. To eliminate the harmful consequences of both Islamophobia and radicalisation, the question of what it means to be a Muslim in the reality of multicultural Britain remains particularly pertinent.

Many historical challenges face British Muslims in the current period. Considerable attention focuses on questions of race, ethnicity, loyalty, belonging and local and global identities. Importantly, however, the impact of policy and practice on questions of Islamophobia and radicalisation in particular is largely absent from this debate. The following chapter explores the problems of far-right and Islamist extremism as interrelated notions with similar drivers, including mutually reinforcing forces centring on identity, belonging and representation.

8

FAR-RIGHT VERSUS ISLAMIST EXTREMISM

In late July 2016, an eighteen-year-old German, Ali David Sonboly—the son of Iranian parents who had sought refuge in Germany in the early 1990s—fatally shot nine young people in a fast-food restaurant and a shopping mall in Munich. As the news reports first came in, the immediate response was to suggest that the incident was yet another example of an Islamic State-related act of terrorism. After a spate of attacks in Brussels, France and Germany earlier in the same year, the Sonboly killings appeared to be another instance of radical Islamism acting as a forerunner to violent extremism. There was, however, a crucial difference. Due to various personal, psychological and political motivations, the Munich shooter, Sonboly, had subscribed to a 'pure racial identity', one that transcended his co-ethnic cultural, immigrant and minority background. A 'lone actor', Sonboly idolised Anders Behring Breivik, a convicted far-right violent extremist terrorist,[1] and even carried out these tragic shootings on the fifth anniversary of the Breivik attacks in Norway on 22 July 2011 that killed seventy-seven people. The reality was that Sonboly did not feel comfortable in his own skin: he murdered others because of his own insecurities regarding his ethnic and cultural identity. The Sonboly episode can consequently be seen as stemming from the twin issues of radicalisation and far-right extremism in an individual who was born into a Shia Muslim household but went on to reject his past. It confirms how identity formation and the self-realisation journeys of a few young people exist within various modes of deep conflict. This incident was a glaring reminder of how similar issues affect a variety of young people experiencing a sense of insecurity in their local and global identities at the margins of society.

Anti-Muslim sentiment plays a part in radicalising far-right extremists.[2] In Britain, the EDL operates as an ethnic nationalist group with historical links to the BNP and football hooliganism.[3] The group's activities reflect the wider notion of 'reactive co-radicalisation'[4] or 'cumulative extremism',[5] which is a response by states, organisations, groups and individuals to the apparent threat of Muslims in the West. These responses have also become a defining feature of Islamophobia,[6] much of which is also linked to the rise of populism and nationalism.[7] Today, the extremism of the far right has undergone a shift from focusing on ethno-racial issues to cultural–ideological ones. Breivik's objections, for example, were not merely ethnic and religious in nature, as they also encompassed the ideologies and philosophies of multiculturalism and diversity that underpin them—his actions should be seen as an assault on the very idea of difference itself. Breivik was also hostile to other traditions of political thought, such as Marxism and liberalism.[8] But in thinking through radicalisation, it is important to situate the debate within the wider economic, political and cultural contexts of post-industrial urban centres. The way these extremisms are conceptualised indicates how identities conflict due to the simultaneously moving terrains of localisation and globalisation. This chapter is an attempt to explore the theoretical and conceptual nature of the symbiosis that defines and characterises far-right and Islamist extremism. It synthesises current knowledge on the similarities and differences between these two extremisms, which are based on a disjuncture between the interplay of social structure and identity, the knowledge gaps in existing research, and the implications for policy and practice in this area.

In some respects, radicalisation refers to pathways, while in others, it relates to outcomes. But radicalisation does not always equate with terrorism.[9] This lack of clarity over what radicalisation actually means has distorted existing understandings of violent extremism,[10] in particular where confusion reigns over clearly problematic social outcomes that are high-priority security threats. No two countries define 'radicalisation' in the same way. For some, violence is the main concern. For others, an ideology that may or may not produce violence is the primary focus. All definitions nevertheless recognise the notion as a highly individualised and largely unpredictable process.[11] For the purposes of this discussion, radicalisation refers to both the processes and outcomes of violent extremism.

Far-right and Islamophobic attacks inspire Islamist terrorism, reflecting a shift within broader right-wing extremism, with many groups and individuals—including Breivik—condemning Nazism, fascism and anti-Semitism while defining their main cause as a defence against the perceived threat from Islam.[12] Pavlo Lapshyn, a Ukrainian far-right terrorist convicted for the murder of eighty-two-year-old Mohammed Saleem from Small Heath in Birmingham, claimed he carried out the murder because Saleem was a Muslim and because there would be no witnesses. Saleem had been walking home from his local mosque in the late hours of 29 April 2013. In June and July 2013, Lapshyn attempted to bomb three mosques in Walsall, Wolverhampton and Tipton during Friday afternoon prayers, the busiest time of the week.[13] His devices failed on all three occasions. Although a significant proportion of 'lone actor' terrorists are preoccupied with neo-Nazi symbolism and the idolisation of far-right figureheads and their ideologies, there is relative underreporting and under-analysis of the threat from right-wing extremism in North America and in Western Europe.[14]

Western European societies and economies have experienced a profound transformation since the deregulation of the financial sector and the ensuing dominance of privatisation and economic neoliberalism that began in the 1980s.[15] This has had repercussions for youth identity, particularly in urban spheres.[16] The inner-city areas, oft-forgotten by urban planners and policymakers, frequently house diverse communities concentrated in a particular space through no real choice of their own.[17] The minorities that arrived in Britain after the Second World War are clustered in specific urban areas for social, economic and cultural reasons. Simultaneously, the spatial concentration of deprived marginalised minorities is also an opportunity to protect group norms and values associated with the group identity, which perceives a threat from the dominant other. The general overriding discourse, however, presents 'self-styled segregation' among ethnic minorities as a self-induced rejection of integration. This discourse, however, is harmful for many minorities who are on the receiving end of vilification, alienation and discrimination.[18] Majority white communities also suffer from the predicaments of extremism, radicalisation and violence, but the media and political discourse tends to concentrate less on such groups, markedly skewing the debate.[19] Deindustrialisation, post-industrialisation and globalisation have consequently affected Muslim minority groups in the inner-city areas of Western Europe, but these concerns have also affected members of majority groups, some of whom can be susceptible to far-right political views.[20] In general, there has only been limited discussion of the links between extremist far-right and radical Muslim groups. Developments to such thinking would help to explore the synergies between two parallel and similar radicalisation and violent extremism outcomes.[21]

The separation between white indigenous and Muslim minority groups reflects differences in identity formations at local and global levels, revealing a distinct layer of conflict and locking both groups into an intense struggle, often for the least in society. A crucial feature in the radicalisation of far-right and Islamist extremists is, therefore, the search for an alternative, 'purer' identity.[22] Although both groups have had a certain impact at the political level, their electoral successes have largely been negligible, at least until recently[23] and the Brexit vote in the UK, motivated to a large degree by negative discourses on immigration, refugees and questions of national political identity.[24]

At the individual level, various social, psychological, economic and structural issues can cause problems in the formation of identities, introducing the need for self-actualisation, which is the realisation of individual potential. This applies equally to Muslim minorities and the 'left-behind' white working classes. In both cases, there are fears over multiculturalism, dislocation and identity. A lack of hope creates psychological problems, leaving countless young men vulnerable, exposed and susceptible to nefarious external influences. With limited educational and employment opportunities due to entrenched patterns of structural disadvantage, the uncertain futures facing young people, both minority and majority alike, in inner-city areas create additional challenges.[25] Notably, these anxieties affect young people of all backgrounds.

Part of the reason for the radicalisation of both European-born Muslims and far-right youth is an aspect of their coming to terms with hegemonic masculinity in the context of an intergenerational disconnect combined with economic insecurity.[26] Such dominant male aspirational qualities include notions such as being heterosexual, attractive and earning significant amounts of money. Britain First, the EDL and radical Islamic organisations such as Al-Muhajiroun and Islam4UK have all proven attractive to young men with limited education, employment or social status. These men are outraged and simultaneously embittered by the spiritual or material challenges of their existence, and many of the recruits to ISIS who heralded from the inner-city areas of Western Europe shared similar anxieties and aspirations.

Minorities with specific cultural characteristics may also feel particularly disconnected from broader society. Research into Pakistani and Turkish communities, for instance, suggests that patriarchy plays a particularly important role in familial relations, which derives from a cultural reading of the role of the male head of the household.[27] This in turn serves to reproduce patterns of masculinity within the home. In wider society, however, the same people who are heads of their respective households often experience racialisation and subjugation in the workplace, while their sons face downward social mobility combined with acute anxiety over their identity. Accordingly, it would appear that patriarchal practices reinforce internal issues within the home, but this takes place in the context of a situation where Muslim minorities face ethnic and religious discrimination in the labour market, further affecting income levels,[28] status and the persecution felt by Muslim men of different generations. The local, regional and transnational interconnects the spaces in which these masculinities are constructed and deconstructed.[29] British South Asian Muslims, for example, have at various points been viewed as either effeminate or hyper-masculine. In the early phases of post-war migration and settlement, these men were ascribed feminine characteristics. Yet at the same time, they were also regarded as a threat because of their 'dark and handsome' appearances,[30] which ensured that employers, often with the assistance of unions, did not allow minority men to share workspaces with white English women. Today, however, in the post-9/11 climate, these British Muslim men are presented as posing a significant threat to society owing to their masculinity.[31] Intergenerational disconnect and the importance of the socioeconomic and sociocultural context are important considerations in the experiences of 'white' groups as well as Muslim minorities. The phenomenon of 'convert radicalisation' among white groups, however, is associated with a lack of suitable grounding in community values or the adoption of Islam as a method of rebellion.[32]

In the midst of the material challenges facing young men and women in Western European and North American societies, particular concerns have arisen over hyper-masculinity and hyper-sexuality (an over-concentration on sexual activity).[33] These fears stem from the unrealistic expectations placed upon young people, creating fear, anger and anguish, rather than a smooth transition from youth to adulthood. Here, 'jihadis' and far-right young men experience equivalent challenges, where differences in religion and culture regarding 'the other' become politicised. In a number of ways, hyper-masculinity diminishes the confidence of young people in Britain, with the consequence that young people are increasingly encouraged to prove themselves, to seek recognition, to become somebody, by using all means necessary. A crisis of masculinity and femininity is at the centre of many of the predicaments facing marginalised communities. It has been created by a lack of social mobility, persistent unemployment, growing anomie and political disenfranchisement, fuelling a national identity crisis. The effects are anger, fear, loathing, intimidation and violence. In reality, when trying to understand radicalisation among young Islamists and far-right extremists, one needs to look at the role of the individual, social structure and the question of anomie. Islamist radicals are opposed to globalisation, while far-right extremists are anti-localisation, but both are pro-totalitarian. These groups wish to instil a sense of purist identity politics and both have a utopian vision of society. Furthermore, both have a narrowly defined vision of the self, one that is exclusive of the other. In the case of far-right groups, much of their motivation stems from a counter-jihadist discourse. But radical Islamists also experience status inconsistency. Both groups are the structural and cultural outsiders of society who are directly opposed to each other. As new forms of tribalism emerge, radicalised groups point to the core narrative at the heart of their newfound tribalisitic radicalisation.[34] Membership of this new tribe is both ascriptive and aspirational, shaped by how the young are using the internet as an instrument in their radicalisation.[35]

Research suggests that far-right extremism is becoming increasingly widespread. Two concerns emerge from this. First, when far-right extremism does occur, it is often underreported or misreported. Furthermore, when a discussion does take place, it is often claimed that the violence was carried out by loners or someone suffering from a mental illness. Conversely, when it comes to young Muslims involved in acts of serious violence, unconscious associations are nearly always made with jihadism, Islamic radicalism or even ISIS. There is a particular reporting bias in the coverage of such crimes in the media (see Chapter 4).[36] As we saw earlier, in the case of the murder of Jo Cox MP, while evidence was emerging relatively quickly that the assailant had direct associations with far-right groups, most media and political commentators were slow to highlight these links. This ultimately serves to confirm the bias against far-right extremism while maintaining an overt focus on Islamist radicalisation. But two sets of 'left-behind' groups are now in direct competition with each other, one racialised and alienated and the other marginalised and alienated, yet both have emerged in the context of neoliberalism and economic restructuring in post-industrial urban settings. As social divisions grow ever wider, these groups become increasingly angry, voiceless and underrepresented. Far-right groups seek to respond to this by holding on to a sense of identity presented to them as at-risk due to the emergence of other groups in society that may be diluting the purity of this identity. Such representations are ideological, selective and political. But the idea of being a Briton is to be one in a nation of immigrants, a strongly held view until 9/11, after which multiculturalism was increasingly criticised. Due to the conservative politics of anti-Europeanism and ethnic nationalism, however, being English is closely associated with Anglo-Saxon blood. Race is the signifier here, but an imagined race, as is perennially the case when it comes to ethnic nationalism (see Chapter 2).[37]

Since the end of the Cold War, global politics has shifted to the Muslim world, while in Western Europe, Muslim minorities are increasingly seen in religious rather than ethnic or cultural terms. All of this has given Muslims more exposure, much of which has been negative and in some cases overtly hostile and violent. Political elites have often used local area tensions for political gain. As some young men express hyper-masculinity, combined with self-realisation, and engage in acts of violence and extremism, automatic associations are made with a global phenomenon, further legitimising an invasive foreign policy together with a regressive domestic policy on integration and immigration. With the securitisation of multiculturalism now the norm, where Muslim cultural and religious differences are seen as problematic for matters of security, Muslim minorities have been receiving even more attention.[38] As the levels of frustration among young Muslim men reach a point of no return, they vent their anger at the global level, rendering their local area realities invisible. Many Muslim men do not fight for their local communities, but for an imagined global project, forming a vacuum at the local level, filled by the machinations of right-wing politics, fermented locally but curated nationally.

The question of the associations between two sets of similar experiences, therefore, points to local area considerations. The failures of successive governments to introduce policies that bring about equality and fairness have done little to limit the negative consequences of neoliberalism, which has also led to the loss of the imagination of the nation in a global climate of inequality and competition, where national elites hold on to an imagined notion of the nation as well its peoples. Concerns about social justice and equality have increasingly been supplanted in policy thinking by an emphasis on vacuous notions such as 'values', which have no direct role in bringing communities together as such conceptions are exclusive rather than inclusive. In groups that are already facing downward pressures on social mobility, there are intense levels of competition and conflict within local communities, which has the potential to result in violence and, ultimately, terrorism. Thus, both sets of violent extremism are the result of the biopolitics of the state, but among groups in opposition to each other due to narrow definitions of identity. Whereas far-right groups project their angst nationally, jihadists project it globally. These realities have emerged in various spatial formations, reflecting the search for self-actualisation due to their 'left-behind' status with few or no alternative routes to empowerment or status. It is therefore important to consider issues of social structure and identity politics when attempting to understand the nature of radicalisation and extremism among those who engage in far-right extremism, as well as those drawn to Islamist extremism.

To address the problems of Islamist extremism, Western governments have identified 'Muslim communities' as the most 'vulnerable' to radicalisation compared with other groups. Muslim groups are the main target group of countering violent extremism (CVE) policy, the latest manifestation of which is Prevent in the UK context.[39] As such, far-right groups have been notably absent from the wider discourse on Prevent, although referrals from far-right groups are increasing in number each year. While prevent focuses on disengagement from radicalisation and reintegration at a community level while building resilience, engagement and participation in society, it is underscored by maintaining community cohesion through 'shared values'.

There has been fierce resistance to the Prevent policy among community actors, many of whom argue that the policy is intrusive. Viewed by some as an attempt to delegitimise criticism of politics and policy while maintaining the status quo in foreign policy, Prevent has been accused of ignoring the role of domestic policies in the integration of ethnic minorities. A broad sense of alienation has accordingly emerged among certain communities due to the political, religious and cultural transformations of the social milieu that has occurred because of wider developments to thinking and practice on localisation and globalisation. All of these young people variously enter into the theatre of radicalisation and violence due to emotional, psychological, ideological and sociological factors. Measures targeting such crimes must recognise the multi-layered nature of the processes involved in radicalisation, and hence introduce joined-up policy thinking at a much earlier stage of the process. It is thus vital to understand the intersecting paths towards Islamist and far-right radicalisation in order to adopt the correct policies in response. As a result, it is of fundamental importance that the dynamics of radicalisation are viewed as embedded in social processes at the structural level, stemming from concerns over identity, belonging and self-realisation.

Far-right and Islamist extremism are similarly problematic yet distinctly related issues, as the path towards radicalisation is local and urban in nature and outcome in both cases. These kinds of extremisms need to be recognised as two sides of the same coin. Both forms of extremism feed off the rhetoric of the 'other', compounded by an elite discourse that seeks to divide and rule when it comes to dealing with differences in society, combined with the issue of the diminished status of white working-class communities in general. It is therefore crucial that there is greater understanding of the linkages, interactions and symbiosis between these two oppositional but related extremisms. This is especially true in the current climate, where a post-truth, post-normal world has gained ascendancy, with expertise derided and where the status quo prevails. It is also important to examine how understanding these concepts can determine how they can feed into policy development. An effective approach to these issues will need to engage with extremism as a wider societal issue, not simply as a task for particular communities, ultimately placing accountability on the government and local authorities to arrive at solutions to violent extremism. In the current political climate, the projection is that violent radical Islamism is a reality of Muslim communities, in which exist all the problems and all the solutions. The following chapter builds on this discussion by exploring how the generation and spread of online content has fed into different kinds of radicalisations.

9

PLUGGED INTO THE RAGE

The radicalisation of vulnerable youths has had a number of consequences for securitisation, policing and intelligence, particularly online, and any attempt to understand the processes of mutually reinforcing radicalisation will inevitably need to grapple with the role of the internet in exacerbating this radicalisation. However, the precise nature of the processes that entice young people and 'activate' their radicalisation requires greater understanding.[1] It is not possible to argue that the internet increases the rate or intensity of terrorism, as many studies have demonstrated that it merely plays a facilitating and enabling role.[2] Thus, despite the internet's ability to connect people and ideas, the offline world remains important in connecting the real with the virtual. Importantly, young people susceptible to radicalisation are the products of a particular social, cultural and political context in which the restructuring of the economic base, from manufacturing to services, has created a 'left-behind' generation of marginalised, disenfranchised, alienated young people, both indigenous citizens and minority groups. In Western Europe, the growth of far-right and Islamist extremism has been directly associated with economic and social transformations that have resulted in groups feeling unable to contribute to their individual existence, creating alienation and anomie. In this context, anger and resentment has been directed against the perceived 'other'. For far-right groups, theirs is a 'counter-jihad' narrative that uses the rhetoric of ethnic nationalism, anti-immigration and anti-religion, specifically a concentration on anti-Islam (see Chapter 8), for instrumental ends.[3]

This online world of the far right is an alternative reality that enables people to promote their own political views while also providing information on how to construct devices that can be used for terrorist acts. The individuals attracted to such forums are often reclusive and difficult to identify.[4] The online world is a space for exploring identities, learning more about the 'other' and questions of being and becoming in a much wider space than previously understood.

Social media has grown immensely as an information and communication tool. The medium provides regular updates on activities as well as commentaries on various topics and themes, some of which relate to sensitive areas. Print and television media still affect perceptions, but it is increasingly vital to consider the role of the internet, and particularly social media, when seeking to understand how opinions and behaviour are shaped. Social media can be used in a systematically organised way, as in the case of 'astroturfing', where armies of hired hands post comments on online articles and on social media, giving the impression of being random members of the public rather than part of a highly organised and well-funded campaign. This practice has often taken place during election periods.[5] Due to the lack of stringent regulations, together with the ability to hide behind a *nom de plume*, social media has allowed different individuals and groups to support and participate in radicalised activities,[6] while those seeking to encourage others to adopt radical ideas have used social media to 'groom' vulnerable young people online.[7]

Twitter is one of the easiest social media platforms to use, and it has been a popular platform for individuals and organisations seeking to lure potential foreign fighters willing to join ISIS,[8] which was able to organise its online propaganda despite temporary setbacks to operations, with back room developers putting together tweets with YouTube videos and other documentation in an ongoing process of communication, indoctrination and recruitment. Much of this online activity took place behind the scenes—not as acts of random online messaging but as highly regulated output: 'Twitter is used to propagandize for core *Jihadist* tenets that are translated into symbolic images for a generation of social media users who prefer pictures to text.'[9]

The media in the West tends to focus on ISIS beheading videos as the main output of its propaganda, frequently ignoring the group's other areas of content[10] such as the perverse utopian vision of the Caliphate, which appealed to some Muslims based on the lure of authoritarianism. The *Inspire* magazine, produced by Al-Qaeda from July 2010 until November 2016, which is thought to have played an important role in the radicalisation and the participation of Muslims in violent jihad, is a case in point. Aiming to resonate with Western audiences, much of its content focused on instances of terrorist violence in the name of 'jihad', but the magazine also contained wider discussions on the idea of jihad as mastery of the ego.[11] The content of *Inspire* changed in response to various events and themes, in particular the Arab Spring, when *Inspire* would often focus on regional and local matters.[12]

The complex and multi-layered structure of the Islamic State's social media output showed that it was designed to tap into the aspirations of otherwise alienated and disconnected Muslims facing similar concerns around the world. In its prime, ISIS delivered a message that was acceptable to a number of conservative Muslims, many of whom would nevertheless reject the need to engage violence or terrorism. Policymakers working to eliminate the threat from such attempts to motivate young Muslims therefore operate within a framework containing a huge canvas of opinion, and intervention will only be effective if 'counter-narrative strategies' use 'reverse engineering' to undermine the 'strategic logic' of the kinds of information campaigns created by groups such as ISIS.[13] Such strategies need to first dismantle the messages and then work with messengers who can reach out to a diverse body of people.[14] A possible counter-narrative strategy would involve adopting a 'jihadi cool' narrative that seeks to nullify, but then also provide a direct alternative to an aggressive masculinity promulgated by the nuances of the digital media in question.[15] This can take different configurations depending on the different opportunities for doing so.

Research on the experiences of Islamists who have been radicalised online points to a number of underlying concerns. The following is a summary of the main approaches that were employed by ISIS to recruit foreign fighters through the digital superhighway. Each is a specific mechanism through which young minds were enticed to join the cause:

> *Humanitarian*: at some basic level, a sense of duty motivates jihadis with reference to the emphasis in Islam on the responsibility to help in humanitarian causes, especially but not exclusively in Syria.
>
> *Democracy*: radicalisers are able to argue that an inherent, unbridgeable and permanent divide exists between Islam and democracy, where incompatibility is the norm. Such perspectives extend this argument to underscore the notion that living in *dar-al-kufr* (the land of the unbelievers) is un-Islamic and that the only answer is aggressive jihad.
>
> *Identity*: radicalising groups propel a sense of the perfect Muslim who seeks to migrate to the utopian vision of an absolute society, created for Muslims to flourish as the ideal types.
>
> *Eschatology*: groups promulgate the view that the religious and political ideology of the 'end of times' is upon Muslims, and that it is a duty upon Muslims over the world to defend the Caliphate established for precisely this purpose.

The appeal of radical Islamist online magazines such as *Dabiq* (2014–16) and *Inspire* (2010–16) can be traced to the idea that Islam is under attack and in a state of crisis, which calls for a violent jihad against apostate regimes in the MENA region, with a message compelling people to join the 'vanguard of believers' as part of their individual duty in Islam. Unlike ISIS, Al-Qaeda did not seek to become the sole leader of the global Islamic community but simply a catalyst for change. In line with this aim, *Inspire* urged Muslims to carry out attacks against Western targets, acting through the use of 'lone wolf' terrorist acts. ISIS, in contrast, sought to create and maintain the Caliphate, emulating the perfect city (Medina), and emphasising the importance of migration to it (*hijra*). This is somewhat analogous to Al-Qaeda, whose core ideas are binary but also virtual, unlike ISIS, which, through the existence of war between existing Al Qaedaaffiliate groups, instrumentalised the idea of the founding of a state. In particular, *Dabiq*, until its final issue in July 2016, presented the formation of the Islamic State as a success story—a perfect place for Muslims, delivering a supreme vision of the ideal home for Muslims from across the world, portrayed as having efficient services, excellent living conditions, bountiful food and total freedom. The aim was to attract new citizens to the state. All the while, it also hailed the cause as a triumphant victory while demonising the enemy, including Shias as well as all 'others'.[16]

In general, ISIS took a mixed approach to its social media strategy, using many different platforms. Messaging ranged from general content conveyed via popular sites such as Twitter, to one-to-one targeted approaches using such applications as Telegram and the online forum Ask.fm. In many cases, Twitter was the gateway entry point; however, in more recent periods, the website has faced pressure from governments to remove problematic content, which has created challenges for it and other major social media outlets, while also raising questions about the legitimacy of government interventions to influence independent private companies seeking maximum profits.[17] ISIS drafted social media content and disseminated it widely to the public. For example, when a terrorist attack happened. The group promoted videos of terrorist acts for shock value, then lionised the attackers and pushed the message to attract people to do the same, ultimately using the attacks for later propaganda purposes in a bid to continue to rouse others. This media output was of a professional quality: no more grainy VHS recordings carried out in caves. ISIS also produced videos re-enacting popular content such as scenes from the *Hunger Games* or *Saw* films. It attempted to engage target audiences through media messages, using references that were already familiar to consumers of contemporary Hollywood-quality production techniques.

Much analytical thinking, as well as evidence obtained from young people and research, continues to argue that many European-born Muslim youth have been drawn to radicalisation in far-off lands because their own countries have not done enough to integrate them as citizens of the state. Such thinking, however, excludes the role of catalysts or accelerators, and while the internet has clearly played a role in this, it is not clear how the radicalisation process actually takes place.[18] Existing research fails to address the link between the availability of Islamist digital media and its popularity. As yet, there has been no methodical way to measure this influence directly. While the existence of online radicalisation is undeniable, how it links to offline radicalisation has yet to be explained. Furthermore, the notion of 'lone actor' terrorism is a misnomer, as others are inevitably involved. The lone actor is not a single detached offender but an individual who is part of a wider network of similarly minded individuals—the 'digital tribe'.[19] However, while the internet is an echo chamber for Islamist thinking, it did not in and of itself create radical Islamism, nor does Islamism necessarily result in violent outcomes,[20] which has further implications for those seeking to police this echo chamber as a space that spreads messages of hate and targets vulnerable groups.[21]

'Lone actor' terrorism is an important consideration in the study of radicalisation, but when anyone supports the rhetoric of any particular online ideology that gives rise to violent extremism, they do so through digital tribalism. That is, group identities take on a new meaning in the context of individuals connected through various nodes. The virtual space helps to distil not merely the content of the message and the impact it has on perceptions but also the processes behind the generation of these messages and what they mean for a digital presence. This affects Islamist groups as well as far-right groups, with the appeal of both traceable to a sense of identity loss that such groups seek to reclaim at all costs. Whereas far-right groups tend to project their grievances locally and nationally, while promoting anti-immigration sentiment, Islamist groups do the same nationally and globally, with reference to resisting integration in the West, opposing Western foreign policy and the idea of regaining a 'golden past'.

Since the inauguration of Donald Trump in January 2017, observers around the world have been disturbed by his many negative utterances, provocative put-downs of other countries and wanton dismissal of those he has appointed to run important government departments. The result has been a global outcry led by women, the young, minorities and liberal-minded people at the narcissism and self-centred nature of Trump's words and actions. Right-wing extremists have felt empowered by a triumphalism reflected in the repeated mantra of 'Make America Great Again'. The impact this has on minority communities of all backgrounds, but especially Muslim and Jewish groups, is all too clear as reports of rising anti-Semitism run alongside growing Islamophobia.[22] A general sense of intimidation towards a whole host of groups is rife, from students daubing swastikas on campus walls to graves being desecrated, bomb threats at mosques and attacks against individuals. The discourse of the far right, alt-right and other groups whose *modus operandi* is to direct hate, indignation and intolerance towards minority groups is the seed of this symbolic and actual violence. This hate speech is not singularly pointed at specific groups in North America or Western Europe but at all those who seek to uphold religious, cultural and community norms seen as un-American, un-British or un-European.[23]

Many political elites around the world are leveraging the power of authoritarian majoritarianism—a form of populism—with the aim of achieving two simultaneous outcomes. The first is to safeguard a belief in the existence of internal and external enemies who pose a threat to the nation, keeping majority populations under the grip of the ruling authority. The second is to create an ethnic (and religious) nationalism that seeks to promote the purity of the people and of the nation. This is especially the case because nativist traditionalism is increasingly becoming the central ideology behind the current wave of populism sweeping Western and once-liberal nations.[24] Many people in these nations are concerned that capitalism has failed them, with 'metropolitan elites' taking full advantage of all opportunities for themselves, leaving the rest behind. Those who have been 'left behind' are now rising up against the system and embracing populist politicians, riding a wave of traditionalism that has swept America, Britain and mainland Europe. In its path, traditionalism exposes the exceptionalism, or racist parochialism, underscoring Western and some Eastern European nationalisms that have systematically eroded the ability of the people to appreciate or respect differences among their ranks.[25]

Islamophobia and far-right nationalism have taken hold among numerous politicians-turned-demagogues throughout Europe, and elsewhere in countries that have consistently grown richer but are increasingly divided between rich and poor. Prime Minister Narendra Modi in India and President Tayyip Erdoğan in Turkey regularly evoke religious and nationalistic sentiments. Islam is also used for authoritarian ends throughout the MENA region. Seen against this context, President Trump is not the cause of the malaise but a symptom of many different forces that are threatening democratic systems all over the world.

In these heady times, many who are protected by governmental policies still feel alienated from the progressive forces that championed them. Those policies did not end unemployment, huge inequalities in wealth and power, or address the underlying value system that has shaped everyday life in competitive capitalist societies. Those most marginalised feel that they lack a stake in society and believe that those they put in power have forgotten them. These marginalised groups gain satisfaction from 'kicking' the establishment because they feel they have nothing to lose and everything to gain by shaking the system to the core. But powerful elites have leveraged these frustrations by channelling them into pseudo-populist rebellions that are under their control, directing anger away from themselves and towards other marginalised groups.

In this dystopian world, elites and those hoping to become part of the elite are increasingly dismissive of the needs of all others, in the process turning themselves into a cadre of uber-wealthy people whose principal political interest is to find ever-more resilient ways to shore up their wealth even further. But, in many cases, they also seek more than this, going as far as to change the cultural fabric of the countries in which they operate. In the case of Trump's United States, for instance, the interests of white Christian evangelicals are increasingly prioritised above all others, flourishing as the vanguard of a nation reborn. This has emboldened disaffected majority groups, whose new mantra is protectionism moulded by plutocrats that pull the strings of a man who is the front-facing mode of white supremacy (Trump has admitted his preference for selective breeding in past interviews, rendering him a eugenicist in all but name).[26] There has been a post-West era for quite some time—some would argue as early as the late 1970s.[27] For this reason, everything experienced since then should be understood in the context of the long tail of Western decline. Neoliberalism aimed to stop the declining power of the United States by cutting back the frontiers of the state, with rampant individualism replacing collective notions of community, fraternity or belonging. Multiculturalism is alive and well among the multitudes that live within diverse communities, but elites present it as not merely deficient but also a risk to the identity and well-being of the nation.

It is important to note that the emergence of the far right does not necessarily coincide with the rise of Donald Trump. White supremacy has been in play in the United States since the prospering of the Ku Klux Klan in the 1920s. Forced underground over the years, it has now found itself able to appeal to the mainstream due to a wider political and cultural malaise in which the failings of the prevailing economic system have coincided with a wave of populism, authoritarianism and xenophobia. As much as Trump's rhetoric has focused on speaking for the 'left behind', galvanised around a white supremacist political project, if they eventually feel let down, severe consequences are likely to follow.[28] The ability of the far right to move from the fringe into the mainstream is perturbing. In doing so it has taken subjects previously discussed discreetly and projected them into the public sphere as popular discourse.[29]

Islamist extremists use the internet to radicalise vulnerable young men and women, but the far right has also sought to take advantage of the opportunities the medium provides, with Brexit and the Trump victory generating concerns over the sources of electoral financing and the role played by IT companies in micro-targeting political advertisements via social media. Much has been said about the toxic masculinity of members of far-right organisations (i.e. aspects of masculine behaviour that are problematic with respect to women and young children). The characteristics of such behaviour include individualism, hyper-competitiveness, chauvinism, sexism, a belief in patriarchy, entitlement, misogyny, objectification and the infantilisation of women. The left recognises the implications this has for women as victims. The right, or rather the alt-right, is hostile to women because women form part of the threats to their identity, thereby motivating them to defend it.[30] The alt-right is a community of discourse[31] that came to prominence during the election campaign of Trump in 2016. It responded to the failures of neoliberalism and the left in establishing a political project able to unite the people against the inequities of global capitalism, internalising both biopolitics and cultural globalisation. It is akin to fascism—an ideological formation that seeks to maintain authoritarian nationalism. In many ways, alt-right groups have similar designs to ISIS, which can also be seen as a discourse and a narrative, demonstrating the 'agile interplay of coded and idiosyncratic styles combined with studied public performances of disclosure'.[32] The militarisation of the alt-right has coincided with the tendency of some in the United States to assert that it is white and Christian, returning to the supposed historical paradigms that originally defined the nation. This radicalisation has had harmful consequences for a range of different groups, and specifically Muslims, who are the target of most of the hate. The way the United States is now perceived around the world has undergone a profound transformation, partly due to the realities found on the streets of urban areas in cities facing the challenges of global capitalism. A clear correlation exists between the hate presented by President Trump and the rise in racism that has become all too evident in US society.[33]

One characteristic shared by both ISIS and the alt-right groups is the nature of their opposition to feminism. It is a perspective on ideology motivated by a response to the challenges of the neoliberal economy, which has led to the transformation of traditional modes of work. Simultaneously, the presence of women in the labour market and the importance of equality for people of colour have also shifted the narrative to the role of men and their position in society. The desire to challenge these developments has led to the emergence of this 'manosphere'—a digital tribalism associated with such networks, virtual and real.[34] But while conflicts between different heterosexual masculinities are taking place within this space, the common mode of resistance is against feminism and ethnic diversity. The particular nature of this anti-female discourse comprises a misogynistic network of angry, disillusioned and hateful men purporting to speak out against feminism in particular.[35] Within these spaces, subcultures manipulate news content through the use of 'fake news', distracting less informed people from the central issues they face in their daily lives. The ability to propagate problematic ideas and influence opinion is a growing concern as the mainstream media also uses the online social media space as a way to promote, promulgate and present their own news stories. Although there are many differences between the various alt-right manifestations of the manosphere, each of the respective groups has a clear ability to influence the online space. Islamophobia, racism, intolerance and bigotry spread easily, especially when such ideas are able to target susceptible young men. These ideas serve to generate mistrust of news even further, encouraging the most distrustful to seek alternative views as a way in which to find common norms.[36] Journalists face a particularly difficult task in ensuring objectivity in the space dominated by 'fake news', alternative facts and downright lies as trust in news media is an increasingly rare commodity.[37]

A crisis of masculinity is at the heart of the malaise facing young men all over the world. Both radical Islamists and the far-right fringes have galvanised in the online space in resistance to neoliberal globalisation, their loss of identity and the increasing prominence of women in society. Unreconstructed patriarchy, in the form of an anti-feminist discourse grounded on selective aspects of conservative Islamic and Christian norms, is finding a new voice on the internet, coupled with hate towards the 'other' more generally, presented as a common enemy to the collective male 'self'. The internet has become a safe haven for men struggling to come to terms with the loss of traditional male life. The language, culture and discourse of violence towards women and 'others' dominate the manosphere and the world of online radical Islamists. From the fringes to the mainstream, Trump and other authoritarian nationalists legitimise fascism in all but name. Islamists, promoting a utopian, if perverse, world vision, promote a narrow scriptural reading of the texts in order to approbate their need for revenge for years of enslavement through colonialism and the post-war migration history of racism and discrimination in their new homes. Trump has successfully instrumentalised the politics of hate that has been festering under the tentative surface of a fragmented United States. Abu Bakr al-Baghdadi, leader of Islamic State, is a similar hate-filled figure of power, someone whose views are based on contempt for previous experiences of political and cultural uncertainty. The victims in both cases are young men who are angry, enfeebled and distrustful of one another, now morphed into a cyber-realm where their rage finds a voice online, where their digital tribalism gives them new meaning in an otherwise broken and divided world. The following chapter returns to a focus on the British Muslim, in particular exploring the contemporary themes of Islamophobia and radicalisation that have afflicted British Muslims in their pursuit of recognition, belonging and status as citizens of the state.

10

VANQUISHING FALSE IDOLS

The transatlantic slave trade led to advances in industry, trade and commerce, sustaining an international political economy in which capitalism was king. Today, the world is starkly divided between the haves and the have-nots, between the empowered and disempowered, and not solely between black and white but also between the Muslim world and the rest of the world. Since the fall of the Berlin Wall and the end of the Cold War, this Muslim/non-Muslim binary has become increasingly noticeable economically, politically, culturally and ideologically.[1] This chapter delves into the world of British Muslims who have experienced a whole host of interconnected challenges at the national and local levels, with the perils of Brexit sowing deep divisions. It also explores the so-called 'Trojan Horse' affair of 2014, which demonstrated that Islamophobia had reached the highest levels of government.

As we have seen, many Muslims who came to Western Europe after the end of the Second World War did so in order to fill employment vacancies for roles shunned by indigenous populations who were seeking better prospects in the labour market. Employers and policymakers invited guest workers to take up these jobs in the hope their sojourn would be temporary. But this proved not to be the case, with the outcome an aspect of policy but also design. Employers benefited by keeping wages down, while Western economies as a whole gained from a pliable and insecure workforce. Minority Muslim communities were law-abiding in seeking their cultural wants and needs while maintaining loyalty to their new nations. But the racism inherited by their host societies due to colonialism, Orientalism and cultural ethnocentrism did not dissipate upon their arrival, nor as they settled over time. Instead, racism adapted by centring on colour, before focusing on race, ethnicity and, eventually, religion.[2] Current generations of Western European-born Muslims, as distinct ethnic, cultural and linguistic groups, continue to face the brunt of discrimination, vilification and isolation but largely on anti-Muslim terms, where religious identity trumps all other categories of differentiation.[3]

Around 30 million Muslims of various backgrounds live and work in Western Europe.[4] The vast majority originate from once-colonised lands, originally migrating to their 'mother countries' in order to take up work in declining industrial sectors. Over the years, however, their ability to integrate has been hampered by discrimination, racism, xenophobia and vilification, so much so that it required Western governments to legislate in order to protect the rights of citizens of different cultural and religious backgrounds.[5] But despite the efforts of policymakers, similar problems continue to persist. Present-day Muslim minorities face limited opportunities for social mobility through education and employment. The social discontent this generates plants the seeds for radicalisation for all groups, but particularly for Muslims, as they suffer disproportionately from the 'othering' of groups in various societies.

In this milieu of insecurity and indifference Western European societies have narrowly determined what it is to be a good citizen. The conversation over differences, however, focuses on Islam as antithetical to the needs and aspirations of nations with long histories of contact with the religion over the centuries. This prevailing discourse does not reflect questions of diversity or pluralism, but instead focuses on how to curb the supposedly excessive Muslim demands that Europe once accommodated. These nations are increasingly defining citizenship in a narrow and exclusive way, promoting a neoliberal outlook that is also anti-social democratic in reality. Western European nation states sustain their economies via questionable economic and political practices in far-flung corners of the world, from interventionist policies in the MENA region in the name of 'democracy' and 'freedom' to a narrow focus on the financial sectors as the wealth creators for countries as a whole. Connecting these concerns is a discourse on Muslims as a predicament for the globe as a whole, with a particular focus on terrorism and extremism acting as unifying topics to sustain the status quo.[6] The forces of neoliberal market economics ravage societies, leaving many struggling, in particular those at the margins of society, namely former working-class communities, minority communities from once-colonised lands and new immigrant groups placed at the bottom of society irrespective of colour or religion. Globalisation, which in reality refers to global financial flows, is not always about trade and commerce—rather, globalisation simply accelerates these processes.[7] The role of powerful internet and media actors helps to take attention away from other concerns around climate change, the problems of the food industry, the power of 'big pharma', the unevenness of national and international economic development or the tax avoidance of the rich and the most successful of corporate actors.[8] In the past, people of colour faced exploitation by the Western world. Today, Muslims are centre stage within Western powers, where an 'othering' process continues to re-invent itself. The dominant view is that Muslims are dangerous, menacing, misogynistic, lecherous, inferior, backward and primitive.

Considerable contact, exchange and intercultural relations between Islam and Europe helped to define and shape each other's character.[9] During the period in which Islam was in the ascendency, it absorbed European Christianity, but as Islam waned, Christian Europe disdained Islam even though it had benefited from it considerably. As Europe grew, it split into nation states competing aggressively with each other until the conflict was unsustainable. The ideals of the European Union were harnessed as a response to internal challenges, but European harmony remains fragile, as the 2016 Brexit vote has demonstrated. For some, Europe has become blinkered and inward-looking, focusing on exclusivity and a particular historical narrative. The failures of European ideas today are the ignominies of its imagination in the twenty-first century, but they have also resulted from the disappointments of the past. In effect, Western European inventiveness has stagnated due to the need to uphold the designs of hyper-capitalism at the expense of all other social and philosophical systems. Free market principles have triumphed. While this approach has clear limitations, it seems the whole world has signed up to this neoconservative, neoliberal creed when it comes to thinking through economy and society.[10] As such, Muslims, entombed in a cultural and intellectual vacuum, live in dominant societies seeking only to reproduce the economic status quo. Unable to go forward, they sometimes withdraw. Those farthest away at the peripheries are the most vulnerable to internal conflict and external persuasion.

For many, capitalism remains a highly effective means to pursue self-interest, despite the many checks made by governments to curb the powers of monopoly corporations, to prevent firms from colluding and price-fixing, and to ensure fair taxation to facilitate a welfare state. However, the dominant economic model is turning a small body of the world's population into a self-sustaining elite while much of the rest of the world lingers behind.[11] Traditionally, a left-leaning standpoint in societies worked as a means to check the workings of dominant capital and its effects on media, politics and the nature of social relations. The left, however, has all but relinquished authority, save for a recent resurgence in socialist thinking, some of which is even rejuvenating aspects of the Labour Party in the UK.[12] Liberals have always been inclined to waver with the mood music of the time and still do so today[13]—especially those who do not 'do God'.[14] A long and bloody struggle attempted to overcome the discernible discriminations of white racism towards black groups, but Muslim objectification is so deeply structured and cultured in the present day that overcoming it will take a mammoth effort on the part of all in society.[15]

So-called ethnic ghettos, where specific Muslim groups are sometimes concentrated—though rarely out of choice—are not usually a reflection of communities choosing to live among themselves. Instead, their experience reflects the failure of government to implement policies promoting integration and equality.[16] At the same time, former 'white' working classes have also suffered because of deindustrialisation, technological innovation and globalisation. They face ongoing cultural, economic and political disenfranchisement.[17] Most Muslims retain their ethnic, faith and cultural norms and values as forms of solace, which some majorities may regard as a retreat into regressive practices. Though they also suffer from marginalisation in society, ostracised 'white' groups have the history of their nation, whether imagined or real, and the co-ethnic partisanship of the dominant hegemonic order at their disposal.[18] The dominant political discourse continues to blame those who radicalise as a response to the failures of capital as losing their 'values' or having a 'crisis of identity', rarely scrutinising the workings of wider society to appreciate the holistic character of social conflict. Issues to do with freedom of expression, or categorising values as alien, are routinely instrumentalised to ensure the focus is on the victims, who are then tricked into blaming these 'others' for the shortcomings of wider society as a whole.[19] Attacks from 2015 to 2017 by *takfiri*-jihadis in London, Paris, Berlin, Nice, Barcelona and Sydney were all carried out by the sons of immigrant minorities caught between cultures. Rather than being supported and developed as individuals and communities in society, the far fringes of marginalised groups vent their frustrations at the centre. All of the attackers were the insiders/outsiders of society, but rather than ameliorating matters, certain illiberal political actors can generate capital from their plight.

Writing in early 2019, anti-Muslim sentiment has been normalised across wide sections of Western Europe. Far-right groups are increasingly targeting individuals, groups and institutions associated with Islam, including mosques and Islamic centres, with numerous accounts of some firebombed or daubed with hateful graffiti. Large numbers of Muslims face being subject to random attacks on the streets of cities all over Western Europe almost on a daily basis. All the evidence suggests that the situation is deteriorating for Muslims in Western Europe, as levels of violence against Muslims are on the rise— coupled with increasing levels of anti-Semitism.[20] At the same time, aspects of the so-called Islamophobia industry are preventing Muslims from raising concerns or dealing with profound questions emanating from their religious and cultural experiences. Bridges have yet to be established between the enlightened and secular standards of free enquiry, coupled with critical investigation and a spiritual humanism that is intellectually and philosophically driven by Muslim groups from within.[21] The need for 'Muslimness' to be owned and developed by Muslims is still in process. What does exist has emerged independently of affected communities. It is benign but ultimately creates polarised opposites, fuelling extremisms on all sides (see Chapter 8).

—•—

As the local and global inextricably combine, nation states are prone to infection by ethno-nationalist ideas, which are seen as a means to protect national identities on the world stage. An essentialist discourse divides societies, placing emphasis on a repackaged national 'brand' in order to compete effectively within the global marketplace. Existing impoverished, dispossessed, marginalised and minority groups find their positions further instrumentalised in this race to success.[22] Increasingly authoritarian nations adopt policies of securitisation, 'muscular liberalism' or anti-multiculturalism as a way to ensure the permanent 'othering' of some of the most 'othered' groups in society.[23] The emphasis of much of this othering has centred on ISIS, but other historical paradigms and contemporary political contexts in sites of conflict have also come into focus. But while global Islamic militancy remains a problem, it is also important to remember that this militarised form of Islam largely emerged because of the vacuum left after states had failed—especially those facing external pressures and internal strife, including Syria and Iraq.[24] ISIS was partly successful due to its use of different kinds of methods in its violence, combining both conventional and guerrilla tactics. It also made rapid territorial gains because it had its own income, which was key to its initial emergence. Using social media to promote the cause and encourage others to join the group, ISIS was able to become a revolutionary movement with a particular theological framework, capable of using technology and in particular the internet to expand its reach. What was novel about ISIS were its aspirations to the end of times thesis, combined with a specific notion of Islamist ideology. Its initial success acted as a pull factor for those who experienced the greatest levels of marginalisation, alienation, disenfranchisement, subjugation and frustration due to the ineffectiveness of the nation states in which they lived. ISIS successfully exploited existing grievances and prevailing narratives, using the fear and insecurity Muslims experience, combined with the history of the Muslim world's interaction with the West to encourage the *hijra* to Iraq and Syria, cleverly fusing together an array of disparate complaints.

A range of structural crises afflict groups in the Muslim world and in the West, with many of the pre-migration sending countries remaining politically unstable and economically underdeveloped. The vulnerability of young people in these Western societies feeds into an ever-growing level of rage at the status quo, leading to insurrection or simply the desire to join insurrectionary forces. Many of the young men and women who ended up in the Islamic State had little or no real appreciation of Islam, and their actions should instead be seen as an act of rebellion against their own societies. In this respect, a specific form of political Islam often appeals to young people because it provides a pre-prepared model and way of making sense of their lives. Attention is dedicated to the view that this conflict is not about Islam or Muslims at all; however, this perspective would be to deny the mask of Islam few right-thinking Muslims anywhere in the world would recognise as Islamic. It is therefore necessary to accept how the lived experience in the West contributes to pushing young people towards extremism.[25] It is vital to look at the structure of societies and popular culture, where structural disadvantage is measurable, conflated by the absence of a stable centre within the political spectrum, which pushes dissenting voices to the periphery. Opportunities are limited in a climate where the 'us and them' dichotomy, designed by the powerful, affects the most powerless in the most intense of ways. Those placing the full spotlight on Islam and Muslims aim to give the impression that everything else affecting people associated with these categories is insignificant in determining both the push and the pull factors associated with radicalisation.

Young people who gravitate towards zones of conflict in the Middle East do so because of push and pull factors, but it is nevertheless dangerous to make generalisations about their motivations. Many other struggles affect Muslim communities across the globe, and misinformation fuels protestations on all sides. In reality, Muslims face far more important struggles than violent extremism alone, given that the percentages of those involved in violent extremism are incredibly small. The more pressing reality is that around the world today Muslims are the victims of violent extremism more than any other group. Religion provides the justification, but the effects of integration, alienation, power, authority and social class should not be underestimated. Ill-informed policymaking has consequences. In numerous instances of Muslim-originated violence found in Western Europe, many of the young people involved were already on the radars of the intelligence and police services, and in some cases they had been picked up and allegedly mistreated by the authorities.[26] In the meantime, Britain continues to supply weapons and logistics support to a whole host of Middle Eastern countries:

> Britain's foreign policy making system is far removed from promoting the public interest. Rather, Whitehall's secret affairs with radical Islam have increased the terrorist threat to Britain and the world; a distinctly immoral aspect of foreign policy that has made Britain, the Middle East and much of the rest of the world deeply insecure.[27]

After the 2008 global financial crash, the UK government introduced a policy of austerity in public spending as a way to reduce public debt. In effect, the policy originated from the failures of the banks. But it went against the advice of the IMF and many leading economists, further dividing a battered Britain already reeling from the consequences of thirty years of deindustrialisation and neoliberalism. The 2011 English riots that led to looting and unrest in numerous towns and cities were acute illustrations of the lack of awareness of what was really happening in communities.[28] In 2016, the EU referendum in Britain reflected the angst of vast swathes of Britain who were no longer willing to accept being left behind. Brexit was in many ways a response to austerity, as many of the older members of the population voted to leave, not just the middle-aged but also pensioners. Meanwhile, the young mainly voted to remain.[29] The irony is that the people who voted for Brexit as a 'kick' to the establishment in London could find themselves in a worse-off position after Britain leaves the European Union.

As of 2019, Britain is a divided nation where questions of Islamophobia, violent extremism and radicalisation are at the fore.

Much of this can be traced to the politics of the moment—the intolerance, bigotry and selfishness that characterises the idea of the self or one's nation as promoted by political elites underqualified to appreciate the nuances of community-level divisions. Structural inequalities result from the unfettered workings of capitalism. If those who own the means of production do not pay their taxes, there is no 'trickle down'.[30] The economic divisions this generates are also contributing to a notion of English ethnic nationalism that has now become the dominant paradigm in British politics, as Britain, led by the political centre in London, which voted overwhelmingly to remain in the European Union, seeks to distance itself from the EU.[31] The leave–remain separation began as a spat between two right-wing elements of the Conservative Party, eventually leading to a campaign in which the political elite cajoled the population one way or another through propaganda and, in many cases, sheer falsehoods. Many of these elites believe they can return to a golden age where Britannia ruled the waves. Yet migration is and will continue to be necessary for survival in a globalised world—no nation that wants to grow and compete can endure without it. The Brexit vote weakened the pound and forced investors to turn elsewhere. Leaving the EU will not lead to improved wages or greater economic opportunities for most in British society, save for business elites who will avoid EU tax regulations. Withdrawing from the European Union will widen divisions in society while isolating Britain from its neighbours. It clears the way for the potential break-up of the UK, with England left alone and isolated. No discernible long-term benefits to leaving the EU exist.

The vote to leave the EU has exposed the divisions in Britain between working-class communities in deindustrialised areas and the urban educated metropolitan and wealthier groups in the South. Somewhat paradoxically, many of those who voted to leave will be the most badly affected by its consequences. In harking back to a bygone age that can never return, narrow-minded politicians were successfully able to whip up fear and hate based on misinformation and xenophobia. Brexit exposed patterns of deeply held racism in Britain, exacerbated further by the poor economic conditions many face.[32] The EU is far from perfect, but it has nevertheless provided numerous benefits to workers, as well as grants to researchers, protections on human rights, and a collective economic, political and cultural spirit that aims to meet the interests of the many rather than a small elite. In leaving the EU, Britain risks becoming an isolated, detached and irrelevant entity in European affairs. Brexit has brought to the surface layers of racism and the 'ghosts of empire'. In many ways, the UK has given into hate and bigotry, shunning openness and tolerance. Immigration remains necessary at both ends of the labour market, from Egyptian heart surgeons with specialist skills to Estonian cleaners working in hospitals. London will become more dominant compared to the rest of England, not less, as a result of Brexit. Instead of being a key player in the game of world affairs, Britain has decided to watch from the side-lines.

In this climate of austerity and Brexit, Muslims are facing growing levels of bigotry, hate and intolerance.[33] There is little room in the prevailing national discourse for an acceptance of differences, even though these differences are very small indeed. Most people are content with trying to do their best as citizens of the state despite feeling voiceless, inhibited and even silenced by the workings of society, as a pervasive mean streak affects individuals and institutions. At the start of the twenty-first century, diversity and differences were increasingly seen as enhancing, rather than challenging, a collective sense of the nation—one that was inclusive and forward-looking yet self-assured and poised to take on the world by embracing globalisation. Fast-forward two decades, and Britain is now seen by many as bigoted, reactionary, inward-looking, intolerant, spiteful and blind to all criticism and oblivious of all that has shaped the post-war experience—a history of immigration, diversity and difference. Seen from this perspective, Brexit is a retreat to 'little Englandism'. This dark and disturbing sense of national identity is based on a woeful ignorance of the history and contributions of once imperial subjects and others in the development of British society today.

The leadership in charge of schools at Birmingham City Council have historically overlooked the realities facing young Muslims in education. Decade upon decade of underachievement, in particular among men, inevitably led some to enter into a life of criminality and even extremism. Birmingham's schools were mismanaged, leaving the aspirations of young people unmet. In 2014, an alleged 'Trojan Horse' plot to Islamise education in a number of schools attended predominantly by Muslim pupils in the inner-city wards of Birmingham raised questions over the integrity of Muslims who had been given the freedom and power to educate their young with public money. The Office for Standards in Education (Ofsted) investigated twenty-one of the city's schools in its efforts to explore these concerns at the behest of the then secretary of state for education, Michael Gove. As part of the government's counterterrorism policy, the accusations of the Islamisation of education within these Trojan Horse schools foreshadowed the additional securitisation of all sectors of education. But there was neither evidence nor any legal justification for ratcheting up the anti-extremism education measures that eventually followed, namely the Counter-Terrorism and Security Act of 2015. The consequences of the negative attention heightened existing levels of Islamophobia while also limiting the opportunities for de-radicalisation through education.[34]

When the matter first entered into the public domain, Birmingham's local authority was keen to dispel fears over Islamism, largely because it wanted to protect the city's reputation. The Trojan Horse schools were attended by poor, marginalised young Muslims whose parents did not want their children to grow up in a culture of failure. The pupils in these schools were instilled with a sense of purpose, as well as being helped to resolve pressures on identity and to open up their thinking on Britishness and belonging. The leadership of the schools placed considerable emphasis on empowering young Muslims by learning about their religion, thereby equipping them to appreciate its depth and nuances.[35] Doing so bestowed young people with the courage and wisdom to counter the narratives propounded by the likes of ISIS, which has been able to capitalise on the lack of Islamic awareness among disaffected youth, filling the vacuum with a sense of belonging, knowing and self-actualisation. In the context of the racism, discrimination, inequality and marginalisation facing many British Muslim groups in inner-city areas today, a programme of self-awareness in education was an effective solution in a climate that sought to present all the problems of society as the problems of

Muslims. The controversy surrounding the schools merely uncovered the fear and loathing of conservative Islam and pious Muslims in certain sectors of society.[36]

The Trojan Horse saga, as a case study of Muslim minority experiences of ethnic and religious identities in Britain, confirmed that the perceptions of the 'other' held by the dominant group remain crucial sources of anxiety.[37] After seventy years of post-war immigration, settlement and adaptation to society, many Muslim minority communities continue to face racism, prejudice, intolerance, bigotry and discrimination, affecting educational outcomes and their sense of identity.[38] Dominant notions of race and nation have thrust Muslims into the limelight as the most racialised, objectified and 'othered' group in education, but adaptation and social integration has simply not occurred because of the workings of wider society. This is not to argue that social and cultural integration is the solution, but rather to assert that various external factors are forcing communities apart rather than bringing them together. The episode led to a vast array of new counterterrorism practices—including promoting 'British values'. The presumption that promoting 'British values' will somehow eliminate the structural inequalities that result from modern racism is nonsensical, as it will simply reproduce the status quo, recreating the conditions for disadvantage and discrimination. It is an attempt to preserve ethnic nationalism in the face of its ongoing disintegration. Projected as representing all that is least desired about the 'self', the irony is that British Muslims, in reality, are more a part of British life than ever.

The rise of anti-Muslimism, culturally, economically and politically, is not confined to specific Western nation states but is seen across vast swathes of the Global North. In many cases, forms of structural exclusion within these communities prevent European-born Muslims from resisting the allure of criminality, contributing to the normalisation of anti-Muslim and Islamophobic racism and radicalism, combined with fear and myopia on the part of Muslims themselves. All of which is taking place at the same time as the collapse of the Western European imagination, placing pressures on both the Muslims in Western Europe, and the states in which they reside, to draw inwards, narrowing the terms of engagement and ultimately handing further powers to governments to legislate and police without always considering human rights or civil liberties. Simultaneously, Muslims facing the brunt of exclusion in society in the current period, run the risk of further isolation and 'othering'. The following chapters explore questions relating to the education of Western European Muslims in further detail by examining the kind of knowledge that may help with de-radicalisation measures.

11

TOMORROW BELONGS TO THOSE ...

As seen in the previous chapter, in the summer of 2014 Michael Gove launched an investigation into a supposed plot to Islamise the education provided to predominantly Muslim pupils in a number of state schools in the city of Birmingham. In response, certain political actors and sections of the media were quick to adopt an Islamophobic narrative that demonised those who adhere to a conservative form of Islam. These negative sentiments operated within a framework that shapes political identities through a narrow spectrum of supposed British values, with the defining parameters presented in exclusivist terms, namely: (a) those who do not espouse particular (cultural) values are somehow upholding extremist views and (b) are a threat to democracy (political values) and, as such, to the status quo.[1] This chapter continues to focus on education, in particular as a means to challenge Islamophobia and radicalisation.

The prevailing post-war paradigm on education and social class was based on a direct association between these two concepts, such that they are inseparable in the minds of many.[2] That is, education leads to class mobility as a direct result of the education system. In extending this argument, the idea that minority children underperform in education due to their ethnic and class characteristics should hold sway, but research has also claimed that stronger schools can raise the average performance levels of pupils from weaker backgrounds, while weaker schools tend to reduce the average performance of pupils from lower-class backgrounds. The idea of the 'school effect'[3] suggests that the school makes all the difference, and if weak schools improve their management, leadership and organisation and adopt a curriculum that enhances the pupil–teacher–school interaction, dramatic changes to educational outcomes occur. In the 1980s and 1990s, the move to the New Right in education—with pedagogical practices based on the belief that the state is unable to meet all of people's needs, which should instead be met by the private sector—furthered the process of marketisation in education. It provided parents and children with greater choice and thus, in theory, greater opportunity.[4] The role of school governors in steering the management and leadership of schools meant that parents and community members played a greater part in the running of schools than they ever had before. The process also ensured that too much power did not rest in the hands of head teachers or local authority policymakers. These changes supposedly met the needs and demands of a competitive education system that allowed for greater independence at the school level.

Educational underperformance among young Muslims is seen by many as an intractable problem. However, in reality, the poor educational performance of young British Muslims is often due to policy decisions made at a local or national level. This is particularly true in the case of Birmingham, as a number of schools were closed in the city from the mid-1980s onwards, severely damaging the life chances of young people in inner-city areas, leading to further deprivation and disadvantage.[5] Further mismanagement and poor leadership in these same schools was also highlighted in the 1990s. The current generation of young Muslims in inner-city areas of Birmingham are in exactly the same schools based in precisely the same areas; little seems to have changed since the 1980s. During this period, the education system has failed tens of thousands of young Muslim children in schools in the inner-city areas of Birmingham. Beyond the realm of education, there is a wider problem where the city is incorrectly labelled a 'hotbed' of radicalisation and violent extremism, an issue that came to the fore as a result of the Westminster attacks on 22 March 2017, given that the assailant had lived in Birmingham for a period.

The situation is further compounded by the obstacles to career progression that many Muslim teachers experience,[6] as well as the tendency for the young Muslims they teach, especially boys, to struggle to reconcile their faith-based identities with their national, ethnic or cultural allegiances.[7] New Labour began funding faith-based schools, including Muslim ones, in 1997 as means to foster a diverse, multicultural society, yet its policy largely ignored the views of Muslims themselves, for whom being a minority is a charged and contested issue. It is also loaded with complexities beyond the simple divisive rhetoric of Muslim or non-Muslim.[8] Although British Muslims in education generally want to emphasise coherence and interdependency between their identities as Muslim and British,[9] it would be far too simplistic to place all Muslims into a single category, as there are myriad differences between and within groups.[10] These differences also exist between and within generations,[11] and elsewhere in Muslim diasporas across the Western and Eastern worlds.[12] All the same, there is still an opportunity to mobilise 'Muslimness' as a bottom-up political identity that contests the negative paradigms, in the process expanding the reach of the concept of 'Muslim' among both empowered and marginalised groups.[13] The 'Trojan Horse' schools demonstrated how it was possible, but in a charged political context driven partly by Islamophobia and neoliberalism, they encountered severe resistance.

Education can undoubtedly play a highly important role in preventing radicalisation and de-radicalising those who have been attracted to extremist views.[14] The administration and management of the Trojan Horse schools discussed in the previous chapter placed considerable emphasis on empowering young Muslims to know more about their religion and their religious identity. The schools sought to equip pupils with the ability to appreciate the depth and nuances of Islam, bestowing young people with the courage and wisdom to counter the narratives propounded by the likes of ISIS.[15]

In the wake of the controversy, Ofsted took over the administration of twenty-one schools, placing outstanding schools under special measures. As well as facing the wrath of government, with administrative bodies changed and senior staff replaced, five teachers were also forced to go through disciplinary procedures over their alleged role in the so-called Trojan Horse Affair to Islamise state secondary schools. For nearly three years, these five teachers were subject to an investigation that was often delayed. Ultimately, however, because government lawyers withheld valuable evidence, all the charges against the teachers, with one sole exception, were eventually withdrawn. Yet the events nevertheless provided a useful background for the introduction of the 2015 Counter-Terrorism and Security Act, which greatly increased the power of the state with regard to counterterrorism and de-radicalisation. One of the act's provisions was designed to strengthen the Prevent policy mentioned earlier in the book by making it law for up to 500,000 public sector workers to take the Workshop to Raise Awareness of Prevent (WRAP) and to implement safeguarding on a large scale. Ultimately, the act formalised the securitisation of a 'pre-crime' space, where groups are policed, regulated and modulated before anyone commits a crime. In the end, the battle over this issue was not about young people and their schooling but about power and politics at the top of government. The victims were the young people studying and the professionals working in these schools whose lives were never the same again.

One of the questions that emerged as a result of the controversy concerns educational leadership. The directives introduced by Ofsted allowing schools greater autonomy feed into the neoliberal agenda that manifests in education policy, a continuation of school policies that were first introduced in the late 1980s and early 1990s, which were designed to introduce market forces into education; however, in such circumstances, the tendency is for the free market to enhance existing divisions between stronger and weaker schools. But it is also possible to introduce innovative educational methods to encourage and motivate children in schools to improve their performance in examinations. In this space, the Trojan Horse schools became a victim of their own success in that they took the opportunity to use the system to change seemingly cemented performance patterns. Yet doing so evoked the twin concerns of radicalisation and extremism at a time when these concepts carry considerable weight.[16]

The education of British Muslims has evolved in the context of the policies of post-war immigration, integration and diversity policy. In reality, in situating these groups, popular systems of multiculturalism endorse notions of tolerance and secularity through the popularisation of a multiculture that racialises the civilised, modern or backward in the construction of national identities.[17] By centring on cultural boundaries while de-emphasising structural disadvantage or racism, the phenomenon of Islamophobia sets limits to how differences within societies can be recognised. The retreat of multiculturalism has coincided with the increasing dominance of neoliberalism in education, where the individual is not merely a learner but also a customer, where satisfaction is the measure of success rather than explicit learning outcomes. In the post-9/11 war on terror culture, this performance-orientated approach is problematic, as it views Muslims through the lens of surveillance and suspicion, as 'suspect communities'. The idea of integration today centres on the expectation that minority communities will assimilate into wider society while ignoring the impact of changing socioeconomic and sociocultural dynamics for Muslim and ethnic minority groups in various British towns and cities—no longer a two-way street between the state and Muslims but a cul-de-sac. In reality, adaptation to and incorporation into society is restricted. As racism persists, ethnic minority groups respond to marginalisation and exclusion with actions that might disconnect them further from the mainstream.

The supposed secular neutrality of British society belies a disproportionality in approaches to non-Protestant faiths. Throughout a history of orientalism and Islamophobia, the greatest focus of moderation is on Islam. Neoliberalism as the hegemonic hyper-capitalistic world order is the setting of rampant globalisation that rips apart both nations and neighbourhoods. In this context, appreciation of the value of Islam for Muslims has surfaced as a form of resistance through re-reading and re-application. But for migrant, diasporic and transnational communities, problematising Muslim minorities in education evokes complexities beyond the simple dividing rhetoric of Muslim or non-Muslim. Persistent negative societal, attitudinal and behavioural attention challenges a diverse minority community of communities who are persistently on the receiving end of sustained and disparaging attention.[18] Fears over resource investment in educational infrastructure, curricula and pedagogical anxieties affecting British Muslims in education create uncertainties. This not only affects young children but also parents, teachers and education managers. In rationalising the political and sociological milieu in these contexts, the themes of religion, ethnicity and gender are as significant as ideology, culture and policy. They are set within the frameworks of secularisation, de-secularisation, sacralisation and the re-sacralisation of Islam in the public sphere. Generating a philosophical, spiritual and intellectual evaluation of British Muslims in education requires a suitable approach that synthesises the sociological, educational, political and cultural apprehensions that are internal and external, local and global.

Education is merely one stream of activity in these changing dynamics during a period of around four decades of social and economic policy. The liberalisation of educational markets, the importance of globalisation and localisation in shaping identity politics, and the significance of the counterterrorism and securitisation agenda raise new concerns, challenges and questions. But it would be wrong to suggest that there is no room for progress. While the neoliberal securitisation framework on the education of young British Muslims has created an emphasis on Muslims as the 'suspect community', it is important to note that educational settings can also be a space in which youth masculinity and femininity can be redefined and reshaped. This includes challenging the status quo in a way that results in progressive and integrative forms of national belonging. Questions over Muslim identities are an opportunity for positive change in curricula, pedagogy and assessment—specifically in critical opposition to the UK government's Prevent agenda that tends to focus on young Muslim men solely due to their religion.[19] The notion of a culturally responsive pedagogy is important because of the general removal of discussions of diversity or multiculturalism in educational settings. Teachers should move beyond the simple notion of schoolchildren as consumers or potential customers, instead emphasising the importance of cultural inclusiveness and thereby re-introducing notions of self-esteem and confidence vigorously taken away by a concentration on secular identity. One potential way to do so would involve looking at the mother tongue as an opportunity for enhanced teacher–pupil interaction, or refocusing on the hijab as a form of female self-empowerment. An engaged, inclusive curriculum can help to bridge the divisions created by the hyper-marketisation of education where individual performance defines the measure of successful learning. The role of the teacher in this regard is crucial.[20]

The idea of empowerment through individuality to release young Muslim women from the bondage of cultural repression is to revert to existing dominant stereotypes concerning the need to protect these minorities from themselves. The net result is reinforced neoliberal individualisation, seen as a route to success for disaffected working-class communities but also Muslim minority women, considered especially susceptible to the risk of regressive cultural practices. It is somewhat dispiriting that these powerful notions persist despite years of alternative thinking and practice, but at the same time, it is also unsurprising given the context in which these dominant themes materialise, namely the securitisation agenda that signals a wholesale retreat from multiculturalism, inter-culturalism and respect for diversity. A radical black feminism, in response to patriarchal policies and the post-feminist discourse of the white female liberal standpoint, allows young Muslim women to come to terms with this subjugation and, crucially, find ways to challenge it holistically and systematically through a form of individual agency that both re-engages and empowers the 'self'.[21] Important progress has also been made in female education due to the role of British Muslim parents in determining and validating the aspirations of their daughters, particularly in higher education. Young Muslim women are progressing and achieving well in education, especially when compared with young Muslim men.[22] This suggests that reflexivity, particularly after secondary school education, encourages and motivates young Muslim women, with their parents' support, to achieve optimal educational outcomes.

A series of new challenges is currently affecting young Muslims in British schools. After many years of post-war immigration, settlement and adaptation, many British Muslims continue to face racism, prejudice, intolerance, bigotry and discrimination in wider society.[23] These outcomes shape concerns over identity politics, where dominant notions of race and nation thrust Muslims into the limelight as the most racialised, objectified and 'othered' group in education in the current climate.[24] Young Muslims are often viewed as a potential security threat, and teachers and educational professionals, without adequate training, have been mandated to identify, isolate and process those seen as 'at risk', ultimately producing deeper inequality, social divisions and additional disaffection.[25] Since the end of the Cold War, counterterrorism and the securitisation agenda have seeped into educational policy, negatively affecting British Muslims in educational settings.

At the heart of the problem of global inequality is the formation of capital and wealth creation based on the neoclassical economic theory of the free market, which affects the nature and output of the media, and aspects of Orientalism, which help to propel certain propaganda. It supports modes of geopolitical competition, enhancing internal divisions by maintaining the framework in which elites seek to realise external geopolitical goals. The power of the elites is also maintained through aspects of the knowledge and information economy.

Where does this leave Muslim minorities? Where does it leave the role and position of Islam in the public sphere? Since the Rushdie Affair and the fall of the Berlin Wall, there has been a desire to regard differences as bounded by culture, ethnicity and even heritage, but not by religion, or specifically Islam. Islam is simply alien. Socioeconomic inequalities affect all, yet they have the greatest effect on poor, alienated, marginalised and voiceless white and Muslim groups who are left to clash with each other for the least in society.

12

THE POSTCOLONIAL SUBJECT'S DISCONTENT

Islamophobia existed well before 9/11. Although it emerged as a concept used by academics and policymakers in the 1990s, the reality of Islamophobia is as old as Islam itself. It is based on a reimagining of the Orient, a reconceptualising of the 'other', and a reframing of the discourse of difference across societies that emphasises an 'us' and 'them', the civilised and the uncivilised, the familiar and the unfamiliar, the insider and the outsider, the West and the rest. Events have also had a role in reshaping the discourse. Much of the current discourse surrounding Muslims can arguably be traced to the Rushdie Affair in Britain in the late 1980s,[1] an event that raised to the fore concerns over the apparent reluctance of Muslims to assimilate.[2] This accusation has continued to persist, but it has also taken on a new lease of life. Since 9/11, not only have reported incidences of violence and aggression towards Muslims in Britain increased but there is also increasing evidence that a large proportion of the population holds prejudicial views about Muslims.[3] This has real implications for the Muslim experience and perceptions of Muslims by the dominant 'other'. The events of 9/11 did not fundamentally change the world. Rather, they confirmed an existing set of prejudices and discriminations, in the process transforming binary identities into rigid categories of self and 'other', Muslim and non-Muslim, Islam and the West.[4]

Islamophobia is undoubtedly important and real, in the sense that it affects minority Muslim lived experiences. However, it is also an instrument of oppression used by those in positions of power as a means to stifle debate and by a few minorities themselves to place artificial parapets around their community interests. Islamophobia establishes binaries and polarises groups, and in doing so it marginalises Muslims further. The tendency for binaries reproduces itself in a much-misused theory that recreates the conditions for exoticisation, exploitation, subjugation and oppression.[5] In countering Islamophobia, Muslim groups are building mechanisms for conflict reduction, social cohesion and ultimately social mobility and equality. Here, Islamophobia is being reconceptualised by the postcolonial subject in order to re-appropriate it as a discourse of integration and inclusion. This chapter is an attempt to reconceptualise the reality of Islamophobia by coming to terms with its true nature. Different aspects of the realisation of Islamophobia can lead to its eventual overcoming, largely based on the efforts of Muslim communities to challenge these modes of oppression effectively and purposefully by taking ownership of the notion and its implications.

Before 9/11, Muslim misrepresentation in media and political discourses centred on culture. In the post-9/11 and post-7/7 climate, this negative representation has continued, but with securitisation as the dominant paradigm. At the heart of these transformations is the neoliberal restructuring of the global economy, where minority groups, including Muslims, are central to the idea of managing national differences. In this framework, the 'Muslim' has become a politicised category within the British discourse on diversity. As the war on terror raged on after 2001, it became incumbent upon New Labour to foster positive relations with Muslim organisations, specifically those considered the voice of most Muslims in the country.[6] Government policy under New Labour effectively institutionalised Muslim politics by establishing a formal relationship with the MCB.[7] The perspective of engagement was through religion rather than ethnic, cultural, social or wider political factors. Using the interaction to engage with religious communities or addressing religious fundamentalism, however, has led to subdivisions, polarisations and ineffectiveness.

THE POSTCOLONIAL SUBJECT'S DISCONTENT

Historically, local authorities in Britain, operating under the national policy rubric of 'community cohesion', have had only limited autonomy. Their ability to re-narrate the local policy of multicultural language was limited.[8] The politicisation of Islam, compounded by party politics, regarded immigration as a source of 'religious fundamentalism', conflating notions of race and nation with the demonisation of Muslims. Viewed through this lens, Muslims are seen as responsible for all the ills of society, seemingly traversing the boundaries of acceptable difference as well as shunning their assimilation into a secular liberal Britain. It was during the 2000s that 'faith based multiculturalism [took] on a profoundly oxymoronic role, where it [was] both something to be feared, and simultaneously something to be celebrated; as though policy [appeared] to veer between seeing the multicultural polity as the problem at one moment, and the solution in the next'.[9]

The experiences of Muslim communities in Britain are characterised by internal and external ethnic, social and cultural capital, with multiple layers of meaning and action.[10] These are far more nuanced and deeply experienced than is often assumed. An explicit impression that Islam is incompatible with secularism and democracy persists, such that Muslims are seen as a threat to the well-being of European nations and their social and political order.[11] Anti-Muslim racism has established itself within a liberal and secular post-Enlightenment discourse that discriminates based on 'values'.[12] The everyday, however, provides a degree of messiness concerning European secularism, where the boundaries of appreciating or valuing difference in society, particularly as it refers to religion, are yet to be fully articulated. Nor is this disarray entirely consistent across a far-ranging demographic and political Western European milieu. In this wider space, there has been a discernible shift to the political right in Western Europe since the 1990s, and no less so in the British context. This transformation has led to anti-immigration, anti-welfare and anti-Muslim sentiment as the dominant approach. It has also generated a mushrooming of the Islamophobia industry, presenting an opportunity for some to implicate Muslims as the cause of their own problems. Simultaneously, politically correct liberalism has sought to evade the accusation of Islamophobia by challenging Islamic cultural practices.

Prominent political voices have also encouraged the normalisation of Islamophobia in contemporary Britain. In January 2016, for example, David Cameron delivered a speech focusing on the need to fund the teaching of the English language to British Muslim women who have been left behind by 'progress', but the backdrop to his statements was deeply problematic. In the 1950s, British 'coloured immigrants', as they were referred to at the time, were not integrating, supposedly because of some cultural deficiency due to a lack of competency in the English language. This view dominated throughout the 1960s and 1970s. Similarly, after the British race riots of 2001, Home Secretary David Blunkett argued that the lack of English among mothers had created divisions within the home, leading young Muslims to become hostile, antisocial and even engage in criminality. In 2016, Cameron associated the lack of English proficiency among Muslim mothers as one of the reasons why young Muslims join ISIS, where lack of English not only represented 'backwardness' but also a cultural threat. The outcome of this rhetoric from the top was to foster community tensions and place the onus back on Muslim groups as both the cause and the solution to a range of problems, all defined by narrow and inward-looking rhetoric, not by evidence or research.

Genuine concerns have been raised about the patriarchal nature of many Muslim homes and its effects on Muslim women. However, the vast majority of Muslim women play a significant role within their households. Many Muslim women are the primary homemakers because employment in the labour market would make childcare unaffordable.[13] But if a Muslim woman desires to learn the English language, there are only limited opportunities to do so because of cutbacks to the funding of language training and development, which disproportionately affect poorer urban areas.[14] The entirely spurious links between English-language acquisition and radicalisation is not only condescending and patronising but also damaging for community relations already facing pressures due to the misguided utterances of political elites. Women belonging to other minority groups do not face being targeted by a policy of integration through language. No other groups have experienced similar levels of attention on their potential for radicalisation. In this case, some of the most isolated, marginalised and racialised groups in society, people who are also most likely to face violence and intimidation in public spaces due to the ever-growing phenomenon of violent Islamophobia (as opposed to passive Islamophobia), are also victims of an Orientalist, exoticised dominant male gaze.[15] This prevailing focus on the English language reflects a similar colonial mind-set to that which defined the British Empire. At the same time, the focus on values has further entered into the debate on de-radicalisation, where a lack of English equates with the potential for extremism. These statements reaffirm the patterns of the 'securitisation of integration' and their association with Islamophobia.

Another case in point concerns Trevor Phillips, a man who rarely shies away from outspoken commentary. Since leaving his post as chairman of the Commission for Racial Equality, Phillips has increasingly turned his attention to British Muslims, asking a variety of questions on integration, loyalty and identity in a programme entitled *What British Muslims Really Think*, which aired on Channel 4 on 13 April 2016. These questions are important in a climate of fear and misunderstanding, but Phillips's programme simply stoked the fires of hate and bigotry. The programme focused on the relatively higher within-group marriage rates for Muslim groups, leading him to draw all sorts of conclusions—from the impact on school demographics to the consequences for social cohesion. Analysis of the 2011 Census indicates that a within-group marriage dynamic exists among some South Asian Muslims, but that over time, as opportunities for integration and participation improve, groups marry out at greater rates. At some level, relationships and marriage between majority and minority groups is the truest indicator of integration, but in this case, additional factors must also be taken into consideration. Lack of confidence in social institutions combined with a desire to uphold particular cultural characteristics prevent groups from marrying outside of the group, particularly among Bangladeshis and Pakistanis. For Indian Muslim groups, far higher rates of out-group marriage occur. Poorer, marginalised and isolated Muslim communities are less likely to marry out compared with their aspirational and more successful middle-class South Asian Muslim counterparts.

In a speech given a few days after 7/7, Phillips interpreted the existence of local area geographical concentrations as confirmation of 'sleepwalking into segregation' and asserted that the reluctance of

Muslim communities to integrate presented risks to national security.[16] In making his case, Phillips drew spurious links between cultural preferences and violent radical extremism, but the reality is that segregation is not a choice but the result of a lack of choice based on social immobility, disadvantage and direct and indirect racism. This is especially so in parts of towns and cities experiencing severe economic decline. By alluding to this discredited cultural values thesis, Phillips's speech was supporting the neoliberal agenda that wholeheartedly ignores the wider workings of society.

Liberalism is not under attack from Islam and Muslims in British society; instead, internal divisions transpire within liberalism, which bring to the fore anxieties over differences in society and how best to manage them. These forebodings also point to questions of Europeanisation and immigration. The problems facing liberalism also relate to questions of the role of religion in society, in communities and within the family. Isolated examples of members of ethnic and religious minority groups who are seemingly at odds with majority society cannot defeat a confident liberalism. Few would agree that the integration of British Muslims is complete. But these are socioeconomic issues in the main—the political and cultural usually follow once communities have a strong foundation. In reality, where problems of Muslims not wishing to be part of wider society do exist, they are isolated cases in specific local area contexts. As such, these concerns are situational. It is impossible to compare communities in the Midlands and the North with those in London or the South East. A multiplicity of opinions, attitudes and behaviours, as well as ethnicity, religious diversity and cultural adaptation, needs to be taken into consideration. Inferring social trends from methodologically flawed data is tantamount to sensationalising for ideological purposes.

Phillips alludes to the importance of absorbing minorities of Muslim backgrounds into a society that has accepted many other minority groups over the course of its history. Numerous examples appear in the twentieth century alone. One can look to Jews, African Caribbeans and South Asians. Presently, new groups have made Britain their home as the EU expands and Britain is seen as a refuge for those fleeing persecution in their countries of birth. However, though Britain has managed to integrate various minorities over time, it has always had a dominant 'other' on which to project its deepest fears about itself, and no other group in society has had as much attention paid to it in recent years as British Muslims. The attitudes of Muslims in Europe have been extensively researched—where they live, what they watch on television, what they wear, what they eat, what they believe in, which parties they support and what their beliefs are with respect to an assortment of social, cultural, political and religious questions. Such 'ground-breaking insights' as presented by Phillips in this regard serve only to enhance existing prejudices by misunderstanding Muslims. Contributions such as his do not simply add to the Islamophobia industry; they also prevent the industry from being unpacked or debunked. These sentiments suggest a set of biases and prejudices that have, unfortunately, become ingrained in liberal thinking—they are exaggerated, ideologically loaded, methodologically defunct and entirely obstructive.

Despite the growth of 'Islamophobia studies' as a field of research, the term itself continues to be afflicted by problems of classification, categorisation and generalisation. Some regard the term as a process, while others see it as a product. The former relates to prejudice and marginalisation measured as distinct patterns of racial, cultural and religious discrimination, while the latter manifests itself in history as well as contemporary politics, revealing an analytical gap between conception, perception and ultimately realisation.[17]

Islamophobia is not only a lived social and political experience facing British Muslims. It is conflated by a paradigm of anti-multiculturalism, which has sought to abandon a critical acceptance of differences in society and replace it with an outmoded, reductive and exclusive notion of English nationalism, especially in the post-EU referendum era.[18] It reflects the normalisation of anti-Muslim hatred, which has grown exponentially since the outset of the war on terror that began after 9/11,[19] a period that has witnessed growing intolerance, bigotry and the development of far-right, radical left and religious extremist groups. Cumulative extremisms at the margins of society incubate the discourses of intolerance and hate that allow these subgroups and their ideas to foment. Islamophobia and radicalisation are intimately tied up with each other.[20] In an attempt to theorise Islamophobia further, the following perspectives are an attempt to move beyond a general set of characteristics. They outline specific cultural and ideological differences affecting the negative representation of Islam in popular contemporary discourses:

- *Postcolonial*: Islamophobia is seen as a continuation of the historical exploitation, exoticisation and 'othering' that have plagued Western cultural and intellectual framing of Islam and Muslims. An example of this is the idea of needing to 'protect' Muslim women from Muslim men.
- *Racism*: Islamophobia is effectively a form of anti-Muslim racism or anti-Muslimism. It suggests that Islam is only relevant in understanding the nature of discriminatory practices that affect visible minorities because it creates a unifying target for wider-ranging racist sentiment. Patterns of racism and discrimination that are well documented and understood in academic and policymaking terms exist to act as a focus on Islam as a singular concept. Islamophobia here does not refer to Muslims in reality.
- *Political*: Islamophobia is form of systematic and ideological political control and authority that maintains the idea of ideological differences between group norms and values that are incompatible with majority society. For example, attacks on multiculturalism are, in effect, a direct critique of the Muslim presence in society.
- *Social Conflict*: Muslim groups have become subservient to dominant modes of economic exploitation, that is, Muslim groups have suffered disproportionately as ethnic and religious minorities in social outcomes such as education, employment, representation and participation in politics, which affects social mobility.
- *Policy*: the removal of policy directives that concentrate on the specificities of dialogue, exchange and social interaction between Muslim and non-Muslim groups in societies, where misunderstanding, misrepresentation and demonisation is the norm, is a distinct form of Islamophobia that seeks to eliminate Muslim ethnic–cultural differences in the discourse on Islam itself.

THE POSTCOLONIAL SUBJECT'S DISCONTENT

Without considering the context, there is a risk of conflating different Islamophobic realities, some of which clearly operate at the same time. Whether it is political, cultural or ideological, different groups experience Islamophobia to different degrees. For example, while there may be coherence concerning equality and social cohesion, secular groups may have a greater aversion to the religious dimension within Islam, even though they would wish to oppose discrimination against Muslim groups as a whole. Therefore, a fundamental problem is that Islamophobia is simply irreducible to a discussion about the experiences of Muslims and Islam without specifying a context, situating the experience within a particular economic, cultural and political paradigm. The problem here is one of identities. The faith of Islam acts as a unifying identity for Muslims across the world who share its value systems, faith principles, rites of passage and spiritual and legalistic frameworks, but there are a whole host of other layers of meaning people have in their lives that exist in addition to or despite religious norms and values. These distinctions add to the difficulty of homogenising Muslimness through sweeping assertions.[21] A generalised view of Islam and Muslims creates the conditions for attacks on the entire religion. By maintaining the view that Islamophobia is indivisible, opponents of Islam criticise it using similar, single-minded definitions of the faith. In all instances, the gradation is lost, thereby reproducing a dichotomy between Muslim and non-Muslim, Islamophobe and anti-Islamophobe, and reducing the possibilities for those Muslims who wish to criticise Islam as understood by certain Muslim groups based on perfectly rational and measured justifications. In each instance, peripheral voices that may have genuine contributions to make to the debate face marginalisation as the dominant view takes precedence, further dividing communities and minimising the opportunities for constructive dialogue.

There are other challenges when considering new categories of meaning and belonging. In the United States, the category 'brown' has traction as a means to reflect the concerns of a body of people who do not necessarily fit into the political or cultural category of 'black', even though this definition reflects the processes of oppression, subjugation and marginalisation of people of all colour at a general level.[22] In places such as Western Europe and the United States, Islamophobia is a critique of Muslim norms and values seen as antithetical to those of majority society as a whole. For some in Turkey, Islamophobia stems from the view that Islamism is a danger to the secular state, where Islam equates with power and authority, undermining the secular traditions of a post-Ottoman Turkish Republic. After the Arab Spring that began in 2011, many Middle Eastern states became increasingly fearful of Islam because of the critique it provided of existing power structures and the potential for the faith to act as a means to reorganise society along strictly religious and theological principles. In South Asia, many of the problems faced by nations such as Afghanistan, Pakistan, India and Bangladesh can be traced to politicised Muslims with limited political opportunities who regard terrorism and extremism as valid interpretations of Islamic texts. In all these cases, the problem is less about the faith as a whole than about Muslim interpretations and actions that stem from aspirations that have political and sociological relevance.

The nature of globalisation, neoliberalism and capitalism in Middle Eastern and Asian Muslim societies invariably fosters social divisions and political polarities that destabilise nations and create the conditions for social conflict and problematic ethnic relations. Part of this is a consequence of a wider global historical trepidation about the nature of relations between groups based on colour and power. For the last few decades, Muslims across the world have increasingly been seen as 'victim communities' that suffer from patterns of oppression and underdevelopment attributed to systems of the West. Recruiting sergeants for those at the centre of the violence-creation often refer to examples of Islamophobia to influence vulnerable young people. Concentrating on the religion adds weight to the argument that the West is reductive, essentialist and narrow-minded in relation to Islam in general and the Middle East in particular. For many susceptible to these voices, the West perpetuates neo-colonialism, concomitantly protecting regional interests for economic and political gain. Meanwhile, the reality is that many Muslim countries are mired in underdevelopment, corruption, tribalism, militarism and elitism.

In the present climate, it is non-Muslims who generally instigate Islamophobia against Muslims. But in terms of radicalisation and extremism in the context of the Middle East, both the victims and the perpetrators are often Muslims. Islamophobia is far too multifaceted to project the problem entirely on to the 'other' or to disassociate it from a whole host of issues concerning a religious community that has myriad concerns at a number of different internal levels. At the same time, it is not up to 'others' to set the limits of the debate or the frames in which it is understood or accepted. Islamophobia is not a given or an absolute. It is a relative experience dependent on context, opportunity and design.

Accepting differences between groups clearly raises challenges for those who regard such differences as a threat to wider society. Yet, for others, these differences are an asset. This is where politics enters the fray and helps to explain why the idea of 'multicultural societies' has caused so much confusion. It is possible to think about the 'management' of differences in society. The following, penultimate chapter explores a range of vignettes of different spaces and places across the world that reflect on the problems of ethnic, racial and religious inequality in which the 'Muslim question' has emerged as an important feature. These experiences reflect on notions of civilisations, or their end, and the ways in which the twenty-first century has revealed a particular set of challenges facing the globe as a whole.

13

FEAR AND LOATHING AT THE END OF HISTORY

Britain's post-war approach to multiculturalism has differed from the other countries comprising 'Old Europe', such as France and Germany, for example. All three countries once had empires but later had to reach out to their once-colonised peoples to reduce employment gaps created by the loss of men and infrastructure during the Second World War. The indigenous populations that either remained or returned after the war were reluctant to be employed in what were increasingly seen as menial jobs. The UK is an amalgamation of four separate nations, as well as being a nation of immigrants. Subjects of the UK Commonwealth were invited to the country to take up the roles shunned by the indigenous workforce, but they ended up staying permanently, contrary to the expectations of the host society and, in many cases, the immigrants themselves.[1] Hence the current make up of Britain can partly be traced to the post-war period, in which communities settled permanently in Britain despite the official claim that these groups were merely temporary 'guest workers'. But as these workers' employment and educational outcomes were limited, they found themselves trapped in poor working conditions and dilapidated housing in impoverished areas. Ethnic minorities who possessed social and cultural capital in the sending regions before migration also experienced all sorts of downward pressures on their mobility,

153

including being confined to the same poor inner-city areas containing other minorities from less privileged backgrounds.

The UK's approach to multiculturalism has also differed from that of other, non-European countries. In Canada, for example, different motivations have been in play, as Canada needed migrant labour in the 1970s. Singapore has had to 'manage' a hugely diverse population differentiated by ethnicity as well as religion, while also dealing with its own colonised historical legacy.[2] These are important developments, as Canada's immigration policy has been largely successful, yet integration nevertheless remains a pertinent issue, despite the absence of a colonial history for the incoming groups, in contrast to the situation in Britain.[3] Indeed, to some extent, it seems that intolerance and ethnic nationalism is as much a problem for Canada as it is for other countries. The model in Britain closely resembles the Dutch case, which is based on the idea of 'pillarisation',[4] that is, 'we' as a state will give recognition to all groups, religious and ethnic, but 'we' will do little to bring these groups together in a diverse society. The UK does make a reasonable effort, but the messages from policymakers have been inconsistent. In 1967, for example, Roy Jenkins made an astonishing speech in which he described integration as 'not a flattening process of assimilation but equal opportunity accompanied by cultural diversity in an atmosphere of mutual tolerance'.[5] But the Labour Party of the time rushed through the 1968 Commonwealth Immigrants Act in just three days.[6] In the 1980s, the proponents of multiculturalism talked of the need to celebrate aspects of migrant culture.[7] But while a school in some rural backwater might hold an international food event one day in the year, for all the other days, diversity was an afterthought, if it featured at all.

In 2011, David Cameron talked of 'muscular liberalism', a clear attempt to wholly disassociate the Conservatives from the apparent failings of New Labour, much of which was code for the view that 'Muslims killed multiculturalism = Muslims are a danger = We must eliminate the danger that is multiculturalism.'[8] In London, however, globalisation and cosmopolitanism are thriving. It is a vibrant and fast-moving city, but one in which the national agenda-setters are London-centric. The North has experienced significant deindustrialisation and job losses but with little inward investment or regional development.[9]

Once-bustling industrial towns have been left to decline. Most have not sufficiently redeveloped as service sector economies. Ever since the monetary policies of Margaret Thatcher in the 1980s and Reaganomics across the Atlantic, the financial services sector of the economy has become the main component of GDP. This structural imbalance in the economy, combined with a lack of political imagination, helped to foster the discontent that gave rise to the Brexit vote and a profoundly divided Britain.

Today, Britain faces a range of questions: what kind of society is desirable? Is it a form of unity within diversity or diversity within unity? The aspirations of members of a multicultural society are inevitably prone to political manipulation, with short-term thinking usually linked to public opinion of a particular issue giving rise to certain policies, such as the banning of minarets in Switzerland in 2010, for example.[10] The public, deceived by dubious news stories and sensationalist television reports, do not trust their politicians but continue to vote for them nevertheless.[11] The interests of individuals in multicultural societies are also affected by the economic cycle. As societies continue to suffer from the consequences of the 2008 economic crisis, poorer minorities have been easy targets, particularly in those West European countries that have begun to move to the political right. In terms of the social context, bogeymen are occasionally used to project an ominous fear of the 'other' when doing so is politically expedient. Examples in Britain include the Jews in the 1930s, the Irish in the 1950s, black people in the late 1970s, Asian gangs in the 1980s and the 'Muslim terrorist' of today—all used for instrumental ends until another bogeyman replaces them. Others do come to the fore from time to time, such as 'asylum seekers' in the 1990s or the 'hoodies' of the 2000s, but presently the 'Muslim terrorist' or the 'Islamic extremist' are the categories 'we' all 'hate' or must 'fear' the most.[12]

There was a time when many Britons thought of themselves as unique, representing a particular culture, heritage, language, ethnicity and even religion defined in collective terms. However, today, it is increasingly the case that Britain is defined in negative terms, where 'who we are' is defined in terms of 'who we are not'.[13] Those who resolutely hold on to their ethnic or religious identifies do so due to the pressures put on those identities by others who wish to hold on to their own in competition with them. This is a given anywhere in the world, but all these tensions play out greatest when inequalities are at their highest. Reducing inequality helps to build cohesive, multicultural societies.[14] Minor changes will not result in permanent solutions. A stable model of multiculturalism requires equality and opportunity, as well as equality of outcomes, for all. In a complex world, memories are short and selective, political interests are immediate and social divisions are increasingly wide and getting worse. A perfect multicultural society does not exist. As much as it is important to have an informed debate and to discuss alternative theories and observations, an idealised multiculturalism is a philosophical dream, as the creation of any such society will invariably be subject to the interests and manoeuvrings of those who hold power vis-à-vis those who seek power. In reality, positive progressive multiculturalism is never an enduring entity, but rather than seeking to get the policy right, politicians have been quick to abandon the idea altogether.

Since the 1990s, the Eastern world has gradually been returning to a position of global dominance, as was the case many thousands of years ago. In the 1990s, the so-called Asian tiger economies were booming. Countries such as Indonesia and Malaysia have experienced exceptional levels of economic development and growth. China and India are now able to rival and compete with the United States and Western Europe economically. China holds a large part of the debt of the US, giving the country leverage over particular currency and trade issues. The ability of nations such as Brazil to compete at the global level has also placed considerable pressure on the Western economic model. This change to the world economic order is likely to continue, such that in the next few decades India, China and Brazil will be among the primary world economies.[15] It places particular pressure on the United States and its role as a global watchman, something it emphasises through its activities as part of the UN, IMF, World Bank, NATO as well as through its cultural influence over the world through institutions such as Hollywood.[16]

Seen against this context, the global economic dominance of the United States is entering a period of relative decline. In an effort to promote freedom, liberty, democracy and capitalism to the rest of the world, the United States has found itself on the verge of being unable to compete in the way that it had in the past. Inside the United States, inequality is increasingly becoming a problem, resulting in the dominance of the few who work towards fulfilling their self-interests at all costs while being increasingly out of touch with the rest of society. With other economies across the world now capable of demonstrating their capacity for efficiency, the Americanisation of global society is in retreat.[17] Though many hoped that the presidency of Barack Obama would arrest this decline, the industrial-military complex and the power of corporate elites to determine policy dominated his term.[18] The United States reached into the Middle East for the better part of the twentieth century for various reasons to do with the need to penetrate additional markets and to control the availability of fossil fuels should the reserves in the United States become susceptible to depletion as well to prevent others from capitalising on them.

In the 2000s, US foreign policy was ostensibly focused on bringing about 'freedom' and 'democracy' in various parts of the world. But the events of the Arab Spring demonstrated that young Arabs across the MENA region were not prepared to endure further abuses of power, injustice, illegitimate authority and the social divisions that had been created between elites and the masses. The upheavals the Arab Spring preceded led to a demographically young Middle East effectively dislodging the existing power structures, some of which had been in place for four decades. For a time, many Middle Eastern countries were no longer in the hands of leaders favoured by the United States.[19] The end of history thesis paradoxically revealed the end of American history. The availability of new information communication technologies has permitted citizens access to different media, creating a sense of awareness that would otherwise have been unattainable (although the ability of governments to manipulate social media, especially during elections, has also become evident). Hegemony through economic, military, political and cultural power concentrated in the hands of the few is now challenged by the availability of media in a range of different forms, further accelerating the breakdown of US influence. The institutions and mechanisms established by the Western economic neoliberal framework have created opportunities for the Eastern part of the world to respond to the challenges raised by them, rendering obsolete the very foundations of the Western economic and political model.[20]

As mentioned in an earlier chapter, in late 2015 I spent a semester as a visiting scholar at New York University, a renowned institution of higher learning in the United States, where I was afforded the distinct luxury of being allocated NYU housing on West Fourth Street. The entrance to the block was at the foot of Fifth Avenue. The buildings of New York University surround its unofficial quadrangle of Washington Square Park, with the park's arch commemorating the 1789 inauguration of President George Washington. Using a long-zoom lens, the arch is visible from the eighty-sixth-floor observatory of the Empire State Building. The park was not always a popular destination for tourists, skateboarders honing their skills, musicians practising their tunes or pot smokers exchanging their vibes. Farmland until the late 1700s, the area was a burial site for slaves and immigrants and later for the victims of yellow fever. As many as 20,000 dead bodies are buried under the park.[21]

Today, a newly placed fountain draws the attention of visitors to the centre of the park, with the concentric circles of people looking in reflecting both New York City and the United States in microcosm. To the centre are tourists and the elite students of NYU. They sip coffee, listen to live music and watch or take part in the entertainment, absorbing the atmosphere. However, at the corners of the park, the homeless wander dispossessed and outcast. They linger at the fringes during the day and sleep rough at night. In many ways, this is the United States. In at least two of the corners, cannabis is available for sale late at night, as has been the case since the 1960s.

Washington Square Park was at the heart of old New York. In the early 1600s, Dutch settlers and freed slaves turned a patch of marshland into pastures. They called it Noortwyck (North district), renamed Greenwich later in the 1600s, quite possibly due to an English settler from an area in London where the notion of Greenwich Mean Time originates. Washington Square and Greenwich merged during the nineteenth century to become Greenwich Village. It was home to intellectuals, writers, musicians, artists and designers, and to residents and visitors, it was known as 'The Village'. It was also home to famous actors and writers and artists before they were all priced out by the super wealthy. The Village has appeared in numerous films since the 1950s, including *Barefoot in the Park* (1967) and *Serpico* (1973). The 2013 Cohen brothers film *Inside Llewyn Davis* highlighted the development of the folk music scene in New York, with most locations in the film set in a depiction of Greenwich Village in the early 1960s. Bob Dylan and Leonard Cohen lived in the area. It is even the place of work for the fictional superhero Wonder Woman. Caffe Reggio served the first cappuccino in the United States in 1927. This coffee house still operates on MacDougal Street.

In 1632, the native Indians sold Manhattan, an island, to the Dutch settlers for the equivalent of 1,016 USD. In 1664, the English conquered the city and colonised it as their own without a single shot being fired. In 1783, George Washington, however, forced the British out. New York subsequently became the first capital under the Constitution of the United States. Soon after, it began to thrive on manufacturing, trade and commerce, especially after the opening of the Erie Canal in 1825, which connected the city to the US mainland, greatly enhancing the city's national and global economic importance. The needs of capital required labour, and this encouraged the migration of people from across the United States as well as, crucially, from across the world. Wave after wave of migrants came from Ireland, Eastern Europe and Southern Europe, establishing the city as a hotbed of ethnic, religious and cultural diversity. Today, the skies are replete with skyscrapers, but the minorities who work in the offices and buildings of the city live in the greater New York City area: the Bronx, Queens, Brooklyn and Staten Island, along with Manhattan.[22]

The people who made the city also made its history. Successful entrepreneurs built edifices to mark their fortunes and contribute to the city's vibrancy. Architects and designers erected magnificent towers at the behest of wealthy benefactors. Reaching for the skies became emblematic of the city. The completion of the Empire State Building in the early 1930s coincided with the height of the Great Depression, but it did not stop the developers completing a remarkable art deco structure that sits at the heart of Manhattan. As Wall Street became the centre of finance, banking and insurance, the midtown area of Manhattan housed the jet-set and sought to meet their needs for luxury goods and services. On either side of Central Park, these tall constructions are a reminder of the opulence and wealth of those who came and conquered. Americans who wanted to get to the top did so in Manhattan. There persists a glowing energy in the city to this day. It is the city of light. It is the stuff of dreams for those who care to dream. Tourists spanning every corner of the globe match the great diversity of the city's residents. But it is also a city of contradictions, as much like all global cities. From London to Paris to Istanbul, there is always a dark underbelly. Centuries of history lie underneath the pavements of Manhattan, with places and people long forgotten and written over.[23] Wealth and tradition abound but also poverty and disadvantage. New York City is profoundly racialised, as is Washington, DC, Chicago and significant parts of Los Angeles.

New York has always been the scene of political resistance. Home to the suffrage movement, it was also an important site during the civil rights movements of the 1960s. In more recent periods, it has been at the forefront of the fight for LGTB rights. While Republican presidential candidates in the run-up to the 2016 elections spewed bigotry and intolerance towards those regarded as most dangerous, from Mexican immigrants to Muslims from outside of the country, New Yorkers stood firm. After the Paris shootings of November 2015 and the San Bernardino homicides in December 2015, American Muslims faced racist and Islamophobic attacks across the country. But Jews, Christians and people of no faith openly supported their fellow citizens. Senior politicians with eyes on their electorate, not on sound policymaking, emitted hatred, breeding ignorance and intolerance. Their misguided utterances only fuelled the rise of Islamophobia and radicalisation. American exceptionalism, so championed over the years, has turned into fear and loathing. What was noteworthy in the United States and for the rest of world until the 1970s, namely public education, technology, science and research, is increasingly becoming the preserve of the privileged few. Reaganomics, much like Thatcherism in Britain, undermined the welfare state and introduced individual success as the overriding measure of the performance of societies.[24] Without a robust alternative, it is how the rest of the world has also reconfigured itself in the twenty-first century.

In early 2012, I had the opportunity to spend five weeks in Jerusalem. The Holy Lands are a strange place. They are full of thousands of years of history, principally from the ancient Jewish, Roman and Muslim periods onwards. Yet outside the country, apart from devotees of the faiths, many people associate Israel with a state that occupies the lands of others. For the nearly 2 million Palestinian Arabs who are Israeli citizens, the feeling of occupation is inescapable. A tiny percentage is doing well through business and trade, but the vast majority feel the pressure of containment in a security state that is conservative, centralised and racist. But it would be wrong to paint a blanket picture here. Not all Israeli Jews are the same—far from it. Around 15 per cent are ultra-orthodox. They make the most noise and are heard the loudest. Among these few, around 150 different factions exist, and all deeply divided. Israeli Jews range from liberal-moderates to staunch secularists. These latter groups have a great deal in common with their Muslim counterparts, but few fully appreciate it, with those on the right of politics being those who tend to disagree with such notions the most. These Jews are wealthier, are highly educated and well travelled, but often they are also reactionary and fundamentalist. Jews on the political left tend to be tolerant and open but also critical of authority. This applies in Jerusalem as it does everywhere else in the world.

Many matters disturbed me as I looked upon the city. Occupational and residential segregation are major concerns. Palestinians and Jews rarely share the same spaces in schools, neighbourhoods or in employment settings. But ethnicity, class, politics and religiosity from within also divides Jews. Aspects of the machinery of the state are also problematic: laws are discriminatory and enacted by biased judges, from those that prevent Arabs and Jews from marrying to those that prevent Arab–Israeli political parties from forming if they are not outwardly loyal to Zionism. Then there is the wall—that confounded wall. Standing up close to it made me think of one thing—a prison. Centuries-old Arab villages were razed in order to erect this homage to dehumanisation. Many families face up to ninety minutes of travel to the nearest checkpoint to get to the other side of the wall in order to visit their loved ones who were previously a ten-minute walk away.

My natural instinct is to take the side of the oppressed, the dispossessed and the marginalised and to look at social systems and all of their failings.[25] The experience of the period from 1948 to 1967 to two Intifadas has led many Palestinian Arabs to the view that resistance is futile, as it simply irritates the bear who crushes the irritating fly with one clean swoop of its giant paws. At the same time, Israeli Jews are not one voice. The country is home to critical and progressive voices that want to build sustainable peace, but they face crowding out by the regressive tendencies of influential ultra-religious and neoconservative groups. In my time there, I came to learn about an Israeli female soldier who had refused to sit at the front of a particular bus after being commanded to do so by ultra-orthodox men sitting at the back. As she objected, they violently attacked her. Stories of ultra-orthodox Jewish women described as the 'Israeli Taliban' also emerged. These women do not work, rarely leave the home, do not use contraception and wear layer upon layer of black clothing. No part of their skin is visible, including the hands and ankles. Their young daughters dress in the same way.

During my time in Israel, I gave a number of presentations to graduate and postgraduate students as well as to academic staff in Jerusalem, talking about my work on Islamophobia and radicalisation. On these occasions, I reminded people that however much we stir up opinion about our identities and wish to protect and nurture them in the context of internal and external challenges and opportunities, as human beings, we are all the same. East and West are constructions of each other, and it is no accident that at the intersections of these points, such as in Jerusalem, it is the differences that are emphasised rather than similarities. Strip away the extremist religious codes, the inward-looking politics, notions of a memory around an identity and we are all the same. This went down well with some and badly with others, including Palestinian students who looked more shocked than their Jewish classmates, such was the palpable inequity between the groups in reality.

The idea of history as a dialectical process, propounded by Friedrich Hegel and later enhanced by Karl Marx, was challenged by Francis Fukuyama, who obtained notoriety during the early 1990s for his end of history thesis, which suggested that Western capitalism had championed in the conflict between communism and free market economics. In the fourteenth century, Ibn Khaldun also wrote about the rise and fall of civilisations.[26] At the time, the Islamic world was facing decline from within and competition from without. Because of invasions by the Mongols from the East and the Christian powers of the West, various Islamic kingdoms were beginning to collapse. Ibn Khaldun's general theory proposed that the needs of human beings formed the nature of humankind. Once man has met his basic needs for food and a roof over his head, he will inevitably seek more. His desires turn to furnishing his intellectual development through the acquisition of knowledge and expertise, establishing a set of secondary needs, namely the tools to improve the proficiency of humankind to develop and enhance its existence. The next step is to develop civilisation, but in order to create a civilisation, humankind needs to relinquish its desires for luxury goods, substituting immediate consumption for the re-development of the tools of human civilisation.[27] It is through these processes that great civilisations advance. As part of the processes of building civilisations, it is important that members of the community fulfil reciprocal obligations in order to meet the needs of production, introducing specialisation and interdependence. This occurs in a cyclical dynamic when members of rural societies move to the urban sphere, which then leads to a concentration of specialisation and interdependence, all of which calls for greater intellectual and organisational development. Through the leadership of the people, a balance emerges between the needs of society as a whole and the desires of the few, but in enjoying increasingly luxurious goods, the leadership loses its connectivity with the greater majority. This results in the breakdown of the relationships between humankind, which can lead to resistance and, eventually, renewal. For Ibn Khaldun, spiritual connectivity binds people together in an effort to attain the greater good. Though these spiritual directives emerged from an Islamic perspective, conceptually and theoretically they also apply to any other religious community. He was able to conclude that societies represent the characteristics of ecological existence, where living beings experience birth, development, degeneration and eventually death due to natural causes. The height of any particular form of social existence is based on the balance between luxury and necessary goods, but with decline setting in at the point at which leaders disconnect from the masses, and when they then seek luxury goods for themselves.[28] The relationship between groups and group feelings understood as social cohesion creates the conditions for the emergence of new civilisations and the associated power structures they contain.

Western European powers developed a particular set of sophisticated tastes and preferences that emerged out of the colonial process, including the consumption of exotic foods and a desire for luxuriant clothing, exclusive housing and other material wants.[29] The Western European model peaked at the turn of the twentieth century, but this desire for luxury goods failed to diminish. Given the inequalities across the world and the particular power structures that are concentrated in the West, political authorities are elected to maintain existing levels of consumption and use the physical and human resources of the once-colonised world in order to maintain existing patterns of conspicuous consumption. The essential model has not changed, and the rest of the world is now one with it. This singular approach to existence has its downside, creating problems within nations due to deep-seated inequalities and class conflict, while across nations competitive strategies are carried out by major international corporations that pit nation against nation in the pursuit of profits. One of the reasons for the ongoing underdevelopment of parts of the world is precisely because of the behaviour of large international corporations that engage with state actors to determine preferential treatment while exploiting human and physical capital.[30]

This 'machine brain' model of economic growth and development is stuck in the late nineteenth-century mode of being. Even the terms used to describe its 'functions' arise from a mentality that grew out of the reliance on industry. Economies 'overheat', resulting in the need to 'gear' finance or for fiscal 'pumping', or the constant reference to 'oiling' the 'machinery' of industry. It is useful in such a context to return to the ideas of Ibn Khaldun, in which he likened societies to gardens. In his analogy, it is possible to have large trees in one corner, which may make the garden look enchanting, but they draw up most of the water in their roots, leaving the rest of the garden barren. The idea of a progressive tax system applies here. Sometimes, the weeds need pulling out, as they are poisonous to the other plants in the garden. This is business regulation. Attention to the aesthetic focuses on the diversity of various shrubs, plants and flowers that create a culture of their own. A garden needs constant attention and balancing, but in the current climate, the garden of the world is in complete disarray. One of the main reasons for this is the constant focus on the economic rather than the social, cultural or spiritual aspects of human existence. As internal divisions become acute, those who have want more. Those who do not have anything barely have their existence.

The planet is suffering on a global scale. Environmental catastrophes are looming due to the burning of fossil fuels at ever-growing rates. Animal species are disappearing at an unprecedented pace. The climate is changing forever as the world is reaching the end of its history. Democratic systems are in danger, with plutocracy, autocracy and oligarchy now the norms in the United States and parts of Western Europe. The will of the people is subdued, critical thinking is supressed and polarising ideological perspectives push the electorate in one way or another as great inequalities ensue. Governments take power away from the people and act on their whims. Wealth is concentrated in the hands of the very few. Violence is hyper-normalised in an egotistical self-serving world largely run by white men. Populations across the world are growing faster than ever, but the resources available have been diminished despite rapid technological developments and the discovery of new energy sources. The crises of civilisations are man-made, but they are not inevitable.

The final chapter now returns to the core themes of this book—Islamophobia and radicalisation—to suggest some possible ways forward in breaking down this formidable cycle of hate, intolerance and cruelty.

14

IN CONCLUSION

In 2017, five UK terrorist attacks killed thirty-five and injured many others. The security services thwarted nine further potential attacks, including one targeting Downing Street and Prime Minister Theresa May. At the same time, Islamophobia became more virulent and aggressive than ever. While investment goes into counterterrorism and countering violent extremism, attacks keep on happening. Islamophobia and radicalisation have become normalised, yet we are no closer to solving either of them. With expertise derided, and critics of all hues silenced, the average citizen is left with more questions than answers. Perhaps this is deliberate. We live in an age of rampant disinformation from which there seems to be no escape.

This concluding chapter summarises the primary messages of this book, which have concentrated on establishing the sociological, political and ideological associations between two important concepts in the current period—Islamophobia and radicalisation. The main contribution of this book has been to outline how they are interrelated but also mutually reinforcing due to the interaction of global, national and local forces. In this process, the nature of Muslimness is being moulded by the state, which seeks to generate a moderate Muslim amenable to an idea of an identity based on 'values'. In an uncertain future, the only inevitability is change itself.

The current wave of anti-Islam 'fake news' or disinformation began immediately after 9/11, although Orientalism and Islamophobia have a much longer history in the West. These weapons of mass distraction led to the illegal invasion of Iraq, despite the protests of millions in cities all over the world. After numerous pressures derailed the Arab Spring in Egypt, the attacks on Libya and Syria led to the disruption of the entire MENA region and the emergence of ISIS, the origins of which lie in Western attempts to arm Sunni rebels in opposition to Bashar al-Assad. In the English post-industrial city of Birmingham, the supposed Trojan Horse plot exposed all sorts of failings, including the reality that no one from London had dared to question the authenticity of the original letter that suggested a plot to Islamise state schools in the city was well under way. The investigation into the allegations negatively affected the lives of thousands of young Muslim schoolchildren. The era of fakery reached a new peak during the Brexit campaign. Based on huge distortions of fact, the campaign divided a nation into two, leaving a country stranded. Across the Atlantic, a narcissistic businessperson made it his goal to delegitimise President Obama by any means necessary. President Trump retweets fake videos, including reposting the vile iconography of Britain First, whose numbers temporarily swelled because of the unprecedented coverage they received.

The most striking of all this dissimulation is the view that radicalisation is caused by ideology derived from an interpretation of religion, while far-right terrorism is often explained as a mental health issue. The 'Muslim problem' is at the centre of all this misrepresentation. All this suggests a conspiracy to alter the truth—a disinformation propaganda exercise to divide societies. The 1 per cent has all the power in the world, but those belonging to the 1 per cent are invisible in wider cultural circles or in politics—they are simply untouchable. The very powerful have reshaped the world in their own image to suggest an endless dystopian worldview that only they can save the rest of the world from, with Islamist radicalism the main foe. The truth of our social world is quite different. The planet is burning. Social mobility is at an end. Income disparities are wider than ever. Welfare redistribution is seen as a throwback to a gloomier age of social(ist) policy. With the poor and the infirm forgotten, the wealth created by neoliberal hyper-capitalism does not 'trickle down' to the rest of society. The inevitability of radicalisation is that poverty, alienation and disempowerment are its major causes, compounded by scarcity, disadvantage, racism and marginalisation. These are the factors facing both far-right and Islamist extremists—they are two sides of the same coin.

The certainty of Islamophobia is that it creates racism and anti-Muslim discrimination, which produces radicalisation, both of an Islamist nature and that associated with the far right. At the heart of this problem are the social conditions facing both groups, made to feel poles apart, yet fighting for the same issues: self-actualisation, self-realisation, an opportunity to become someone, to have a stake and a place in society. The authorities evoke security, terrorism and focus on cultural relativism as a threat to the liberal secular order of British-ness or European-ness—and then sprinkle the idea of progressive liberalism, swallowing 'enlightened' Muslims seduced by the trappings of selective inclusion. A once left-leaning majority of young people enter into the fray only to find themselves turned into cardboard cut-outs of themselves, they are silenced into submission by the governmentality of the war on terror culture. Senior British politicians such as Michael Gove and Boris Johnson outline their own theories of Islamist extremism in speeches delivered to select audiences. These persuasive speakers rarely discuss institutional and structural factors as the root causes of extremism and violence, instead focusing on the supposed ideological or religious factors they subjectively place to the fore as the primary drivers.

The gloomy truth is that most victims of violent extremism are Muslims themselves, invariably killing each other, and, yes, something is very wrong with the Muslim mind that allows this or even encourages it. But the reasons for the violence in parts of the Muslim world are not entirely different from those that drive British-born or other Western European-born young men and women to the theatres of war. Both experiences are born out of disenfranchisement. Institutions have failed them. Society has forsaken them. Deep-seated inequalities combined with selfish interests at the top and the instrumentalisation of exploitative power compound the matters further. As authorities define radicalisation as specific to Muslims as a group, they absolve themselves from any direct association or responsibility. It enthrals proud nationalists, wavering liberals and diehard conservatives. As this distance grows, the narratives become believable, and the greater the discombobulation. And we are back to square one.

—•—

The work of the UK Commission for Countering Extremism, headed by the Home Office, has raised a number of questions. Many within the Muslim community argue that its existence sends a chilling signal that the status quo will remain, perpetuating the existing dominance of the pro-Prevent, pro-assimilation model on relations between Muslims and the state. History tells us that these kinds of commissions rarely challenge the existing policies of the government and in some cases simply act as a rubber stamp. As one of the most pressing concerns that affect the entire country on matters of cohesion, identity and security, the question of radicalisation and its elimination affects us all. If the dominant paradigm does not change the stupefying assumption that ideology is the driving force in radicalisation, there is a real possibility that the discourse will become ever more divisive. The problem with extremism thinking in Britain—and elsewhere in Western Europe—is the assumption of a single cause of extremism in the form of the ideological misinterpretations of a particular religion. Context, history, memory and the underlying implications of existing policy, ideology and their normalisation in the everyday imagination rarely generate any consideration in practice. Prevent is a policy that generates division and infighting but produces very little change.

Despite many years of academic, social and community criticism, Prevent continues to rumble on with little or no adaptation in response to these concerns. The lack of an alternative in the form of rounded, indigenous, organic measures that empower communities, make them resilient, protect the youth and develop a forward-looking vision of inclusion and growth is also a major concern, although it is slowly being addressed despite government reservations in respect of certain organisations engaging in this work. This is because government rhetoric focuses on ideology, regressive interpretations of Islam, anti-integration sentiment, resistance politics, anger and disaffection towards failed Western foreign policy and lumps them all together as elements of a problem that has a singular solution, which is to modify and moderate Islam and Muslim behaviour. This has been at the heart of the problem for at least the last decade and a half. Research suggests that radicalisation because of a religious interpretation is a later-stage process, and that it is the sociological, political and cultural pressures that act as the initial push factors in radicalisation. If policymakers are serious about eliminating radicalisation, should the primary focus not be the structural and cultural issues that drive vulnerable people who have no recourse but to kill themselves in order to realise themselves? Surely, this is a failure of society as a whole. If we were honest about the problems we face, we would not be talking about commissions, appointments of particular individuals or the immense divisions that exist between policymakers, scholars, activists and the community at large.

Do the authorities truly want to understand radicalisation and extremism for what it is objectively, accurately and verifiably? There seems to be no appreciation of independent rigorous scholarly research unless carried out by the government or through projects delivered by sympathetic organisations that do not challenge the status quo. The Home Office routinely funds institutions to deliver particular outputs to help with the existing agenda. The Research Information Communications Unit of the Home Office is a propaganda operation that uses various tools, in particular social media, to sway vulnerable young people away from radicalisation. This is an admirable goal, but the mechanisms are somewhat dark and sinister. Various think tanks associated with the world of counterterrorism and anti-radicalisation fixate not on addressing the social and cultural issues but on talking up the problems of ideology while talking down the reality of structural disadvantage. I have been walking through the hallowed corridors of Whitehall and through the doors of institutions that either talk up or talk down radicalisation for far too long. The reality is that many different sides of the equation simply do not want to talk to each other but talk past each other because the policy agenda driving this is stuck in the past and is too hollow and shallow to be reformed.

British Muslims are on the receiving end of the intense gaze and scrutiny of media and political institutions. Sadiq Khan, the mayor of

London, has consistently been subjected to attacks in the press due to his religion. Routinely presented as one of the 'bad' Muslims and a threat to democracy and liberty because of his apparent associations with extremists in the past, Khan has proven to be an effective 'community leader'. So who are the 'good' Muslims? 'Good' here is not the worldly, spiritual or conservative (with a small c). Rather, political elites would have us believe that these are 'bad' Muslims. They would prefer to regard 'good' Muslims as actors involved with think tanks and non-government organisations who espouse the need to do away with Islamism (without carefully defining what the concept means in reality). They would argue that the problems of extremism reside in the heart of Islam itself, in the very nature of its being, in the essence of its soul. The only kind of 'good Muslim' is an ex-Muslim, a former extremist or a revolutionary reformer whose aims are to depart radically from their once 'bad' positions, all the while playing host to the theory that any kind of political Islam is a problem. Likewise, every Muslim who is a firm believer is a risk because they believe in a set of norms and values that makes them dangerous to society as a whole. This view has resulted from so-called 'good' Muslims or ex-Muslims, now dubbed as experts, speaking openly against Islam or Muslims. Media and political institutions support and fete them in their efforts to demonise, homogenise and essentialise a vast, multi-layered and rich religion while wholly negating its positive aspects. The 'ugly' Muslims are individuals who might be characterised as violent extremists, with the reality that they have radicalised politics, not radicalised Islam. These young Muslims are disaffected and disillusioned, seeking an explanation for their feelings of alienation, which they are no longer able to endure. Many will share this view on the 'ugly' Muslims, but it is quite clear that on far too many occasions 'good' Muslims are labelled as 'bad' and 'bad' Muslims are labelled as 'good', which serves the interests of the dominant hegemon in an effort to placate critics of its foreign policy and the failures of its domestic policy in accepting and valuing differences in society. Muslim minorities in Britain are as normal as the rest of the population—they are normally diverse.

IN CONCLUSION

In thinking through the future of British Muslims, given the particular context of Islamophobia and radicalisation, a number of important issues come to mind. While the past is not a predictor of the future, a range of emerging trends and existing patterns suggests that it is possible to determine, with reasonable certitude, the likelihood of particular outcomes. While the current reality suggests a disheartening future, change is inevitable, and while the powers of particular structural preconditions will predetermine specific outcomes, Muslims are not without agency. We live in post-normal times, and a whole range of issues of a social, political, cultural and geological nature are changing at incredibly rapid rates. They are also moving at a pace beyond our abilities to know the nature of their course with any degree of confidence. Policymakers, communities and individuals across the world have been unable to come to terms with the speed of these changes and the endless uncertainty they bring. But observations of human phenomena can provide us with a view that individuals today can influence the futures of tomorrow—challenging the instruments of power in order to determine positive social change. While we can say with reasonable certainty that many predictions of the future will ultimately be proven wrong, there is one thing that is inevitable, which is that change will always take place.

The Muslim population of Western Europe is experiencing a dramatic transformation to its socioeconomic profile, where increasing residential urbanisation and clustering is observable in some of the older towns and cities across these spaces. In general, Muslim men continue to underachieve educationally, while young Muslim women are relative overachievers. As such, gender equality should clearly be an important priority, but not simply to empower women, which is an urgent issue, but also to empower men who face all sorts of crises of masculinity in the context of neoliberal globalisation and hyper-localisation. The rise in the profile of dual-income middle-class Muslims households, with both heads possessing advanced tertiary education from established universities, is important, but a Muslim brain drain also exists because of the pressures of racism, discrimination and cultural marginalisation that suppress social mobility as individuals form a deep sense of under-appreciation.

Most Muslims in Western Europe are young, with one in three under the age of fifteen, which is consistent with wider Muslim world population profiles. This particular dynamic has not shifted since the early 2000s. Around two-thirds of all the people on the move across the world today are Muslims, and conflicts in the world often take place in the Muslim world. Just as the Muslim world has often been the most affected by capitalism, it is also facing, and will continue to face, the consequences stemming from its destabilisation. It is inevitable that Islamophobia has the ability to drive different forms of radicalisation that create further Islamophobia, but it is important to break this cycle, reverse-engineering the process that leads to the harmful consequences. Before this can happen, however, Muslim communities need to own both concepts and define them from within, which requires engaging with the state in a meaningful dialogue in order to challenge its workings effectively. Speaking truth to power will disrupt the speed, scope and scale of the uncertainty faced today. But we also live in a world of great ignorance.

The problems of the hyper-masculinity of men and the unreconstructed nature of patriarchy within households are at odds with wider society, where improvements to gender equality are taking place. A divide has emerged between the Muslim male mind within the home and the workings of wider society with respect to the role and position of Muslim women *and* women in general. The 'self'–'other' separation remains a powerful force in the minds of people who believe in the absolute truth of their knowledge but without the wisdom or ability to think outside of their own self-contained boxes. This is an issue within all societies and all aspects of society including those with privileged access to power, status and the ability to define an image of society based on their own self-image. These ongoing trends suggest that particular challenges of a socioeconomic and sociocultural nature will continue to endure given the wider forces of hyper-capitalism, and while they remain unchecked, Muslim minorities will continue to face all sorts of internal challenges as well as the ongoing effects of an unreconstructed patriarchy. They are at a real risk of lagging further behind the curve.

The role of Muslim women will become even more important in determining the future of Islam. This is not an afterthought but a reality that already exists. Assimilation is not an inevitability, but further integration is desirable in order to gain the power, position and potential to bring about change to a collective human existence. Revolution can exist within an evolution. As genuine concerns arise over the futures of men, the power of women in providing them with their rebirth is already transpiring.

EPILOGUE
RUMI'S CORNER

Konya is the final resting place of Jalaluddin Rumi. Sufi mystic, poet and lover of music, he is one of the most recognised and respected figures in Islamic world history. The impressive Selimiye Cami (built by famed Ottoman royal architect Mimar Sinan, no less) sits next to the Mevlana, where Rumi rests, as countless visitors from every corner of the world sail past gazing at the reflections of their souls. One can only imagine what goes through people's minds as they pass by, some clambering to take photos, others offering prayers, while many stand statue-like in quiet contemplation. What goes on is a combination of self-reflection and remembrance of a saintly man whose aim in life was to spread love. For Rumi, love made the world go round. The love of Rumi has made people from the world over circle around him every day, over 800 years after he left this earth.

In the thirteenth century, during a time of social turmoil and political upheaval, with the Mongols on the warpath, Rumi drew his ideas inwards, connecting the soul to the cosmos, projecting the importance of maintaining inner well-being in unpredictable situations, even in instances of danger and hostility. *Tawhid* (oneness) is not only a central foundation of Islamic theology but also a testable take on the interrelationships of humankind. Rumi's love does not refer to the fiery and temporary nature of romantic love, but rather the love of all things pure, including family, the dearest of friends, nature, music (or the arts generally) and knowledge itself. Love is the fibre of our interconnectedness as human beings, with each other and to nature. The balance of nature is the balance of love. Heaven is a place not beyond the stars but the truth of our existence that we carry with us on this earth. When it is out of balance, our minds despair, our souls catch fire and our hearts are tainted. This love is brain chemistry that springs into action when one sees and senses love. It is the feeling of love that our hearts witness but our minds do not always know. Hence the fissure of heart or mind that leads to a broken heart or the broken hearted whose mind is frenzied. Inner peace reverberates through the intellectual understanding of the world as a single living organism. When one part is diseased, the other parts of the body are in pain. When an imbalance arises, the body does not stand correctly, nor does it breathe or see clearly. These ideas reflect a spiritual connectivity to the idea of a cosmic coexistence between humans, nature and the universe. In this sense, all monotheistic faiths have the same tenets at their core. Religions teach self-reflection, the love of the world and importance of understanding the nature of our environment and the implications of our actions.

Rumi's teachings have lasted the test of time, underscoring their importance for humankind. The testimony to his legacy is how his central message that 'love makes the world go round' is arguably the only message human beings ever need to learn, understand and follow. When social problems arise, it is often because we as humankind have lost our ability to love others. We lack faith in our social world. The idea of human oneness is no longer dominant in understanding the nature of our existence. This lack of love of others shifts to the love of the self, but this stage of being is in a perpetual state of crisis, as love of the self seeks validation from others who face their own inner needing-to-be-loved demons. This urgency for love becomes a tradable commodity, reduced to an impulsive quick fix, each time blackening our hearts and hollowing our minds as we become ever more distant from our connections to the cosmos.

A belief in the oneness of humankind, nature and God helps to steer many towards the path of piety, and while organised religion may seem objectionable to some, there is no doubt that all humans are inextricably linked to one another, whether we like or not, and whether we believe it or not. Our actions lead to reactions and consequences, intended or unintended. An emphasis on the other instead of the self can give rise to an enriching and rewarding experience of love. Through knowing others, we can know the self. Through knowing the self, we can grow to love others. This is all that matters.

NOTES

PREFACE: A TRYST WITH DESTINY

1. See Bhachu, P. (1985), *Twice Migrants: East African Sikh Settlers in Britain*, London: Routledge.
2. Visram, R. (1986), *Ayahs, Lascars and Princes: Indians in Britain 1700–1947*, London: Pluto.
3. Hyslop, J. (2009), 'Steamship Empire: Asian, African and British Sailors in the Merchant Marine c.1880–1945', *Journal of Asian and African Studies*, 44, 1, pp. 49–67.
4. Words immortalised by Jawaharlal Nehru, the first prime minister of India, on the night of India's independence from Britain on 14/15 August 1947.
5. Sneddon, C. (2012), *The Untold Story of the People of Azad Kashmir*, London: Hurst.
6. Khan, J. (2015), *The Raj at War: A People's History of India's Second World War*, London: Bodley Head.
7. Shaw, A. (2000), *Kinship and Continuity: Pakistani Families in Britain*, London: Routledge.
8. Anwar, M. (1979), *'The Myth of Return': Pakistanis in Britain*, London: Heinemann.
9. Patterson, P. (1965), *Dark Strangers*, London: Pelican.
10. Institute of Race Relations (1985), *How Racism Came to Britain*, London: Institute of Race Relations.
11. A place near the town of Jhelum in Pakistan, not far from the site where, over 2,000 years ago, Alexander the Great, who had conquered

vast regions east of Macedonia, finally met his match across the River Jhelum, at the hands of Porus, a formidable Indian king who defeated Alexander and his men through the use of elephants mounted with archers and spearmen.

12. Burke, J. (2012), *The 9/11 Wars*, London: Penguin.
13. Sardar, Z. and Davies, M. W. (2003), *Why Do People Hate America?*, London: Icon.
14. Hiro, D. (2003), *Iraq: A Report from the Inside*, London: Granta.
15. Hutchinson, R. (2004), *Weapons of Mass Destruction: The No-Nonsense Guide to Nuclear, Chemical and Biological Weapons Today*, London: Weidenfeld & Nicolson.
16. Amin, A. (2002), 'Ethnicity and the Multicultural City: Living with Diversity', *Environment and Planning A*, 34, 6, pp. 959–80.
17. Dorling, D. (2014), *Inequality and the 1%*, London: Verso.
18. Akhtar, P. (2013), *British Muslim Politics: Examining Pakistani Biraderi Networks*, Basingstoke: Palgrave Macmillan.
19. Abbas, T. (2005) (ed.), *Muslim Britain: Communities under Pressure*, London: Zed Books.
20. *Macpherson Report* (1999), 'The Stephen Lawrence Inquiry: Report of an Inquiry by Sir William Macpherson of Cluny', Cm 4262-I, London: Stationery Office.
21. Kundnani, A. (2001), 'From Oldham to Bradford: The Violence of the Violated', *The Three Faces of British Racism, Race & Class*, 43, 2, pp. 41–60.
22. Abbas, T. (2011), *Islamic Radicalism and Multicultural Politics: The British Experience*, London: Routledge.
23. Roy, O. (2018), *Globalized Islam: The Search for a New Ummah*, new edn, New York: Columbia University Press.
24. Abbas, T. (2007), 'Muslim Minorities in Britain: Integration, Multiculturalism and Radicalism in the Post-7/7 Period', *Journal of Intercultural Studies*, 28, 3, pp. 287–300.
25. Janmohamed, S. (2018), *Generation M: Young Muslims Changing the World*, London: IB Tauris.
26. Han, B.-C. and Butler, E. (2018), *Psychopolitics: Neoliberalism and New Technologies of Power*, London: Verso.

1. RACE AND THE IMAGINED COMMUNITY

1. Wilson, C. A. (1996), *Racism: From Slavery to Advanced Capitalism*, London: Sage.
2. Solomos, J. (2003), *Race and Racism in Britain*, Basingstoke: Palgrave Macmillan.

3. Ball, W. and Solomos, J. (1990), *Race and Local Politics*, London: Palgrave Macmillan.
4. Murji, K. (2017), *Racism, Policy and Politics*, Bristol: Policy Press.
5. Rattansi, A. (2007), *Racism: A Very Short Introduction*, Oxford: Oxford University Press, p. 6.
6. Davletov, B. and Abbas, T. (2018), 'Narrating Anti-Semitism in Historical and Contemporary Turkey', in Adams, J. and Heß, C. (eds), *The Medieval Roots of Antisemitism: Continuities and Discontinuities from the Middle Ages to the Present Day*, Abingdon: Routledge, pp. 145–60.
7. Carr, M. (2010), *Blood and Faith: The Purging of Muslim Spain*, London: Hurst.
8. Reisgl, M. (2000), *Discourse and Discrimination: Rhetorics of Racism and Antisemitism*, Abingdon: Routledge.
9. Carr, *Blood and Faith*.
10. Markley, R. (2010), *The Far East and the English Imagination*, Cambridge: Cambridge University Press.
11. Immerwahr, J. (1992), 'Hume's Revised Racism', *Journal of the History of Ideas*, 53, 3, pp. 481–6; Bernasconi, R. (2007), '*Kant as an Unfamiliar Source of Racism*', in Ward, J. K. and Lott, T. L. (eds), *Philosophers on Race: Critical Essays*, Oxford: Blackwell, pp. 145–66.
12. Fryer, P. (2010), *Staying Power: The History of Black People in Britain*, London: Pluto.
13. Thomas, H. (1999), *The Slave Trade: History of the Atlantic Slave Trade, 1440–1870*, London: Weidenfeld & Nicolson.
14. Young, R. (2011), *Colonial Desire: Hybridity in Theory, Culture and Race*, Abingdon: Routledge.
15. Ooomen, T. K. (1997), *Citizenship and National Identity: From Colonialism to Globalism*, London: Sage.
16. Sussman, R. W. (2014), *The Myth of Race: The Troubling Persistence of an Unscientific Idea*, Cambridge, MA: Harvard University Press.
17. Farrall, L. A. (1985), *The Origins and Growth of the English Eugenics Movement, 1865–1925*, New York: Garland.
18. Wray, H. (2006), 'The Aliens Act 1905 and the Immigration Dilemma', *Journal of Law and Society*, 3, 2, pp. 302–23.
19. Montagu, A. (1951), *Statement on Race*, New York: Schuman.
20. Fekete, L. (2009), *A Suitable Enemy: Racism, Migration and Islamophobia in Europe*, London: Pluto.
21. Ahmed, S. (2004), *On Being Included: Racism and Diversity in Institutional Life*, Durham, NC: Duke University Press.
22. Vieten, U. M. and Poynting, S. (2016), 'Contemporary Far-Right Racist Populism in Europe', *Journal of Intercultural Studies*, 37, 6, pp. 533–40.

23. Rattansi, *Racism*, p. 169.
24. Van Dijk, T. A. (1991), *Racism and the Press*, London: Routledge.
25. Ibid., p. 5.
26. Downing, J. H. and Husband, C. (2005), *Representing 'Race': Racisms, Ethnicities and Media*, London: Sage.
27. McGee, D. (2008), *The End of Multiculturalism? Terrorism, Integration and Human Rights*, Milton Keynes: Open University Press.
28. Modood, T. (1990), 'British Asian and Muslims and the Rushdie Affair', *The Political Quarterly*, 61, 2, pp. 143–60.
29. Kundnani, A. (2007), *The End of Tolerance: Racism in 21st-Century Britain*, London: Pluto.
30. Anderson, B. (1983), *Imagined Communities: Reflections on the Origins and Spread of Nationalism*, London: Verso, p. 2.
31. Said, E. (1978), *Orientalism*, New York: Pantheon.
32. Younge, G. (2011), *Who Are We? And Should It Matter in the 21st Century?*, London: Penguin.

2. THE RACISM OF THE RADICAL RIGHT

1. Kimmler, M. (2017), *Manhood in America*, New York: Oxford University Press; Connell, R. W. (1998), 'Men and Globalisation', *Men and Masculinities*, 1, 1, pp. 3–23.
2. Massey, D. B. and Meegan, R. A. (1982), *The Anatomy of Job Loss: The How, Why, and Where of Employment Decline*, London: Methuen.
3. Nayak, A. (2010), 'Race, Affect, and Emotion: Young People, Racism, and Graffiti in the Postcolonial English Suburbs', *Environment and Planning A: Economy and Space*, 42, 10, pp. 2370–92.
4. Wallerstein, I. (1983), *Historical Capitalism*, New York: Monthly Review Press.
5. Rich, P. B. (2010), *Race and Empire in British Politics*, Cambridge: Cambridge University Press.
6. Reeves, F. (2009), *British Racial Discourse: A Study of British Political Discourse about Race and Race-Related Matters*, Cambridge: Cambridge University Press.
7. Eatwell, R. (2000), 'The Extreme Right and British Exceptionalism: The Primacy of Politics', in Hainsworth, P. (ed.), *The Politics of the Extreme Right: From the Margins to the Mainstream*, London: Pinter, pp. 172–92.
8. Gilroy, P. (2002), *There Ain't No Black in the Union Jack: The Cultural Politics of Race and Nation*, Abingdon: Routledge.
9. Solomos, J. (1988), 'Institutionalised Racism: Policies of Marginalisation in Education and Training', in Cohen, P. and Bains, H. S. (eds),

Multi-Racist Britain: Youth Questions, London: Palgrave Macmillan, pp. 156–94.
10. Wilson, C. A. (1996), *Racism: From Slavery to Advanced Capitalism*, London: Sage.
11. Gordon, M. (1998), *Slavery in the Arab World*, New York: New Amsterdam.
12. Oldfield, J. R. (1998), *Popular Politics and British Anti-Slavery: The Mobilisation of Public Opinion against the Slave Trade 1787–1807*, Abingdon: Routledge.
13. Smith, A. D. (1992), 'National Identity and the Idea of European Unity', *International Affairs*, 68, 1, pp. 55–76.
14. Daughton, J. P. (2005), 'A Colonial Affair? Dreyfus and the French Empire', *Historical Reflections*, 31, 3, pp. 469–83.
15. Kenny, K. (2006), 'Violence, Race, and Anti-Irish Sentiment in the Nineteenth Century', in Lee, J. J. and Casey, M. (eds), *Making the Irish American: The History and Heritage of the Irish in the United States*, New York: New York University Press, 354–63.
16. Castles, S. and Kosack, G. (1973), *Immigrant Workers and Class Structure in Western Europe*, London: Institute of Race Relations and Oxford University Press.
17. Layton-Henry, Z. (1984), *The Politics of Immigration: Immigration, 'Race', and 'Race' Relations in Post-War Britain*, Oxford: Blackwell.
18. Phizacklea, A. and Miles, R. (1980), *Labour and Racism*, London, Routledge & Kegan Paul.
19. Klug, B. (2013), 'Interrogating "New Anti-Semitism"', *Ethnic and Racial Studies*, 36, 3, pp. 468–82.
20. Abbas, T. (2017), *Contemporary Turkey in Conflict: Ethnicity, Islam and Politics*, Edinburgh: Edinburgh University Press.
21. Holmes, C. (2016), *Anti-Semitism in British Society, 1876–1939*, London: Routledge.
22. Kuechler, M. (1994), 'Germans and "Others": Racism, Xenophobia, or "Legitimate Conservatism"?', *German Politics*, 3, 1, pp. 47–74
23. Mason, H. L. (1984), 'Testing Human Bonds within Nations: Jews in the Occupied Netherlands', *Political Science Quarterly*, 99, 2, pp. 315–43.
24. Corner, E. and Gill, P. (2015), 'A False Dichotomy? Mental Illness and Lone-Actor Terrorism', *Law and Human Behavior, 39*, 1, pp. 23–34.
25. Husband, C. (1984), *'Race' in Britain: Continuity and Change*, London: Hutchinson.
26. Mason, D. (2000), *Race and Ethnicity in Modern Britain*, Oxford: Oxford University Press.
27. Simpson, L. (2007), '*Ghettos of the Mind: The Empirical Behaviour of Indices of Segregation and Diversity*', *Journal of the Royal Statistical Society A*, 107, 2, pp. 405–24.

28. Bonnett, A. (1998), 'How the British Working Class Became White: The Symbolic (Re)formation of Racialized Capitalism', *Journal of Historical Sociology*, 11, 3, pp. 316–40.
29. Solomos, J. (1989), *Race and Racism in Contemporary Britain*, London: Palgrave Macmillan.
30. Foucault, M. (2007), *Security, Territory, Population: Lectures at the Collège de France, 1977–78*, ed. Michel Senellart, trans. Graham Burchell, London: Palgrave Macmillan.
31. Cox, B. (2017), *Jo Cox: More in Common*, London: Two Roads.
32. Gietel-Basten, S. (2016), 'Why Brexit? The Toxic Mix of Immigration and Austerity', *Population and Development Review*, 42, 4, pp. 673–80.
33. Clarke, J. and Newman, J. (2017), '"People in this country have had enough of experts": Brexit and the Paradoxes of Populism', *Critical Policy Studies*, 11, 1, pp. 101–16.
34. Virdee, S. and McGeever, B. (2017), 'Racism, Crisis, Brexit', *Ethnic and Racial Studies*, 41, 10, pp. 1802–19.
35. On 22 July 2011, the horrific actions of Anders Breivik of Norway led to the massacre of sixty-nine young people who were gunned down on Utøya Island, while eight people were killed by a van bomb outside government buildings in Oslo, with countless maimed for life.
36. Burnett, J. (2017), 'Racial Violence and the Brexit State', *Race and Class*, 58, 4, pp. 85–97.
37. Ott, B. L. (2017), 'The Age of Twitter: Donald J. Trump and the Politics of Debasement', *Critical Studies in Media Communication*, 34, 1, pp. 59–68.
38. Suiter, J. (2016), 'Post-Truth Politics', *Political Insight*, 7, 3, pp. 25–7.

3. MUSLIM ORIGINS AND DESTINATIONS

1. Matar, N. (2009), 'Britons and Muslims in the Early Modern Period: From Prejudice to (a Theory of) Toleration', *Patterns of Prejudice*, 43, 3–4, pp. 213–31.
2. Nielsen, J. S. (1987), 'Muslims in Europe', *Renaissance and Modern Studies*, 31, 1, pp. 58–73.
3. Bald, V. (2006), 'Overlapping Diasporas, Multiracial Lives: South Asian Muslims in US Communities of Color, 1880–1950', *Souls*, 8, 4, pp. 3–18.
4. Cesari, J. (2004), *When Islam and Democracy Meet: Muslims in Europe and in the United States*, Basingstoke: Palgrave Macmillan; Fetzer, J. S. and Soper, C. J. (2005), *Muslims and the State in Britain, France and Germany*, Cambridge: Cambridge University Press.

5. Küçükcan, T. (2004), 'The Making of Turkish–Muslim Diaspora in Britain: Religious Collective Identity in a Multicultural Public Sphere', *Journal of Muslim Minority Affairs*, 24, 2, pp. 243–58.
6. Amiraux, V. (2005), 'Discrimination and Claims for Equal Rights amongst Muslims in Europe', in Cesari, J. and McLoughlin, S. (eds), *European Muslims and the Secular State*, Aldershot: Ashgate, pp. 25–38.
7. Peach, C. and Glebe, G. (1995), 'Muslim Minorities in Western Europe', *Ethnic and Racial Studies*, 18, 1, pp. 26–45.
8. Ahmed, A. S. and Donnan, H. (1994) (eds), *Islam, Globalisation and Postmodernity*, London: Routledge.
9. Phillips, D. (2006), 'Parallel Lives? Challenging Discourses of British Muslim Self-Segregation', *Environment and Planning D: Society and Space*, 24, 1, pp. 25–40.
10. Silverstein, P. A. (2005), 'Immigrant Racialization and the New Savage Slot: Race, Migration, and Immigration in the New Europe', *Annual Review of Anthropology*, 34, 1, pp. 363–84.
11. Hopkins, P. E. (2007), 'Young People, Masculinities, Religion and Race: New Social Geographies', *Progress in Human Geography*, 31, 2, pp. 163–77
12. Anwar, M. (2008), 'Muslims in Western States: The British Experience and the Way Forward', *Journal of Muslim Minority Affairs*, 28, 1, pp. 125–37; Norris, P. and Inglehart, R. F. (2012), 'Muslim Integration into Western Cultures: Between Origins and Destinations', *Political Studies*, 60, 2, pp. 228–51; Schumann, C. (2007), 'A Muslim "Diaspora" in the United States?', *The Muslim World*, 97, 1, pp. 11–32.
13. Allievi, S. and Nielsen, J. S. (2003) (eds), *Muslim Networks and Transnational Communities in and across Europe*, Leiden: Brill.
14. Jacob, K. and Kalter, F. (2013), 'Intergenerational Change in Religious Salience among Immigrant Families in Four European Countries', *International Migration*, 51, 3, pp. 38–56.
15. Voas, D. and Fleischmann, F (2012), 'Islam Moves West: Religious Change in the First and Second Generations', *Annual Review of Sociology*, 38, 1, pp. 525–45.
16. Fleischmann, F. and Phalet, K. (2012), 'Integration and Religiosity among the Turkish Second Generation in Europe: A Comparative Analysis across Four Capital Cities', *Ethnic and Racial Studies*, 35, 2, pp. 320–41.
17. Gest, J. (2012), 'Western Muslim Integration', *Review of Middle East Studies*, 46, 2, pp. 190–9.
18. Jopkke, C. (1996), 'Multiculturalism and Immigration: A Comparison of the United States, Germany, and Great Britain', *Theory and Society*, 25, 4, pp. 449–500, here p. 449.

19. Meer, N. and Modood, T. (2009), 'The Multicultural State We're In: Muslims, "Multiculture" and the "Civic Re-Balancing" of British Multiculturalism', *Political Studies*, 57, 3, pp. 473–97.
20. Mac an Ghaill, M. and Haywood, C. (2015), 'British-Born Pakistani and Bangladeshi Young Men: Exploring Unstable Concepts of Muslim, Islamophobia and Racialization', *Critical Sociology*, 41, 1, pp. 97–114.
21. Mirza, H. S. (2013), '"A Second Skin": Embodied Intersectionality, Transnationalism and Narratives of Identity and Belonging among Muslim Women in Britain', *Women's Studies International Forum*, 36, pp. 5–15.
22. Moghadam, V. M. (2002), 'Islamic Feminism and Its Discontents: Toward a Resolution of the Debate', *Signs*, 27, 2, pp. 1135–71.
23. Lorber, J. (2002), 'Heroes, Warriors, and "Burqas": A Feminist Sociologist's Reflections on September 11', *Sociological Forum*, 17, 3, pp. 377–96.
24. Geaves, R. (1996), 'Cult, Charisma, Community: The Arrival of Sufi Pirs and Their Impact on Muslims in Britain', *Journal of Muslim Minority Affairs*, 16, 2, pp. 169–92.
25. Geaves, R., Dressler, M. and Klinkhammer, G. (2009) (eds), *Sufis in Western Society: Global Networking and Locality*, Abingdon: Routledge.
26. Werbner, P. (2007), 'Intimate Disciples in the Modern World: The Creation of Translocal Amity among South Asian Sufis in Britain', in Van Bruinessen, M. and Howell, J. (eds), *Sufism and the 'Modern' in Islam*, London: IB Tauris, pp. 195–216.
27. Raudvere, C. and Stenberg, L. (2008) (eds), *Sufism Today: Heritage and Tradition in the Global Community*, London: IB Tauris.
28. Shah, P. A. (2013), 'In Pursuit of the Pagans: Muslim Law in the English Context', *The Journal of Legal Pluralism and Unofficial Law*, 45, 1, pp. 58–75.
29. Gill, A. (2004), 'Voicing the Silent Fear: South Asian Women's Experiences of Domestic Violence', *The Howard Journal of Criminal Justice*, 43, 5, pp. 465–83.
30. Modood, T. (2004), 'Muslims and the Politics of Difference', *The Political Quarterly*, 74, 1, pp. 100–15.
31. Grillo, R. (2007), 'An Excess of Alterity? Debating Difference in a Multicultural Society', *Ethnic and Racial Studies*, 30, 6, pp. 979–98.
32. Brubaker, R. (2013), 'Categories of Analysis and Categories of Practice: A Note on the Study of Muslims in European Countries of Immigration', *Ethnic and Racial Studies*, 36, 1, pp. 1–8.
33. Bowen, J. R (2004), 'Beyond Migration: Islam as a Transnational Public Space', *Journal of Ethnic and Migration Studies*, 30, 5, pp. 879–94.

34. Gole, N. (2011), 'The Public Visibility of Islam and European Politics of Resentment: The Minarets–Mosques Debate', *Philosophy and Social Criticism*, 37, 4, pp. 383–92, here p. 388.
35. Salvatore, A. (2004), 'Making Public Space: Opportunities and Limits of Collective Action among Muslims in Europe', *Journal of Ethnic and Migration Studies*, 30, 5, pp. 1013–31.
36. Sinno, A. H. (2012), 'The Politics of Western Muslims', *Review of Middle East Studies*, 46, 2, pp. 216–31.
37. Warner, C. M. and Wenner, M. W. (2006), 'Religion and the Political Organization of Muslims in Europe', *Perspectives on Politics*, 1, 3, pp. 457–79.
38. Ayers, J. W and Hofstetter, R. C. (2008), 'American Muslim Political Participation following 9/11: Religious Belief, Political Resources, Social Structures, and Political Awareness', *Politics and Religion*, 1, 1, pp. 3–26.
39. Peace, T. (2013), 'Muslims and Electoral Politics in Britain: The Case of the Respect Party', in Nielsen, J. (ed.), *Muslim Political Participation in Europe*, Edinburgh: Edinburgh University Press, pp. 299–321.
40. Saeed, A. (2007), 'Media, Racism and Islamophobia: The Representation of Islam and Muslims in the Media', *Sociology Compass*, 1, 2, pp. 443–62.
41. Abrahamian, E. (2003), 'The US Media, Huntington and September 11', *Third World Quarterly*, 24, 3, pp. 529–44.
42. El Hamel, C. (2002), 'Muslim Diaspora in Western Europe: The Islamic Headscarf (Hijab), the Media and Muslims' Integration in France', *Citizenship Studies*, 6, 3, pp. 293–308.

4. FRAMING MUSLIMS

1. Said, E. (1978), *Orientalism: Western Conceptions of the Orient*, London: Routledge & Kegan Paul.
2. Runnymede Trust (1997), 'Islamophobia: A Challenge for Us All', London: Runnymede Trust.
3. Westerlund, D. and Rosander, E. E. (1997) (eds), *African Islam and Islam in Africa: Encounters between Sufis and Islamist*, London: Hurst.
4. Lewis, B. (2004), *The Crisis of Islam: Holy War and Unholy Terror*, London: Weidenfeld & Nicolson; Fukuyama, F. (2012), *The End of History and the Last Man*, London: Penguin; Huntington, S. (2002), *The Clash Of Civilizations and the Remaking of World Order*, London: Simon & Schuster.
5. Bunzl, M. (2005), 'Between Anti-Semitism and Islamophobia: Some Thoughts on the New Europe', *American Ethnologist*, 32, 4, pp. 499–508.
6. Bleich, E. (2011), 'What Is Islamophobia and How Much Is There? Theorizing and Measuring an Emerging Comparative Concept', *American Behavioral Scientist*, 55, 12, pp. 1581–600.

7. Esposito, J. S. and Kalin, I. (2011) (eds), *Islamophobia: The Challenge of Pluralism in the 21st Century*, New York: Oxford University Press.
8. Mavelli, L. (2012), *Europe's Encounter with Islam: The Secular and the Postsecular*, London: Routledge.
9. Fekete, L. (2004), 'Anti-Muslim Racism and the Anti-Muslim Racism and the European Security State', *Race & Class*, 46, 1, pp. 3–29.
10. Kumar, D. (2012), *Islamophobia and the Politics of Empire*, New York: Haymarket.
11. Giddens, A. (1989) (ed.), *Sociology*, Cambridge: Polity, pp. 427–32.
12. Cohen, S. (1972), *Folk Devils and Moral Panics: The Creation of the Mods and Rockers*, London: MacGibbon and Kee; Cohen, S. (2000), 'Some Thoroughly Modern Monsters', *Index on Censorship*, 29, 5, pp. 36–42.
13. Van Dijk, T. (1993), *Elite Discourse and Racism*, London: Sage, p. 10.
14. Bennett, C. (1992), *Victorian Images of Islam*, London: Grey Seal.
15. Ahmed, A. S. (1992), *Postmodernism and Islam*, London: Routledge.
16. Said, *Orientalism*, p. 36.
17. Said, E. (1981), *Covering Islam: How the Media and the Experts Determine How We See the Rest of the World*, London: Routledge & Kegan Paul, p. 4.
18. Van Dijk, *Elite Discourse and Racism*, p. 59.
19. Ibid.
20. Asad, T. (1990), 'Multiculturalism and British Identity in the Wake of the Rushdie Affair', *Politics and Society*, 18, 4, pp. 455–80.
21. Asari, F. (1989), 'Iran in the British Media', *Index on Censorship*, 18, 5, pp. 9–13.
22. Abbas, T. (2000), 'Images of Islam', *Index on Censorship*, 29, 5, pp. 64–8.
23. Appignanesi, L. and Maitland, S. (1989), *The Rushdie File*, London: Fourth Estate, 1989.
24. Asad, *Multiculturalism*, p. 457.
25. Sikand, Y. (1994), 'Muslims and the Mass Media', *Economic and Political Weekly*, 29, 33, pp. 2134–5.
26. Van Dijk, *Elite Discourse and Racism*.
27. Klausen, J. (2009), *The Cartoons That Shook the World*, New Haven: Yale University Press.
28. Berkowitz, D. and Eko, L. (2007) 'Blasphemy as Sacred Rite/Right', *Journalism Studies*, 8, 5, pp. 779–97.
29. Weaver, S. (2010), 'Liquid Racism and the Danish Prophet Muhammad Cartoons', *Current Sociology*, 58, 5, pp. 675–92.
30. Weller, P. (2009), *A Mirror for Our Times: 'The Rushdie Affair' and the Future of Multiculturalism*, London: Continuum.
31. Akhtar, S. (1989), *Be Careful with Muhammad: Salman Rushdie Affair*, London: Bellew.

32. Berkowitz and Eko, 'Blasphemy as Sacred Rite/Right'.
33. Nielsen, J. S. (2010), 'Danish Cartoons and Christian–Muslim Relations in Denmark', *Exchange*, 39, 3, pp. 217–35.
34. Otterbeck, J. and Nielsen, J. S. (2015), *Muslims in Western Europe*, Edinburgh: Edinburgh University Press.
35. Foner, N. and Alba, R. (2008), 'Immigrant Religion in the US and Western Europe: Bridge or Barrier to Inclusion?', *International Migration Review*, 42, 2, pp. 360–92.
36. Al-Rawi, A. (2016), 'Facebook as a Virtual Mosque: The Online Protest against Innocence of Muslims', *Culture and Religion*, 17, 1, pp. 19–34.
37. Altheide, D. L. (2013), 'Media Logic, Social Control, and Fear', *Communication Theory*, 23, 3, pp. 223–38.
38. Saeed, A. (2007), 'Media, Racism and Islamophobia: The Representation of Islam and Muslims in the Media', *Sociology Compass*, 1, 2, pp. 443–62.
39. Kundnani, A. (2007), *The End of Tolerance: Racism in 21st-Century Britain*, London: Pluto.
40. Abbas, T. (2013), '"Last of the Dinosaurs": Citizen Khan as Institutionalisation of Pakistani Stereotypes in British Television Comedy', *South Asian Popular Culture*, 11, 1, pp. 85–90.
41. Goffman, E. (1990), *The Presentation of Self in Everyday Life*, London: Penguin.

5. ISLAMOPHOBIA AS NEW RACISM

1. Abbas, T. (2017), 'Ethnicity and Politics in Contextualising Far Right and Islamist Extremism', *Perspectives on Terrorism*, 11, 3, pp. 54–61.
2. Van Dijk, T. (1992), 'Discourse and the Denial of Racism', *Discourse & Society*, 3, 1, pp. 87–118.
3. Troyna, B. (1987), 'Beyond Multiculturalism: Towards the Enactment of Anti-Racist Education in Policy, Provision and Pedagogy', *Oxford Review of Education*, 13, 3, pp. 307–20.
4. Samad, Y. (1992), 'Book Burning and Race Relations: Political Mobilisation of Bradford Muslims', *New Community*, 18, 4, pp. 507–19.
5. Abbas, T. (2007), 'Muslim Minorities in Britain: Integration, Multiculturalism and Radicalism in the Post-7/7 Period', *Journal of Intercultural Studies*, 28, 3, pp. 287–300.
6. Heath-Kelly, C. (2012), 'Counter-Terrorism and the Counterfactual: Producing the "Radicalisation" Discourse and the UK "PREVENT" Strategy', *British Journal of Politics and International Relations*, 15, 3, pp. 394–415.
7. Abbas, T. (2018), 'Implementing "Prevent" in Countering Violent

Extremism in the UK: A Left-Realist Critique', *Critical Social Policy*, iFirst.
8. Ebner, J. (2017), *The Rage: The Vicious Circle of Islamist and Far-Right Extremism*, London: IB Tauris.
9. Amin, A. (2002), 'Ethnicity and the Multicultural City: Living with Diversity', *Environment and Planning A: Economy and Space*, 34, 6, pp. 959–80.
10. Mishra, P. (2017), *Age of Anger: A History of the Present*, London: Allen Lane; Hirsch, A. (2018), *On Race, Identity and Belonging*, London: Jonathan Cape.
11. Lentin, A. and Titley, G. (2012), 'The Crisis of "Multiculturalism" in Europe: Mediated Minarets, Intolerable Subjects', *European Journal of Cultural Studies*, 15, 2, pp. 123–38.
12. World Policy Institute (2011), 'Anatomy of Islamophobia', *World Policy Journal*, 28, 4, pp. 14–15.
13. Schiffer, S. and Wagner, C. (2011), 'Anti-Semitism and Islamophobia: New Enemies, Old Patterns', *Race & Class*, 52, 3, pp. 77–84.
14. Tyrer, D. and Sayyid, S. (2012), 'Governing Ghosts: Race, Incorporeality and Difference in Post-Political Times', *Current Sociology*, 60, 3, pp. 353–67.
15. Allen, C. (2011), 'Opposing Islamification or Promoting Islamophobia? Understanding the English Defence League', *Patterns of Prejudice*, 45, 4, pp. 279–94
16. Busher, J. (2017), 'Why Even Misleading Identity Claims Matter: The Evolution of the English Defence League', *Political Studies*, 66, 2, pp. 323–38.
17. Anderson, B. (1983), *Imagined Communities: Reflections on the Origins and Spread of Nationalism*, London: Verso.
18. Khalili, L. (2017), 'After Brexit: Reckoning with Britain's Racism and Xenophobia', *Poem: International English Language Quarterly*, 5, 2–3, pp. 253–65.
19. Williamson, M. and Khiabany, G. (2011), 'State, Culture and Anti-Muslim Racism', *Global Media and Communication*, 7, 3, pp. 175–9.
20. Cole, M. (2009), 'Critical Race Theory Comes to the UK: A Marxist Response', *Ethnicities*, 9, 2, pp. 246–84, here pp. 251–2.
21. Kumar, D. (2010), 'Framing Islam: The Resurgence of Orientalism during the Bush II Era', *Journal of Communication Inquiry*, 34, 3, pp. 254–77.
22. El-Haj, T. R. A. and Bonet, S. W. (2011), 'Education, Citizenship, and the Politics of Belonging: Youth from Muslim Transnational Communities and the "War on Terror"', *Review of Research in Education*, 35, pp. 29–59.
23. Thomas, P. and Sanderson, P. (2011), 'Unwilling Citizens? Muslim Young People and National Identity', *Sociology*, 45, 6, pp. 1028–44.

24. Amin, 'Ethnicity and the Multicultural City'.
25. Allen, C. (2010), *Islamophobia*, Farnham: Ashgate.
26. Sayyid, S. and Vakil, A. K. (2011) (eds), *Thinking through Islamophobia: Global Perspectives*, London: Hurst.
27. Esposito, J. and Kalin, I. (2011) (eds), *Islamophobia: The Challenge of Pluralism in the 21st Century*, New York: Oxford University Press.
28. Weller, P. (2006), 'Addressing Religious Discrimination and Islamophobia: Muslims and Liberal Democracies; The Case of the United Kingdom', *Journal of Islamic Studies*, 17, 3, pp. 295–325.
29. Allievi, S. (2012), 'Reactive Identities and Islamophobia: Muslim Minorities and the Challenge of Religious Pluralism in Europe', *Philosophy and Social Criticism*, 38, 4–5, pp. 379–87.
30. Josse, P. (2017), 'Leaderless Resistance and the Loneliness of Lone Wolves: Exploring the Rhetorical Dynamics of Lone Actor Violence', *Terrorism and Political Violence*, 29, 1, pp. 52–78.
31. Amin-Khan, T. (2012), 'New Orientalism, Securitisation and the Western Media's Incendiary Racism', *Third World Quarterly*, 33, 9, pp. 1595–610.
32. Pickel, G. (2018), 'Perceptions of Plurality: The Impact of the Refugee Crisis on the Interpretation of Religious Pluralization in Europe', in Schmiedel, U. and Smith, G. (eds), *Religion in the European Refugee Crisis: Religion and Global Migrations*, London: Palgrave Macmillan, pp. 15–37.
33. Jessop, B. (2017), 'The Organic Crisis of the British State: Putting Brexit in Its Place', *Globalizations*, 14, 1, pp. 133–41.
34. Kundnani, A. (2009), 'Radicalisation: The Journey of a Concept', *Race & Class*, 54, 2, pp. 3–25.
35. Abbas, T. (2011), *Islamic Radicalism and Multicultural Politics: The British Experience*, London: Routledge.
36. Alexander, C. (2004), 'Imagining the Asian Gang: Ethnicity, Masculinity and Youth after "the Riots"', *Critical Social Policy*, 24, 4, pp. 526–49.

6. ISLAMISM *REDUX*

1. Ali, T. (2003), *The Clash of Fundamentalisms: Crusades, Jihads and Modernity*, London: Verso.
2. Mabon, S. (2016), *Saudi Arabia and Iran: Power and Rivalry in the Middle East*, London: IB Tauris.
3. Aarts, P. and Roelants, C. (2016), *Saudi Arabia: A Kingdom in Peril*, London: Hurst.
4. Gerges, F. A. (2015), *Contentious Politics in the Middle East: Popular*

Resistance and Marginalized Activism beyond the Arab Uprisings, Basingstoke: Palgrave Macmillan.
5. Esposito, J. L. (1998), *Islam and Politics*, New York: Syracuse University Press.
6. Abbas, T. (2017) (ed.), *Muslim Diasporas in the West*, Abingdon: Routledge.
7. Communities and Local Government (2016), 'The Casey Review: A Review into Opportunity and Integration Review', London: Crown Copyright; Pew Research Center (2016), 'US Muslims Concerned about Their Place in Society, But Continue to Believe in the American Dream', Washington, DC: Pew Research Centre.
8. Feldman, M. and Pollard, J. (2016), 'The Ideologues and Ideologies of the Radical Right: An Introduction', *Patterns of Prejudice*, 50, 4–5, pp. 327–36.
9. Horgan, J. (2014), *The Psychology of Terrorism*, Abingdon Routledge.
10. Herbert, J. (2015), *Testosterone: Sex, Power, and the Will to Win*, Oxford: Oxford University Press.
11. Abbas, T. (2011), *Islamic Radicalism and Multicultural Politics: The British Experience*, London: Routledge.
12. Maher, S. (2017), *Salafi-Jihadism: The History of an Idea*, London: Penguin.
13. Dawson, L. L. and Amarasingam, A. (2017), 'Talking to Foreign Fighters: Insights into the Motivations for Hijrah to Syria and Iraq', *Studies in Conflict and Terrorism*, 40, 3, pp. 191–210.
14. Han and Butler, *Psychopolitics*.
15. Herbert, *Testosterone*.
16. Hamid, S. (2017), *Sufis, Salafis and Islamists: The Contested Ground of British Islamic Activism*, London: IB Tauris.
17. Bartlett, J. (2017), *The Dark Net*, London: Windmill.
18. Ostrand, N. (2015), 'The Syrian Refugee Crisis: A Comparison of Responses by Germany, Sweden, the United Kingdom, and the United States', *Journal on Migration and Human Security*, 3, 3, pp. 255–79
19. Chomsky, N. (2016), *Powers and Prospects: Reflections on Human Nature and the Social Order*, London: Pluto.
20. Dam, N. V. (2017), *Destroying a Nation: The Civil War in Syria*, London: IB Tauris.
21. ltunişik, M. B. and Martin, L. G. (2011), 'Making Sense of Turkish Foreign Policy in the Middle East under AKP', *Turkish Studies*, 12, 4, pp. 569–87.
22. Piketty, T. (2014), *Capital in the Twenty-First Century*, Cambridge, MA: Harvard University Press.
23 Roy, O. (2004), *The Failure of Political Islam*, Cambridge, MA: Harvard University Press.

24. Lambert, R. and Spalek, B. (2008), 'Muslim Communities, Counter-Terrorism and Counter-Radicalisation: A Critically Reflective Approach to Engagement', *International Journal of Law, Crime and Justice*, 36, 4, pp. 257–70.
25. Arendt, H. (1970), *On Violence*, Boston, MA: Harcourt.
26. Dalacoura, K. (2006), 'Islamist Terrorism and the Middle East Democratic Deficit: Political Exclusion, Repression and the Causes of Extremism', *Democratization*, 13, 3, pp. 508–25.
27. Goodwin, M. J. and Heath, H. (2016), 'The 2016 Referendum, Brexit and the Left Behind: An Aggregate-Level Analysis of the Result', *The Political Quarterly*, 87, 3, pp. 323–32.
28. Schmid, A. P. (2013), 'Radicalisation, De-Radicalisation, Counter-Radicalisation: A Conceptual Discussion and Literature Review', The Hague: International Centre for Counterterrorism.
29. Dawson and Amarasingam, 'Talking to Foreign Fighters'; Saeed, T. (2016), *Islamophobia and Securitization: Religion, Ethnicity and the Female Voice*, Basingstoke: Palgrave Macmillan.
30. Semati, M. and Szpunar, P. M. (2018), 'ISIS beyond the Spectacle: Communication Media, Networked Publics, Terrorism', *Critical Studies in Media Communication*, 35, 1, pp. 1–7.
31. Chatty, D. (2018), *Syria: The Making and Unmaking of a Refuge State*, London: Hurst.
32. Abbas, T. and Awan, I. (2015), 'Limits of UK Counterterrorism Policy and Its Implications for Islamophobia and Far Right Extremism', *International Journal for Crime, Justice and Social Democracy*, 4, 3, pp. 16–29.
33. Bunt, G. R. (2003), *Islam in the Digital Age: E-Jihad, Online Fatwas and Cyber Islamic Environments*, London: Pluto.

7. MULTICULTURAL RADICALISMS

1. Meer, N., Dwyer, C. and Modood, T. (2010), 'Embodying Nationhood? Conceptions of British National Identity, Citizenship, and Gender in the "Veil Affair"', *The Sociological Review*, 58, 1, pp. 84–111.
2. Sayyid, S. (2003), *A Fundamental Fear: Eurocentrism and the Emergence of Islamism*, London: Zed Books.
3. Klausen, J. (2005), *The Islamic Challenge: Politics and Religion in Western Europe*, New York: Oxford University Press.
4. Cesari, J. (2005), 'Mosque Conflicts in European Cities: Introduction', *Journal of Ethnic and Migration Studies*, 31, 6, pp. 1015–24.
5. Amghar, S., Boubekeur, A. and Emerson, M. (2007), *Islam: Challenges for Society and Public Policy*, Brussels: Centre for European Policy Studies.

6. Vertovec, S. and Peach, C. (1997) (eds), *Islam in Europe: The Politics of Religion and Community*, Basingstoke: Macmillan.
7. Wiktorowicz, Q. (2004), *Islamic Activism: A Social Movement Theory Approach*, Bloomington: Indiana University Press.
8. Halliday, F. (2003), *Islam and the Myth of Confrontation: Religion and Politics in the Middle East*, London: IB Tauris.
9. Gilroy, P. (2000), *Between Camps: Nations, Cultures and the Allure of Race*, London: Penguin.
10. Song, M. (2003), *Choosing Ethnic Identity*, Cambridge: Polity, pp. 16–21.
11. Castles, S. (2000), *Ethnicity and Globalization: From Migrant Worker to Transnational Citizen*, London: Sage.
12. Vertovec, S. (2001), 'Transnational Challenges to the "New" Multiculturalism', Paper presented to the Association of Social Anthropologists annual conference, 30 March–2 April, University of Sussex, UK.
13. Parekh, B. (2000), *The Future of Multi-Ethnic Britain*, London: Profile Books.
14. Anwar, M. (1998), *Between Cultures: Continuity and Change in the Lives of Young Asians*, London: Routledge.
15. Ijaz, A. and Abbas, T. (2010), 'The Impact of Intergenerational Change on the Attitudes of Working Class South Asian Muslim Parents on the Education of Their Daughters', *Gender and Education*, 22, 3, pp. 313–26.
16. Bunt, G. R. (2003), *Islam in the Digital Age: E-Jihad, Online Fatwas and Cyber Islamic Environments*, London: Pluto.
17. Fekete, L. (2017), 'Lammy Review: Without Racial Justice, Can There Be Trust?', *Race and Class*, 59, 3, pp. 75–9.
18. Jivraj, S. and Simpson, L. (2015), *Ethnic Identity and Inequalities in Britain: The Dynamics of Diversity*, Bristol: Policy Press.
19. Bagguley, P. and Hussain, Y. (2016), *Riotous Citizens: Ethnic Conflict in Multicultural Britain*, London: Routledge.
20. Abbas, T. (2007), 'Ethnoreligious Identities and Islamic Political Radicalism in the UK: A Case Study', *Journal of Muslim Minority Affairs*, 27, 3, pp. 429–42; Kohlman, E. F. (2004), *Al Qaida's Jihad in Europe: The Afghan–Bosnian Network*, Oxford: Berg.
21. Abbas, T. (2011), *Islamic Radicalism and Multicultural Politics: The British Experience*, London: Routledge.
22. Cole, M. (2011), *Education, Equality and Human Rights: Issues of Gender, 'Race', Sexuality, Disability and Social Class*, London: Routledge.
23. Afshar, H., Aitken, R. and Franks, M. (2005), 'Feminisms, Islamophobia and Identities', *Political Studies*, 53, 2, pp. 262–83.
24. Afshar, H. (2008), 'Can I See Your Hair? Choice, Agency and Attitudes:

The Dilemma of Faith and Feminism for Muslim Women Who Cover', *Ethnic and Racial Studies*, 31, 2, pp. 411–27.
25. Bowen, J. R. (2007), *Why the French Don't Like Headscarves: Islam, the State and the Public Space*, Princeton, NJ: Princeton University Press.
26. Mandeville, P. (2009), 'Muslim Transnational Identity and State Responses in Europe and the UK after 9/11: Political Community, Ideology and Authority', *Journal of Ethnic and Migration Studies*, 35, 3, pp. 491–506.
27. Morgan, G. and Poynting, S. (2016) (eds), *Global Islamophobia: Muslims and Moral Panic in the West*, London: Routledge.
28. Gest, J. (2010), *Apart: Alienated and Engaged Muslims in the West*, London: Hurst.
29. Scarman, L. (1982), *The Scarman Report: The Brixton Disorders, 10–12 April 1981*, London: Penguin; Home Office (2002), 'Community Cohesion: Report of the Independent Review Team', London: Home Office.
30. Appleby, N. (2010), 'Labelling the Innocent: How Government Counterterrorism Advice Creates Labels That Contribute to the Problem', *Critical Studies on Terrorism*, 3, 3, pp. 421–36.
31. Miller, D. and Mills, T. (2009), 'The Terror Experts and the Mainstream Media: The Expert Nexus and Its Dominance in the News Media', *Critical Studies on Terrorism*, 2, 3, pp. 414–37.
32. Gunning, J. and Jackson, R. (2011), 'What's So "Religious" about "Religious Terrorism"?', *Critical Studies on Terrorism*, 4 (3), 369–388.
33. Hickman, M. J. et al. (2012), 'Social Cohesion and the Notion of "Suspect Communities": A Study of the Experiences and Impacts of Being "Suspect" for Irish Communities and Muslim Communities in Britain', *Critical Studies on Terrorism*, 5, 1, pp. 89–106.
34. Jayaweera, H. and Choudhary, T. (2008), 'Immigration, Faith and Cohesion: Evidence from Local Areas with Significant Muslim Populations', York: Joseph Rowntree Foundation.

8. FAR-RIGHT VERSUS ISLAMIST EXTREMISM

1. Berntzen, L. E. and Sandberg, S. (2014), 'The Collective Nature of Lone Wolf Terrorism: Anders Behring Breivik and the Anti-Islamic Social Movement', *Terrorism and Political Violence*, 26, 5, pp. 759–79.
2. Feldman, M. (2013), 'Comparative Lone Wolf Terrorism: Toward a Heuristic Definition', *Democracy and Security*, 9, 3, pp. 270–86.
3. Copsey, N. (2010), *The English Defence League: Challenging Our Country and Our Values of Social Inclusion*, London: Faith Matters.
4. Pratt, D. (205), 'Islamophobia as Reactive Co-Radicalization', *Islam and Christian–Muslim Relations*, 26, 2, pp. 205–18.

5. Feldman, M. (2015), *From Radical-Right Islamophobia to 'Cumulative Extremism'*, London: Faith Matters.
6. Hafez, F. (2014), 'Shifting Borders: Islamophobia as Common Ground for Building Pan-European Right-Wing Unity', *Patterns of Prejudice*, 48, 5, pp. 479–99.
7. Mishra, P. (2017), *Age of Anger: A History of the Present*, London: Allen Lane.
8. Bangstad, S. (2014), *Anders Breivik and the Rise of Islamophobia*, London: Zed Books.
9. Borum, R. (2011), 'Radicalization into Violent Extremism I: A Review of Social Science Theories', *Journal of Strategic Security*, 4, 4, pp. 7–36.
10. Sedgwick, M. (2010), 'The Concept of Radicalization as a Source of Confusion', *Terrorism and Political Violence*, 4, 4, pp. 479–94.
11. Bailey, G. and Edwards, P. (2016), 'Rethinking "Radicalisation": Microradicalisations and Reciprocal Radicalisation as an Intertwined Process', *Journal for Deradicalisation*, 12, pp. 255–81.
12. Archer, A. (2013), 'Breivik's Mindset: The Counterjihad and the New Transatlantic Anti-Muslim Right', in Taylor, M., Currie, P. M. and Holbrook, D. (eds), *Extreme Right-Wing Political Violence and Terrorism*, London: Bloomsbury, pp. 169–86.
13. Awan, I. and Rahman, M. (2016), 'Portrayal of Muslims following the Murders of Lee Rigby in Woolwich and Mohammed Saleem in Birmingham: A Content Analysis of UK Newspapers', *Journal of Muslim Minority Affairs*, 36, 1, pp. 16–31.
14. Koehler, D. (2016), 'Right-Wing Extremism and Terrorism in Europe: Current Developments and Issues for the Future', *Prism: A Journal of the Center for Complex Operations*, 4, 2, pp. 84–104.
15. Ferrera, M. (2014), 'Ideology, Parties and Social Politics in Europe', *West European Politics*, 37, 2, pp. 420–48.
16. Sassen, S. (1998), *Globalization and Its Discontents: Essays on the New Mobility of People and Money*, New York: The New Press.
17. Peach, C. (2009), 'Slippery Segregation: Discovering or Manufacturing Ghettos?', *Journal of Ethnic and Migration Studies*, 35, 9, pp. 1381–95.
18. Peach, C. (1994), 'The Meaning of Segregation', *Planning Practice and Research*, 11, 2, pp. 137–50.
19. Beider, H. (2015), *White Working Class Voices: Multiculturalism, Community-Building and Change*, Bristol: Policy Press.
20. Hans-Georg, B. (2015), 'The Two Faces of Radical Right-Wing Populism in Western Europe', *The Review of Politics*, 55, 4, pp. 663–85; Saull, R. (2015), 'Capitalism, Crisis and the Far-Right in the Neoliberal Era', *Journal of International Relations and Development*, 18, 1, pp. 25–51.

21. Goodwin, M. (2013), 'The Roots of Extremism: The English Defence League and the Counter-Jihad Challenge', London: Chatham House Briefing Paper.
22. Pisoiu, D. (2015), 'Subcultural Theory Applied to Jihadi and Right-Wing Radicalization in Germany', *Terrorism and Political Violence*, 27, 1, pp. 9–28.
23. Pupcenoks, J. and McCabe, R. (2013), 'The Rise of the Fringe: Right Wing Populists, Islamists and Politics in the UK', *Journal of Muslim Minority Affairs*, 33, 2, pp. 171–84.
24. Goodwin, M. J. and Heath, H. (2016), 'The 2016 Referendum, Brexit and the Left Behind: An Aggregate-Level Analysis of the Result', *The Political Quarterly*, 87, 3, pp. 323–32.
25. Sullivan, A. et al. (2014), 'Social Origins, School Type and Higher Education Destinations', *Oxford Review of Education*, 40, 6, pp. 739–63.
26. McDowell, L. (2000), 'The Trouble with Men? Young People, Gender Transformations and the Crisis of Masculinity', *International Journal of Urban and Regional Research*, 24, 1, pp. 201–9.
27. Siraj, A. (2010), '"Because I'm the man! I'm the head": British Married Muslims and the Patriarchal Family Structure', *Contemporary Islam*, 4, 2, pp. 195–214.
28. Khattab, N. and Modood, T. (2015), 'Both Ethnic and Religious: Explaining Employment Penalties across 14 Ethno-Religious Groups in the United Kingdom', *Journal for the Scientific Study of Religion*, 54, 3, pp. 501–22.
29. Hopkins, P. E. (2006), 'Youthful Muslim Masculinities: Gender and Generational Relations', *Transactions of the Institute of British Geographers*, 31, 3, pp. 337–52.
30. Kalra, V. S. (2009), 'Between Emasculation and Hypermasculinity: Theorizing British South Asian Masculinities', *South Asian Popular Culture*, 7, 2, pp. 113–25.
31. Mac an Ghaill, M. and Haywood, C. (2015), 'British-Born Pakistani and Bangladeshi Young Men: Exploring Unstable Concepts of Muslim, Islamophobia and Racialization', *Critical Sociology*, 41, 1, pp. 97–114.
32. Uhlmann, M. (2008), 'European Converts to Terrorism', *Middle East Quarterly*, 15, 3, pp. 31–7.
33. Papadopoulos, L. (2010), 'Sexualisation of Young People: Review', London: Home Office.
34. Furlow, R. B. and Goodall, H. L. (2011), 'The War of Ideas and the Battle of Narratives: A Comparison of Extremist Storytelling Structures', *Cultural Studies: Critical Methodologies*, 11, 3, pp. 215–23.

35. Kaplan, J., Lööw, H. and Malkki, L. (2014), 'Introduction to the Special Issue on Lone Wolf and Autonomous Cell Terrorism', *Terrorism and Political Violence*, 26, 1, pp. 1–12.
36. Awan, I. and Zempi, I. (2017), '"I will blow your face off": Virtual and Physical World Anti-Muslim Hate Crime', *British Journal of Criminology*, 57, 2, pp. 362–80.
37. Anderson, B. (1983), *Imagined Communities: Reflections on the Origins and Spread of Nationalism*, London: Verso.
38. Warsi, S. (2017), *The Enemy Within: A Tale of Muslim Britain*, London: Allen Lane.
39. Elshimi, M. (2015), 'De-Radicalisation Interventions as Technologies of the Self: A Foucauldian Analysis', *Critical Studies on Terrorism*, 8, 5, pp. 110–29.

9. PLUGGED INTO THE RAGE

1. Aly, A. (2016), 'Brothers, Believers, Brave Mujahideen: Focusing Attention on the Audience of Violent Jihadist Preachers', *Studies in Conflict & Terrorism*, 40, 1, pp. 62–76.
2. Gill, P. et al. (2015), 'What Are the Roles of the Internet in Terrorism? Measuring Online Behaviours of Convicted UK Terrorists', Brussels: VOX-Pol Network of Excellence.
3. Ford, R. and Goodwin, M. (2014), *Revolt on the Right: Explaining Support for the Radical Right in Britain*, Abingdon: Routledge.
4. Ravndal, J. A. (2013), 'Anders Behring Breivik's Use of the Internet and Social Media', *JEX: Journal for Deradicalization and Democratic Culture*, 2, pp. 172–85.
5. Vergeer, M., Hermans, L. and Sams, S. (2013), 'Online Social Networks and Micro-Blogging in Political Campaigning: The Exploration of a New Campaign Tool and a New Campaign Style', *Party Politics*, 19, 3, pp. 477–501.
6. Weimann, G. (2015), *Terrorism in Cyberspace: The Next Generation*, New York: Columbia University Press, 2015.
7. Klausen, J. (2015), 'Tweeting the Jihad: Social Media Networks of Western Foreign Fighters in Syria and Iraq', *Studies in Conflict & Terrorism*, 38, 1, pp. 1–22.
8. Carter, J. A., Maher, S. and Neumann, P. R. (2014), '#Greenbirds: Measuring Importance and Influence in Syrian Foreign Fighter Networks', London: International Centre for the Study of Radicalisation and Politics Violence.
9. Klausen, 'Tweeting the Jihad', p. 19.

10. Zelin, A. Y. (2015), 'Picture or It Didn't Happen: A Snapshot of the Islamic State's Official Media Output', *Perspectives on Terrorism*, 9, 4, pp. 85–97.
11. Torres-Soriano, M. R. (2016), 'The Caliphate Is Not a Tweet Away: The Social Media Experience of Al Qaeda in the Islamic Maghreb', *Studies in Conflict & Terrorism*, 39, 11, pp. 968–81.
12. Droogan, J. and Peattie, S. (2016), 'Reading Jihad: Mapping the Shifting Themes of Inspire Magazine', *Terrorism and Political Violence*, 30, 4, pp. 684–717.
13. Ingram, H. J. (2015), 'The Strategic Logic of Islamic State Information Operations', *Australian Journal of International Affairs*, 69, 6, pp. 729–52.
14. Ashour, O. (2010), 'Online De-Radicalization? Countering Violent Extremist Narratives: Message, Messenger and Media Strategy', *Perspectives on Terrorism*, 4, 6, pp. 15–19.
15. Herding, M. (2013), *Inventing the Muslim Cool: Islamic Youth Culture in Western Europe*. Bielefeld: Transcript; Huey, L. (2015), '"This is not your mother's terrorism": Social Media, Online Radicalization and the Practice of Political Jamming', *Journal of Terrorism Research*, 6, 2; DOI: 10.15664/JTR.1159
16. Huey, '"This is not your mother's terrorism"'.
17. Sunstein, C. R. (2017), *#Republic: Divided Democracy in the Age of Social Media*, Princeton, NJ: Princeton University Press.
18. Edwards, C. and Gribbon, L. (2013), 'Pathways to Violent Extremism in the Digital Era', *The RUSI Journal*, 158, 5, pp. 40–7.
19. Kirby, A. (2007), 'The London Bombers as "Self-Starters": A Case Study in Indigenous Radicalization and the Emergence of Autonomous Cliques', *Studies in Conflict & Terrorism*, 30, 5, pp. 415–28.
20. O'Hara, K. and Stevens, D. (2015), 'Echo Chambers and Online Radicalism: Assessing the Internet's Complicity in Violent Extremism', *Policy and the Internet*, 7, 4, pp. 401–22.
21. Gendron, A. (2017), 'The Call to Jihad: Charismatic Preachers and the Internet', *Studies in Conflict & Terrorism*, 40, 1, pp. 44–61.
22. Giroux, H. A. (2017), *The Public in Peril: Trump and the Menace of American Authoritarianism*, London: Routledge.
23. Chakraborti, N. (2010), *Hate Crime*, Abingdon: Routledge.
24. Hell, J. and Steinmetz, G. (2017), 'A Period of "Wild and Fierce Fanaticism": Populism, Theo-Political Militarism, and the Crisis of US Hegemony', *American Journal of Cultural Sociology*, 5, 3, pp. 373–91.
25. Vieten, U. M. and Poynting, S. (2016), 'Contemporary Far Right Racist Populism in Europe', *Journal of Intercultural Studies*, 37, 6, pp. 533–40.
26. Giroux, H. A. (2017), 'White Nationalism, Armed Culture and State

Violence in the Age of Donald Trump', *Philosophy and Social Criticism*, 43, 9, pp. 887–910.
27. Modelski, G. and Thompson, W. R. (1999), 'The Long and the Short of Global Politics in the Twenty-First Century: An Evolutionary Approach', *International Studies Review*, 1, 2, pp. 110–40.
28. Futrell, R. and Simi, P. (2017), 'The (Un)surprising Alt-Right', *Contexts*, 16, 2, p. 76.
29. Barkun, M. (2017), 'President Trump and the "Fringe"', *Terrorism and Political Violence*, 29, 3, pp. 437–43.
30. Sculos, B. W. (2017), 'Who's Afraid of "Toxic Masculinity"?', *Class, Race and Corporate Power*, 5, 3, article 6.
31. Salazar, P. J. (2018), 'The Alt-Right as a Community of Discourse', *Javnost: The Public*, 25, 1–2, pp. 135–43.
32. Ibid.
33. Giroux, H. A. (2017), 'White Nationalism, Armed Culture and State Violence in the Age of Donald Trump', *Philosophy and Social Criticism*, 43, 9, pp. 887–910.
34. Ging, D. (2017), 'Alphas, Betas, and Incels: Theorizing the Masculinities of the Manosphere', *Men and Masculinities*; DOI: 10.1177/1097184X17706401
35. Banet-Weiser, S. and Miltner, K. M. (2016), '#MasculinitySoFragile: Culture, Structure, and Networked Misogyny', *Feminist Media Studies*, 16, 1, pp. 171–4.
36. Marwick, A. and Lewis, R. (2017), *Media Manipulation and Disinformation Online*, New York: Data&Society.
37. McNair, B. (2018), 'From Control to Chaos, and Back Again', *Journalism Studies*, 19, 4, pp. 499–511.

10. VANQUISHING FALSE IDOLS

1. Marranci, G. (2004), 'Multiculturalism, Islam and the Clash of Civilisations Theory: Rethinking Islamophobia', *Culture and Religion: An Interdisciplinary Journal*, 5, 1, pp. 105–17; Goody, J. (2004), *Islam in Europe*, Cambridge: Polity.
2. Peach, C. and Glebe, G. (1995), 'Muslim Minorities in Western Europe', *Ethnic and Racial Studies*, 18, 1, pp. 26–46.
3. Modood, T. (2005), *Multicultural Politics: Racism, Ethnicity, and Muslims in Britain*, Cambridge: Polity.
4. Mohiuddin, A. (2017), 'Muslims in Europe: Citizenship, Multiculturalism and Integration', *Journal of Muslim Minority Affairs*, 37, 4, pp. 393–412.
5. Chakrabarti, S. (2014), *On Liberty*, London: Allen Lane.

6. Kumar, D. (2012), *Islamophobia and the Politics of Empire*, New York: Haymarket.
7. Jones, O. (2014), *The Establishment: And How They Got Away With It*, London: Allen Lane.
8. Ahmed, N. A. (2010), *A User's Guide to the Crisis of Civilization and How to Save It*, London: Pluto.
9. Hellyer, H. A. (2007), *Muslims of Europe: The 'Other' Europeans*, Edinburgh: Edinburgh University Press.
10. Piketty, T. (2014), *Capital in the Twenty-First Century*, Cambridge, MA: Harvard University Press.
11. Dorling, D. (2014), *Inequality and the 1%*, London: Verso.
12. Ali, T. (2015), *The Extreme Centre: A Warning*, London: Verso.
13. Cohen, N. (2007), *What's Left? How the Left Lost Its Way: How Liberals Lost Their Way*, London: Harper Perennial; Goodhart, D. (2014), *The British Dream: Successes and Failures of Post-War Immigration*, New York: AtlanticBooks.
14. Hitchens, C. (2007), *God Is Not Great: How Religion Poisons Everything*, New York: Atlantic Books.
15. Parekh, B. (2001), 'The Future of Multi-Ethnic Britain: Reporting on a Report', *The Round Table: The Commonwealth Journal of International Affair*, 90, 362, pp. 691–700.
16. Phillips, 'Parallel Lives?'; Runnymede Trust (2018), 'Integration for All: Why Race Equality Matters', London: Runnymede Trust.
17. Nayak, A. (2003), 'Last of the "Real Geordies"? White Masculinities and the Subcultural Response to Deindustrialisation', *Environment and Planning D: Society and Space*, 21, 1, pp. 7–25.
18. Beider, H. (2015), *White Working Class Voices: Multiculturalism, Community-Building and Change*, Bristol: Policy Press.
19. Sayyid, S. (2003), *A Fundamental Fear: Eurocentrism and the Emergence of Islamism*, London: Zed Books.
20. Meer, N. (2013), 'Racialization and Religion: Race, Culture and Difference in the Study of Antisemitism and Islamophobia', *Ethnic and Racial Studies*, 36, 3, pp. 385–98.
21. Ramadan, T. (2010), *What I Believe*, Oxford: Oxford University Press.
22. Kundnani, A. (2014), *The Muslims Are Coming! Islamophobia, Extremism, and the Domestic War on Terror*, London: Verso.
23. Gest, J. (2010), *Apart: Alienated and Engaged Muslims in the West*, London: Hurst.
24. Cockburn, P. (2015), *The Rise of Islamic State: ISIS and the New Sunni Revolution*, London: Verso.

25. Roy, O. (2010), *Holy Ignorance: When Religion and Culture Part Ways*, London: Hurst.
26. Curtis, M. (2018), *Secret Wars: Britain's Collusion with Radical Islam*, London: Serpent's Tail.
27. Ibid., p. 426.
28. Clarke, J. and Newman, J. (2017), 'The Alchemy of Austerity', *Critical Social Policy*, 32, 3, pp. 299–19.
29. Clarke, J. and Newman, J. (2017), '"People in this country have had enough of experts": Brexit and the Paradoxes of Populism', *Critical Policy Studies*, 11, 1, pp. 101–16.
30. Obermaier, F. and Obermayer, B. (2017), *The Panama Papers: Breaking the Story of How the Rich and Powerful Hide Their Money*, London: Oneworld.
31. Hobolt, S. B. (2016), 'The Brexit Vote: A Divided Nation, a Divided Continent', *Journal of European Public Policy*, 23, 9, pp. 1259–77.
32. Virdee, S. and McGeever, B. (2017), 'Racism, Crisis, Brexit', *Ethnic and Racial Studies*, 41, 10, pp. 1802–19.
33. Burnett, J. (2017), 'Racial Violence and the Brexit State', *Race and Class*, 58, 4, pp. 85–97.
34. Abbas, T. (2017), 'The "Trojan Horse" Plot and the Fear of Muslim Power in British State Schools', *Journal of Muslim Minority Affairs*, 37, 4, pp. 426–41.
35. Shah, S. 'Educational Leadership: An Islamic Perspective', *British Educational Research Journal*, 32, 3, pp. 363–85.
36. Awan, I. (2014), 'Operation "Trojan Horse": Islamophobia or Extremism?', *Political Insight*, 5, 2, pp. 38–9.
37. Mogra, I. (2016), 'The "Trojan Horse" Affair and Radicalisation: An Analysis of Ofsted Reports', *Educational Review*, 68, 4, pp. 444–65.
38. Tomlinson, S. (2015), 'The Empire Disintegrates', *Ethnic and Racial Studies*, 38, 13, pp. 2208–15.

11. TOMORROW BELONGS TO THOSE

1. Richardson, R. (2015), 'British Values and British Identity: Muddles, Mixtures, and Ways Ahead', *London Review of Education*, 13, 2, pp. 37–48.
2. Halsey, A. H., Heath, A. F. and Ridge, J. M. (1980), *Origins and Destinations: Family, Class and Education in Modern Britain*, Oxford: Oxford University Press.
3. Smith, D. J. and Tomlinson, S. (1989), *The School Effect: A Study of Multi-Racial Comprehensives*, London: Policy Studies Institute.
4. Tomlinson, S. (2008), *Race and Education: Policy and Politics in Britain*, Maidenhead: Open University Press.
5. Abbas, T. (2004), *The Education of British South Asians: Ethnicity, Capital and Class Structure*, Basingstoke: Palgrave Macmillan.

6. Shah, S. and Shaikh, J. (2010), 'Leadership Progression of Muslim Male Teachers: Interplay of Ethnicity, Faith and Visibility', *School Leadership and Management*, 30, 1, pp. 19–33.
7. Bhatti, G. (2011), 'Outsiders or Insiders? Identity, Educational Success and Muslim Young Men in England', *Ethnography and Education*, 6, 1, pp. 81–96.
8. Salih, R. (2004), 'The Backward and the New: National, Transnational and Post-National Islam in Europe', *Journal of Ethnic and Migration Studies*, 30, 5, pp. 995–1011.
9. Meer, N. (2009), 'Identity Articulations, Mobilization, and Autonomy in the Movement for Muslim Schools in Britain', *Race Ethnicity and Education*, 12, 3, pp. 379–99; Miller, J. (2013), 'Resilience, Violent Extremism and Religious Education', *British Journal of Religious Education*, 35, 2, pp. 188–200.
10. Tinker, C. and Smart, A. (2012), 'Constructions of Collective Muslim Identity by Advocates of Muslim Schools in Britain', *Ethnic and Racial Studies*, 35, 4, pp. 643–63.
11. Kashyap, R. and Lewis, V. A. (2013), 'British Muslim Youth and Religious Fundamentalism: A Quantitative Investigation', *Ethnic and Racial Studies*, 36, 12, pp. 2117–40.
12. Adamson, F. B. (2011), 'Engaging or Contesting the Liberal State? "Muslim" as a Politicised Identity Category in Europe', *Journal of Ethnic and Migration Studies*, 37, 6, pp. 899–915.
13. Awan, I. (2014), 'Operation "Trojan Horse": Islamophobia or Extremism?', *Political Insight*, 5, 2, pp. 38–9.
14. Sieckelinck, S., Kaulingfreks, F. and Winter, M. D. (2015), 'Neither Villains nor Victims: Towards an Educational Perspective on Radicalisation', *British Journal of Educational Studies*, 63, 3, pp. 329–43.
15. Davies, L. (2016), 'Security, Extremism and Education: Safeguarding or Surveillance?', *British Journal of Educational Studies*, 64, 1, pp. 1–16, here p. 16.
16. Shah, S. (2006), 'Educational Leadership: An Islamic Perspective', *British Educational Research Journal*, 32, 3, pp. 363–85.
17. Haque, E. (2010), 'Homegrown, Muslim and Other: Tolerance, Secularism and the Limits of Multiculturalism', *Social Identities: Journal for the Study of Race, Nation and Culture*, 16, 1, pp. 79–101.
18. Salih, 'The Backward and the New'.
19. Mac an Ghaill, M. and Haywood, C. (2015), 'British-Born Pakistani and Bangladeshi Young Men: Exploring Unstable Concepts of Muslim, Islamophobia and Racialization', *Critical Sociology*, 41, 1, pp. 97–114.
20. Hoque, A. (2018), 'Third-Generation British-Bangladeshis from East

London: Complex Identities and a Culturally Responsive Pedagogy', *British Journal of Sociology of Education*, 39, 2, pp. 182–96.
21. Mirza, H. S. and Meetoo, V. (2018), 'Empowering Muslim Girls? Post-Feminism, Multiculturalism and the Production of the "Model" Muslim Female Student in British Schools', *British Journal of Sociology of Education*, 39, 2, pp. 227–41.
22. Khattab, N. and Modood, T. (2018), 'Accounting for British Muslims' Educational Attainment: Gender Differences and the Impact of Expectations', *British Journal of Sociology of Education*, 39, 2, pp. 242–59.
23. Casey, L. (2016), 'The Casey Review: A Review into Opportunity and Integration', London: Department of Communities and Local Government; Citizens UK (2017), 'The Missing Muslims: Unlocking British Muslim Potential for the Benefit of All', London: Citizens UK Citizens Commission on Islam, Participation and Public Life.
24. Shain, F. (2013), 'Race, Nation and Education: An Overview of British Attempts to "Manage Diversity" since the 1950s', *Education Inquiry*, 4, 1, pp. 63–85.
25. Sian, K. P. (2015), 'Spies, Surveillance and Stakeouts: Monitoring Muslim Moves in British State Schools', *Race Ethnicity and Education*, 18, 2, pp. 183–201.

12. THE POSTCOLONIAL SUBJECT'S DISCONTENT

1. Weller, *A Mirror for our Times*.
2. Shaffer, G. (2008), *Racial Science and British Society*, Basingstoke: Palgrave Macmillan.
3. Sheridan, L. P. (2006), 'Islamophobia Pre- and Post-September 11th, 2001', *Journal of Interpersonal Violence*, 21, 3, pp. 317–36; Zempi, I. and Awan, I. (2019) (eds), *The Routledge International Handbook of Islamophobia*, Abingdon: Routledge.
4. Poynting, S. and Mason, V. (2007), 'The *Resistible Rise* of *Islamophobia*: Anti-Muslim Racism in the UK and Australia before 11 September 2001', *Journal of Sociology*, 43, 1, pp. 61–86.
5. Meer, N. (2014), 'Islamophobia and Postcolonialism: Continuity, Orientalism and Muslim Consciousness', *Patterns of Prejudice*, 48, 5, pp. 500–15, here p. 515.
6. Jones, S. H. (2013), 'New Labour and the Re-Making of British Islam: The Case of the Radical Middle Way and the "Reclamation" of the Classical Islamic Tradition', *Religions*, 4, pp. 550–66.
7. Adamson, F. B. (2011), 'Engaging or Contesting the Liberal State?

"Muslim" as a Politicised Identity Category in Europe', *Journal of Ethnic and Migration Studies*, 37, 6, pp. 899–915.
8. Jones, H. (2014), '"The best borough in the country for cohesion!" Managing Place and Multiculture in Local Government', *Ethnic and Racial Studies*, 37, 4, pp. 605–20.
9. Singh, G. and Cowden, S. (2011), 'Multiculturalism's New Fault Lines: Religious Fundamentalisms and Public Policy', *Critical Social Policy*, 31, 3, pp. 343–64, here p. 346.
10. Karner, C. and Parker, D. (2011), 'Conviviality and Conflict: Pluralism, Resilience and Hope in Inner-City Birmingham', *Journal of Ethnic and Migration Studies*, 37, 3, pp. 355–72.
11. Gutkowski, S. (2012), 'The British Secular Habitus and the War on Terror', *Journal of Contemporary Religion*, 27, 1, pp. 87–103.
12. Kundnani, A. (2012), 'Multiculturalism and Its Discontents: Left, Right and Liberal', *European Journal of Cultural Studies*, 15, 2, pp. 155–66.
13. Eisenstein, H. (2009), *Feminism Seduced: How Global Elites Use Women's Labor and Ideas to Exploit the World*, London: Routledge.
14. Wiley, T. G., and Wright, W. E. (2004), 'Against the Undertow: Language-Minority Education Policy and Politics in the "Age of Accountability"', *Educational Policy*, 18, 1, pp. 142–68.
15. Zebiri, K. (2008), 'The Redeployment of Orientalist Themes in Contemporary Islamophobia', *Studies in Contemporary Islam*, 10, pp. 4–44.
16. Peach, C. (2007), '*Sleepwalking into Ghettoization? The British Debate over Segregation*', in Schönwälder, K. (ed.), 'Residential *Segregation* and the Integration of Immigrants: Britain, the Netherlands and Sweden', Discussion Paper, no. SP IV 2007-602, Berlin: Social Science Research Center Berlin, pp. 7–40; Kalra, V. S. and Kapoor, N. (2009), 'Interrogating Segregation, Integration and the Community Cohesion Agenda', *Journal of Ethnic and Migration Studies*, 35, 9, pp. 1397–415; Phillips, 'Parallel Lives?'
17. Allen, *Islamophobia*.
18. Abbas, T. (2012), 'The *Symbiotic* Relationship between Islamophobia and Radicalisation', *Critical Studies on Terrorism*, 5, 3, pp. 345–58.
19. Esposito and Kalin, *Islamophobia*.
20. Ebner, *The Rage*.
21. Halliday, F. (1999), '"Islamophobia" Reconsidered', *Ethnic and Racial Studies*, 22, 5, pp. 892–902, here p. 896.
22. Semati, M. (2010), 'Islamophobia, Culture and Race in the Age of Empire', *Cultural Studies*, 24, 2, pp. 256–75, here pp. 257–8.

13. FEAR AND LOATHING AT THE END OF HISTORY

1. Fryer, P. (2010), *Staying Power: The History of Black People in Britain*, London: Pluto; Gilroy, *There Ain't No Black in the Union Jack*.
2. Bokhorst-Heng, W. D. (2007), 'Multiculturalism's Narratives in Singapore and Canada: Exploring a Model for Comparative Multiculturalism and Multicultural Education', *Journal of Curriculum Studies*, 39, 6, pp. 629–58.
3. Phan, M. B. et al. (2015), 'Family Dynamics and the Integration of Professional Immigrants in Canada', *Journal of Ethnic and Migration Studies*, 41, 13, pp. 2061–80
4. Duyvendaka, J. W. and Scholten, P. (2012), 'Deconstructing the Dutch Multicultural Model: A Frame Perspective on Dutch Immigrant Integration Policymaking', *Comparative European Politics*, 10, 3, pp. 266–82.
5. Grillo, 'An Excess of Alterity?'.
6. Hansen, R. (1999), 'The Kenyan Asians, British Politics, and the Commonwealth Immigrants Act, 1968', *The Historical Journal*, 42, 3, pp. 809–34.
7. Donald, J. and Rattansi, A. (1992) (eds), *Race, Culture and Difference*, London: Sage.
8. Joppke, C. (2014), 'The Retreat Is Real: But What Is the Alternative? Multiculturalism, Muscular Liberalism, and Islam', *Constellations*, 21, 2, pp. 286–95.
9. Morgan, K. (2007), 'The Learning Region: Institutions, Innovation and Regional Renewal', *Regional Studies*, 41, 1, pp. 147–59.
10. Wyler, D. (2017), 'The Swiss Minaret Ban Referendum and Switzerland's International Reputation: A Vote with an Impact', *Journal of Muslim Minority Affairs*, 37, 4, pp. 413–25.
11. Uslaner, E. M. and Brown, M. (2005), 'Inequality, Trust, and Civic Engagement', *American Politics Research*, 33, 6, pp. 868–94.
12. Cesari, J. (2013), *Why the West Fears Islam: An Exploration of Muslims in Liberal Democracies*, London: Palgrave Macmillan.
13. Younge, *Who Are We?*
14. Hulse, K and Stone, W. (2007), 'Social Cohesion, Social Capital and Social Exclusion', *Policy Studies*, 28, 2, pp. 109–12.
15. Rodrik, D. (2014), 'The Past, Present, and Future of Economic Growth', *Challenge*, 57, 3, pp. 5–39.
16. Cameron, F. (2005), *US Foreign Policy after the Cold War*, London: Routledge.
17. Wallerstein, I. (1989), *The Modern World-System III*, New York: Academic Press.
18. Chomsky, N. (2017), *Who Rules the World?*, New York: Hamish Hamilton.

19. Lynch, M. (2013), *The Arab Uprising: The Unfinished Revolutions of the New Middle East*, New York: PublicAffairs.
20. Harvey, D. (2007), *A Brief History of Neoliberalism*, Oxford: Oxford University Press.
21. Folpe, E. K. (2002), *It Happened on Washington Square*, Baltimore: Johns Hopkins University Press.
22. Sowell, T. (1983), *Ethnic America: A History*, New York: Basic Books.
23. Glaeser, E. and Vigdor, J. (2012), *The End of the Segregated Century: Racial Separation in America's Neighborhoods, 1890–2010*, New York: Manhattan Institute for Policy Research.
24. Irvin, G. (2008), *Super Rich: The Rise of Inequality in Britain and the United States*, Bristol: Polity Press.
25. Becker, H. S. (1967), 'Whose Side Are We On?', *Social Problems*, 14, 3, pp. 239–47.
26. Irwin, R. (2018), *Ibn Khaldun: An Intellectual Biography*, Princeton, NJ: Princeton University Press.
27. Ibid.
28. Cowley, P. (2012), 'Arise, Novice Leader! The Continuing Rise of the Career Politician in Britain', *Politics*, 32, 1, pp. 31–8.
29. Berg, M. (2004), 'In Pursuit of Luxury: Global History and British Consumer Goods in the Eighteenth Century', *Past & Present*, 182, pp. 85–142.
30. Eisenstein, *Feminism Seduced*.

BIBLIOGRAPHY

Aarts, P. and Roelants, C. (2016), *Saudi Arabia: A Kingdom in Peril*, London: Hurst.

Abbas, T. (2000), 'Images of Islam', *Index on Censorship*, 29, 5, pp. 64–8.

———. (2004), *The Education of British South Asians: Ethnicity, Capital and Class Structure*, Basingstoke: Palgrave Macmillan.

———. (2005) (ed.), *Muslim Britain: Communities under Pressure*, London: Zed.

———. (2007), 'Ethnoreligious Identities and Islamic Political Radicalism in the UK: A Case Study', *Journal of Muslim Minority Affairs*, 27, 3, pp. 429–42.

———. (2007), 'Muslim Minorities in Britain: Integration, Multiculturalism and Radicalism in the Post-7/7 Period', *Journal of Intercultural Studies*, 28, 3, pp. 287–300.

———. (2011), *Islamic Radicalism and Multicultural Politics: The British Experience*, London and New York: Routledge.

———. (2012), 'The Symbiotic Relationship between Islamophobia and Radicalisation', *Critical Studies on Terrorism*, 5, 3, pp. 345–58.

———. (2013), '"Last of the dinosaurs": Citizen Khan as Institutionalisation of Pakistani Stereotypes in British Television Comedy', *South Asian Popular Culture*, 11, 1, pp. 85–90.

———. (2017), *Contemporary Turkey in Conflict: Ethnicity, Islam and Politics*, Edinburgh: Edinburgh University Press.

———. (2017), 'Ethnicity and Politics in Contextualising Far Right and Islamist Extremism', *Perspectives on Terrorism*, 11, 3, pp. 54–61.

———. (2017) (ed.), *Muslim Diasporas in the West*, Abingdon: Routledge.

———. (2017), 'The "Trojan Horse" Plot and the Fear of Muslim Power in British State Schools', *Journal of Muslim Minority Affairs*, 37, 4, pp. 426–41.

———. (2018), 'Implementing "Prevent" in Countering Violent Extremism in the UK: A Left-Realist Critique', *Critical Social Policy*, iFirst.

Abbas, T. and Awan, I. (2015), 'Limits of UK Counterterrorism Policy and Its Implications for Islamophobia and Far Right Extremism', *International Journal for Crime, Justice and Social Democracy*, 4, 3, pp. 16–29.

Abrahamian, E. (2003), 'The US Media, Huntington and September 11', *Third World Quarterly*, 24, 3, pp. 529–44.

Adamson, F. B. (2011), 'Engaging or Contesting the Liberal State? "Muslim" as a Politicised Identity Category in Europe', *Journal of Ethnic and Migration Studies*, 37, 6, pp. 899–915.

Afshar, H. (2008), '"Can I see your hair?" Choice, Agency and Attitudes: The Dilemma of Faith and Feminism for Muslim Women Who Cover', *Ethnic and Racial Studies*, 31, 2, pp. 411–27.

Afshar, H., Aitken, R. and Franks, M. (2005), 'Feminisms, Islamophobia and Identities', *Political Studies*, 53, 2, pp. 262–83.

Ahmed, A. S. (1992), *Postmodernism and Islam*, London: Routledge.

Ahmed, A. S. and Donnan, H. (1994) (eds), *Islam, Globalisation and Postmodernity*, Basingstoke: Routledge.

Ahmed, N. A. (2010), *A User's Guide to the Crisis of Civilization and How to Save It*, London and New York: Pluto.

Ahmed, S. (2004), *On Being Included: Racism and Diversity in Institutional Life*, Durham, NC: Duke University Press.

Ahmed, S. and Matthes, J. (2017), 'Media Representation of Muslims and Islam from 2000 to 2015: A Meta-Analysis', *International Communication Gazette*, 79, 3, pp. 219–44.

Akhtar, P. (2013), *British Muslim Politics: Examining Pakistani Biraderi Networks*, Basingstoke: Palgrave Macmillan.

Akhtar, S. (1989), *Be Careful with Muhammad: Salman Rushdie Affair*, London: Bellew.

Alexander, C. (2004), 'Imagining the Asian Gang: Ethnicity, Masculinity and Youth after "the Riots"', *Critical Social Policy*, 24, 4, pp. 526–49.

Ali, T. (2003), *The Clash of Fundamentalisms: Crusades, Jihads and Modernity*, London: Verso.

———.(2015), *The Extreme Centre: A Warning*, London: Verso.

Allen, C. (2010), *Islamophobia*, London: Routledge.

———. (2011), 'Opposing Islamification or Promoting Islamophobia? Understanding the English Defence League', *Patterns of Prejudice*, 45, 4, pp. 279–94.

BIBLIOGRAPHY

Allievi, S. (2012), 'Reactive Identities and Islamophobia: Muslim Minorities and the Challenge of Religious Pluralism in Europe', *Philosophy and Social Criticism*, 38, 4–5, pp. 379–87.

Allievi, S. and Nielsen, J. S. (eds) (2003), *Muslim Networks and Transnational Communities in and across Europe*, Leiden: Brill.

Al-Rawi, A. (2016), 'Facebook as a Virtual Mosque: The Online Protest against Innocence of Muslims', *Culture and Religion*, 17, 1, pp. 19–34.

Altheide, D. L. (2013), 'Media Logic, Social Control, and Fear', *Communication Theory*, 23, 3, pp. 223–38.

Altunişik, M. B. and Martin, L. G. (2011), 'Making Sense of Turkish Foreign Policy in the Middle East under AKP', *Turkish Studies*, 12, 4, pp. 569–87.

Aly, A. (2016), 'Brothers, Believers, Brave Mujahideen: Focusing Attention on the Audience of Violent Jihadist Preachers', *Studies in Conflict & Terrorism*, 40, 1, pp. 62–76.

Amghar, S., Boubekeur, A. and Emerson, M. (2007), *Islam: Challenges for Society and Public Policy*, Brussels: Centre for European Policy Studies.

Amin, A. (2002), 'Ethnicity and the Multicultural City: Living with Diversity', *Environment and Planning A*, 34, 6, pp. 959–80.

Amin-Khan, T. (2012), 'New Orientalism, Securitisation and the Western Media's Incendiary Racism', *Third World Quarterly*, 33, 9, pp. 1595–610.

Amiraux, V. (2005), 'Discrimination and Claims for Equal Rights amongst Muslims in Europe', in Cesari, J. and McLoughlin, S. (eds), *European Muslims and the Secular State*, Aldershot: Ashgate, pp. 25–38.

Anderson, B. (1983), *Imagined Communities: Reflections on the Origins and Spread of Nationalism*, London: Verso.

———. (1992), *Imagined Communities*, London and New York: Verso.

———. (2006), *Imagined Communities: Reflections on the Origin and Spread of Nationalism*, Revised edn, London and New York: Verso.

Anwar, M. (1979), *'The Myth of Return': Pakistanis in Britain*, London: Heinemann.

———. (1998), *Between Cultures: Continuity and Change in the Lives of Young Asians*, London: Routledge.

———. (2008), 'Muslims in Western States: The British Experience and the Way Forward', *Journal of Muslim Minority Affairs*, 28, 1, pp. 125–37.

Appignanesi, L. and Maitland, S. (1989), *The Rushdie File*, London: Fourth Estate, 1989.

Appleby, N. (2010), 'Labelling the Innocent: How Government Counterterrorism Advice Creates Labels That Contribute to the Problem', *Critical Studies on Terrorism*, 3, 3, pp. 421–36.

Archer, A. (2013), 'Breivik's Mindset: The Counterjihad and the New Transatlantic Anti-Muslim Right', in Taylor, M., Currie, P. M. and

Holbrook, D. (eds), *Extreme Right-Wing Political Violence and Terrorism*, London: Bloomsbury, pp. 169–86.

Arendt, H. (1970), *On Violence*, Boston, MA: Harcourt.

Asad, T. (1990), 'Multiculturalism and British Identity in the Wake of the Rushdie Affair', *Politics and Society*, 18, 4, pp. 45580.

Asari, F. (1989), 'Iran in the British Media', *Index on Censorship*, 18, 5, pp. 9–13.

Ashour, O. (2010), 'Online De-Radicalization? Countering Violent Extremist Narratives: Message, Messenger and Media Strategy', *Perspectives on Terrorism*, 4, 6, pp. 15–19.

Awan, I. (2014,) 'Operation "Trojan Horse": Islamophobia or Extremism?', *Political Insight*, 5, 22, pp. 38–9.

———. (2018), '"I never did anything wrong": Trojan Horse; A Qualitative Study Uncovering the Impact in Birmingham', *British Journal of Sociology of Education*, 39, 2, pp. 197–211.

Awan, I. and Rahman, M. (2016), 'Portrayal of Muslims following the Murders of Lee Rigby in Woolwich and Mohammed Saleem in Birmingham: A Content Analysis of UK Newspapers', *Journal of Muslim Minority Affairs*, 36, 1, pp. 16–31.

Awan, I. and Zempi, I. (2017), '"I will blow your face off": Virtual and Physical World Anti-Muslim Hate Crime', *British Journal of Criminology*, 57, 2, pp. 362–80.

Ayers, J. W and Hofstetter, R. C. (2008), 'American Muslim Political Participation following 9/11: Religious Belief, Political Resources, Social Structures, and Political Awareness', *Politics and Religion*, 1, 1, pp. 3–26.

Bagguley, P. and Hussain, Y. (2016), *Riotous Citizens: Ethnic Conflict in Multicultural Britain*, London: Routledge.

Bailey, G. and Edwards, P. (2016), 'Rethinking "Radicalisation": Microradicalisations and Reciprocal Radicalisation as an Intertwined Process', *Journal for Deradicalisation*, 12, pp. 255–81.

Bald, V. (2006), 'Overlapping Diasporas, Multiracial Lives: South Asian Muslims in US Communities of Color, 1880–1950', *Souls*, 8, 4, pp. 3–18.

Ball, W. and Solomos, J. (1990), *Race and Local Politics*, London: Palgrave Macmillan.

Banet-Weiser, S. and Miltner, K. M. (2016) '#MasculinitySoFragile: Culture, Structure, and Networked Misogyny', *Feminist Media Studies*, 16, 1, pp. 171–4.

Bangstad, S. (2014), *Anders Breivik and the Rise of Islamophobia*, London and New York: Zed.

Barkun, M. (2017), 'President Trump and the "Fringe"', *Terrorism and Political Violence*, 29, 3, pp. 437–43.

BIBLIOGRAPHY

Bartlett, J. (2017), *The Dark Net*, London: Windmill.
Becker, H. S. (1967), 'Whose Side Are We On?', *Social Problems*, 14, 3, pp. 239–47.
Beider, H. (2014), *White Working Class Voices: Multiculturalism, Community-Building and Change*, Bristol: Policy Press.
Bennett, C. (1992), *Victorian Images of Islam*, London: Grey Seal.
Berg, M. (2004), 'In Pursuit of Luxury: Global History and British Consumer Goods in the Eighteenth Century', *Past & Present*, 182, pp. 85–142.
Berkowitz, D. and Eko, L. (2007), 'Blasphemy as Sacred Rite/Right', *Journalism Studies*, 8, 5, pp. 779–97.
Bernasconi, R. (2007), 'Kant as an Unfamiliar Source of Racism', in Ward, J. K. and Lott, T. L. (eds), *Philosophers on Race: Critical Essays*, Oxford: Blackwell, pp. 145–66.
Berntzen, L. E. and Sandberg, S. (2014), 'The Collective Nature of Lone Wolf Terrorism: Anders Behring Breivik and the Anti-Islamic Social Movement', *Terrorism and Political Violence*, 26, 5, pp. 759–79.
Bhachu, P. (1985), *Twice Migrants: East African Sikh Settlers in Britain*, London and New York: Routledge & Kegan Paul.
Bhatti, G. (2011), 'Outsiders or Insiders? Identity, Educational Success and Muslim Young Men in England', *Ethnography and Education*, 6, 1, pp. 81–96.
Bleich, E. (2011), 'What Is Islamophobia and How Much Is There? Theorizing and Measuring an Emerging Comparative Concept', *American Behavioral Scientist*, 55, 12, pp. 1581–600.
Bode, L. (2016), 'Political News in the News Feed: Learning Politics from Social Media', *Mass Communication and Society*, 19, 1, pp. 24–48.
Bokhorst-Heng, W. D. (2007), 'Multiculturalism's Narratives in Singapore and Canada: Exploring a Model for Comparative Multiculturalism and Multicultural Education', *Journal of Curriculum Studies*, 39, 6, pp. 629–58.
Bonnett, A. (1998), 'How the British Working Class Became White: The Symbolic (Re)formation of Racialized Capitalism', *Journal of Historical Sociology*, 11, 3, pp. 316–40.
Borum, R. (2011), 'Radicalization into Violent Extremism I: A Review of Social Science Theories', *Journal of Strategic Security*, 4, 4, pp. 7–36.
Bowen, J. R (2004), 'Beyond Migration: Islam as a Transnational Public Space', *Journal of Ethnic and Migration Studies*, 30, 5, pp. 879–94.
———. (2007), *Why the French Don't Like Headscarves: Islam, the State and the Public Space*, Princeton, NJ: Princeton University Press.
Brubaker, R. (2013), 'Categories of Analysis and Categories of Practice: A Note on the Study of Muslims in European Countries of Immigration', *Ethnic and Racial Studies*, 36, 1, pp. 1–8.

Bunt, G. R. (2003), *Islam in the Digital Age: E-Jihad, Online Fatwas and Cyber Islamic Environments*, London and New York: Pluto.

Bunzl, M. (2005), 'Between Anti-Semitism and Islamophobia: Some Thoughts on the New Europe', *American Ethnologist*, 32, 4, pp. 499–508.

Burke, J. (2012), *The 9/11 Wars*, London: Penguin.

Burnett, J. (2017), 'Racial Violence and the Brexit State', *Race and Class*, 58, 4, pp. 85–97.

Busher, J. (2017), 'Why Even Misleading Identity Claims Matter: The Evolution of the English Defence League', *Political Studies*, 66, 2, pp. 323–38

Cameron, F. (2005), *US Foreign Policy after the Cold War*, London: Routledge.

Cannadine, D. (2011), *Ornamentalism: How the British Saw Their Empire*, London: Allen Lane.

Carr, M. (2010), *Blood and Faith: The Purging of Muslim Spain*, London: Hurst.

Carter, J. A., Maher, S. and Neumann, P. R. (2014), *#Greenbirds: Measuring Importance and Influence in Syrian Foreign Fighter Networks*, London: International Centre for the Study of Radicalisation and Politics Violence.

Casey, L. (2016), 'The Casey Review: A Review into Opportunity and Integration', London: Department of Communities and Local Government.

Castles, S. (2000), *Ethnicity and Globalization: From Migrant Worker to Transnational Citizen*, London: Sage.

Castles, S. and Kosack, G. (1973), *Immigrant Workers and Class Structure in Western Europe*, London: Institute of Race Relations and Oxford University Press.

Cesari, J. (2004), *When Islam and Democracy Meet: Muslims in Europe and in the United States*, Basingstoke: Palgrave Macmillan.

———. (2005), 'Mosque Conflicts in European Cities: Introduction', *Journal of Ethnic and Migration Studies*, 31, 6, pp. 1015–24.

———. (2013), *Why the West Fears Islam: An Exploration of Muslims in Liberal Democracies*, London: Palgrave Macmillan.

Chakrabarti, S. (2014), *On Liberty*, London and New York: Allen Lane.

Chakraborti, N. (2010), *Hate Crime*, Abingdon: Routledge.

Chatty, D. (2018), *Syria: The Making and Unmaking of a Refugee State*, London: Hurst.

Chomsky, N. (2016), *Powers and Prospects: Reflections on Human Nature and the Social Order*, London: Pluto.

———. (2017), *Who Rules the World?*, New York: Hamish Hamilton.

Citizenfour (2014), dir. Laura Poitras. Perf. Edward Snowdon, Glen Greenwald, William Binney et al. Praxis Films.

Citizens UK (2017), 'The Missing Muslims: Unlocking British Muslim Potential for the Benefit of All', London: Citizens UK Citizens Commission on Islam, Participation and Public Life.

Clarke, J. and Newman, J. (2017), 'The Alchemy of Austerity', *Critical Social Policy*, 32, 3, pp. 299–319.

———. (2017), '"People in this country have had enough of experts": Brexit and the Paradoxes of Populism', *Critical Policy Studies*, 11, 1, pp. 101–16.

Cockburn, P. (2015), *The Rise of Islamic State: ISIS and the New Sunni Revolution*, London and New York: Verso.

Cohen, N. (2007), *What's Left? How the Left Lost Its Way: How Liberals Lost Their Way*, London: Harper Perennial.

Cohen, S. (1972), *Folk Devils and Moral Panics: The Creation of the Mods and Rockers*, London: MacGibbon and Kee.

———. (2000) 'Some Thoroughly Modern Monsters', *Index on Censorship*, 29, 5, pp. 36–42.

Cole, M. (2009), 'Critical Race Theory Comes to the UK: A Marxist Response', *Ethnicities*, 9, 2, pp. 246–84.

Cole, M. (2011), *Education, Equality and Human Rights: Issues of Gender, 'Race', Sexuality, Disability and Social Class*, London: Routledge.

Communities and Local Government (2016), 'The Casey Review: A Review into Opportunity and Integration', London: Ministry of Housing, Communities and Local Government.

Connell, R. W. (1998), 'Men and Globalisation', *Men and Masculinities*, 1, 1, pp. 3–23.

Copsey, N. (2010), *The English Defence League: Challenging Our Country and Our Values of Social Inclusion*, London: Faith Matters.

Corner, E. and Gill, P. (2015), 'A False Dichotomy? Mental Illness and Lone-Actor Terrorism', *Law and Human Behavior*, 39, 1, pp. 23–34.

Cowley, P. (2012), 'Arise, Novice Leader! The Continuing Rise of the Career Politician in Britain', *Politics*, 32, 1, pp. 31–8.

Cox, B. (2017), *Jo Cox: More in Common*, London: Two Roads.

Curtis, M. (2018), *Secret Wars: Britain's Collusion with Radical Islam*, London: Serpent's Tail.

Dalacoura, K. (2006), 'Islamist Terrorism and the Middle East Democratic Deficit: Political Exclusion, Repression and the Causes of Extremism', *Democratization*, 13, 3, pp. 508–25.

Dam, N. V. (2017), *Destroying a Nation: The Civil War in Syria*, London: IB Tauris.

Daughton, J. P. (2005), 'A Colonial Affair? Dreyfus and the French Empire', *Historical Reflections*, 31, 3, pp. 469–83.

Davies, L. (2016), 'Security, Extremism and Education: Safeguarding or Surveillance?', *British Journal of Educational Studies*, 64, 1, pp. 1–16.

Davletov, B. and Abbas, T. (2018), 'Narrating Anti-Semitism in Historical and Contemporary Turkey', in Adams, J. and Heß, C. (eds), *The Medieval*

BIBLIOGRAPHY

Roots of Antisemitism: Continuities and Discontinuities from the Middle Ages to the Present Day, Abingdon: Routledge, pp. 145–60.

Dawson, L. L. and Amarasingam, A. (2017), 'Talking to Foreign Fighters: Insights into the Motivations for Hijrah to Syria and Iraq', *Studies in Conflict and Terrorism*, 40, 3, pp. 191–210.

Donald, J. and Rattansi, A. (1992) (eds), *Race, Culture and Difference*, London: Sage.

Dorling, D. (2014), *Inequality and the 1%*, London: Verso.

Downing, J. H. and Husband, C. (2005), *Representing 'Race': Racisms, Ethnicities and Media*, London: Sage.

Droogan, J. and Peattie, S. (2016), 'Reading Jihad: Mapping the Shifting Themes of *Inspire* Magazine', *Terrorism and Political Violence*, 30, 4, pp. 684–717.

Duyvendaka, J. W. and Scholten, P. (2012), 'Deconstructing the Dutch Multicultural Model: A Frame Perspective on Dutch Immigrant Integration Policymaking', *Comparative European Politics*, 10, 3, pp. 266–82.

Eatwell, R. (2000), 'The Extreme Right and British Exceptionalism: The Primacy of Politics', in Hainsworth, P. (ed.), *The Politics of the Extreme Right: From the Margins to the Mainstream*, London: Pinter, pp. 172–92.

Ebner, J. (2017), *The Rage: The Vicious Circle of Islamist and Far-Right Extremism*, London: IB Tauris.

Edwards, C. and Gribbon, L. (2013), 'Pathways to Violent Extremism in the Digital Era', *The RUSI Journal*, 158, 5, pp. 40–7.

Eisenstein, H. (2009), *Feminism Seduced: How Global Elites Use Women's Labor and Ideas to Exploit the World*, London: Routledge.

El Hamel, C. (2002), 'Muslim Diaspora in Western Europe: The Islamic Headscarf (Hijab), the Media and Muslims' Integration in France', *Citizenship Studies*, 6, 3, pp. 293–308.

El-Haj, T. R. A. and Bonet, S. W. (2011), 'Education, Citizenship, and the Politics of Belonging: Youth from Muslim Transnational Communities and the "War on Terror"', *Review of Research in Education*, 35, pp. 29–59.

Elshimi, M. (2015), 'De-Radicalisation Interventions as Technologies of the Self: A Foucauldian Analysis', *Critical Studies on Terrorism*, 8, 5, pp. 110–29.

Esposito, J. L. (1998), *Islam and Politics*, New York: Syracuse University Press.

Esposito, J. and Kalin, I. (2011) (eds), *Islamophobia: The Challenge of Pluralism in the 21st Century*, New York: Oxford University Press.

Farrall, L. A. (1985), *The Origins and Growth of the English Eugenics Movement, 1865–1925*, New York: Garland.

Fekete, L. (2004), 'Anti-Muslim Racism and the European Security State', *Race & Class*, 46, 1, pp. 3–29.

———. (2009), *A Suitable Enemy: Racism, Migration and Islamophobia in Europe*, London: Pluto.

———. (2017), 'Lammy Review: Without Racial Justice, Can There Be Trust?', *Race and Class*, 59, 3, pp. 75–9.
Feldman, M. (2013), 'Comparative Lone Wolf Terrorism: Toward a Heuristic Definition', *Democracy and Security*, 9, 3, pp. 270–86.
———. (2015), *From Radical-Right Islamophobia to 'Cumulative Extremism'*, London: Faith Matters.
Feldman, M. and Pollard, J. (2016), 'The Ideologues and Ideologies of the Radical Right: An Introduction', *Patterns of Prejudice*, 50, 4–5, pp. 327–36.
Ferrera, M. (2014), 'Ideology, Parties and Social Politics in Europe', *West European Politics*, 37, 2, pp. 420–48.
Fetzer, J. S. and Soper, C. J. (2005), *Muslims and the State in Britain, France and Germany*, Cambridge: Cambridge University Press.
Fleischmann, F. and Phalet, K. (2012), 'Integration and Religiosity among the Turkish Second Generation in Europe: A Comparative Analysis across Four Capital Cities', *Ethnic and Racial Studies*, 35, 2, pp. 320–41.
Folpe, E. K. (2002), *It Happened on Washington Square*, Baltimore: Johns Hopkins University Press.
Foner, N. and Alba, R. (2008), 'Immigrant Religion in the US and Western Europe: Bridge or Barrier to Inclusion?', *International Migration Review*, 42, 2, pp. 360–92.
Ford, R. and Goodwin, M. (2014), *Revolt on the Right: Explaining Support for the Radical Right in Britain*, Abingdon: Routledge.
Foucault, M. (2007), *Security, Territory, Population: Lectures at the Collège de France, 1977–78*, ed. Michel Senellart, trans. Graham Burchell, London: Palgrave Macmillan.
Fryer, P. (2010), *Staying Power: The History of Black People in Britain*, London: Pluto.
Fukuyama, F. (2012), *The End of History and the Last Man*, London: Penguin.
Furlow, R. B. and Goodall, H. L. (2011), 'The War of Ideas and the Battle of Narratives: A Comparison of Extremist Storytelling Structures', *Cultural Studies-Critical Methodologies*, 11, 3, pp. 215–23.
Futrell, R. and Simi, P. (2017), 'The [Un]surprising Alt-Right', *Contexts*, 16, 2, p. 76.
Geaves, R. (1996), 'Cult, Charisma, Community: The Arrival of Sufi Pirs and Their Impact on Muslims in Britain', *Journal of Muslim Minority Affairs*, 16, 2, pp. 169–92.
Geaves, R., Dressler, M. and Klinkhammer, G. (eds), *Sufis in Western Society Global Networking and Locality*, Abingdon: Routledge.
Gendron, A. (2017), 'The Call to Jihad: Charismatic Preachers and the Internet', *Studies in Conflict & Terrorism*, 40, 1, pp. 44–61.

BIBLIOGRAPHY

Gerges, F. A. (2015), *Contentious Politics in the Middle East: Popular Resistance and Marginalized Activism beyond the Arab Uprisings*, Basingstoke: Palgrave Macmillan.

Gest, J. (2010), *Apart: Alienated and Engaged Muslims in the West*, London: Hurst.

——. (2012), 'Western Muslim Integration', *Review of Middle East Studies*, 46, 2, pp. 190–9.

Giddens, A. (1989) (ed.), *Sociology*, Cambridge: Polity.

Gietel-Basten, S. (2016), 'Why Brexit? The Toxic Mix of Immigration and Austerity', *Population and Development Review*, 42, 4, pp. 673–80.

Gill, A. (2004), 'Voicing the Silent Fear: South Asian Women's Experiences of Domestic Violence', *The Howard Journal of Criminal Justice*, 43, 5, pp. 465–83.

Gill, P., Corner, E., Thornton, A. and Conway, M. (2015), 'What Are the Roles of the Internet in Terrorism? Measuring Online Behaviours of Convicted UK Terrorists', Brussels: VOX-Pol Network of Excellence.

Gilroy, P. (2000), *Between Camps: Nations, Cultures and the Allure of Race*, London: Penguin.

——. (2002), *There Ain't No Black in the Union Jack: The Cultural Politics of Race and Nation*, Abingdon: Routledge.

Ging, D. (2017), 'Alphas, Betas, and Incels: Theorizing the Masculinities of the Manosphere', *Men and Masculinities*. DOI: 10.1177/1097184X17706401.

Giroux, H. A. (2017), *The Public in Peril: Trump and the Menace of American Authoritarianism*, London: Routledge.

——. (2017), 'White Nationalism, Armed Culture and State Violence in the Age of Donald Trump', *Philosophy and Social Criticism*, 43, 9, pp. 887–910.

Glaeser, E. and Vigdor, J. (2012), *The End of the Segregated Century: Racial Separation in America's Neighborhoods, 1890–2010*, New York: Manhattan Institute for Policy Research.

Goffman, E. (1990), *The Presentation of Self in Everyday Life*, London: Penguin.

Gole, N. (2011), 'The Public Visibility of Islam and European Politics of Resentment: The Minarets–Mosques Debate', *Philosophy and Social Criticism*, 37, 4, pp. 383–92.

Goodhart, D. (2014), *The British Dream: Successes and Failures of Post-War Immigration*, New York: Atlantic.

Goodwin, M. (2013), 'The Roots of Extremism: The English Defence League and the Counter-Jihad Challenge', London: Chatham House Briefing Paper.

Goodwin, M. J. and Heath, H. (2016), 'The 2016 Referendum, Brexit and the Left Behind: An Aggregate-Level Analysis of the Result', *The Political Quarterly*, 87, 3, pp. 323–32.

Goody, J. (2004), *Islam in Europe*, Cambridge: Polity.
Gordon, M. (1998), *Slavery in the Arab World*, New York: New Amsterdam.
Grillo, R. (2007), 'An Excess of Alterity? Debating Difference in a Multicultural Society', *Ethnic and Racial Studies*, 30, 6, pp. 979–98.
Gunning, J. and Jackson, R. (2011), What's So "Religious" about "Religious Terrorism"?', *Critical Studies on Terrorism*, 4, 3, pp. 369–88.
Gutkowski, S. (2012), 'The British Secular Habitus and the War on Terror', *Journal of Contemporary Religion*, 27, 1, pp. 87–103.
Hafez, F. (2014), 'Shifting Borders: Islamophobia as Common Ground for Building Pan-European Right-Wing Unity', *Patterns of Prejudice*, 48, 5, pp. 479–99.
Halliday, F. (1999), '"Islamophobia" Reconsidered', *Ethnic and Racial Studies*, 22, 5, pp. 892–902.
———. (2003), *Islam and the Myth of Confrontation: Religion and Politics in the Middle East*, London: IB Tauris.
Halsey, A. H., Heath, A. F. and Ridge, J. M. (1980), *Origins and Destinations: Family, Class and Education in Modern Britain*, Oxford: Oxford University Press.
Hamid, S. (2017), *Sufis, Salafis and Islamists: The Contested Ground of British Islamic Activism*, London: IB Tauris.
Han, B.-C. and Butler, E. (2017), *Psychopolitics: Neoliberalism and New Technologies of Power*, London: Verso.
Hansen, R. (1999), 'The Kenyan Asians, British Politics, and the Commonwealth Immigrants Act, 1968', *The Historical Journal*, 42, 3, pp. 809–34.
Hans-Georg, B. (2015), 'The Two Faces of Radical Right-Wing Populism in Western Europe', *The Review of Politics*, 55, 4, pp. 663–85.
Haque, E. (2010), 'Homegrown, Muslim and Other: Tolerance, Secularism and the Limits of Multiculturalism', *Social Identities: Journal for the Study of Race, Nation and Culture*, 16, 1, pp. 79–101.
Harvey, D. (2007), *A Brief History of Neoliberalism*, Oxford: Oxford University Press.
Heath-Kelly, C. (2012), 'Counter-Terrorism and the Counterfactual: Producing the "Radicalisation" Discourse and the UK "PREVENT" Strategy', *British Journal of Politics and International Relations*, 15, 3, pp. 394–415.
Hell, J. and Steinmetz, G. (2017), 'A Period of "Wild and Fierce Fanaticism": Populism, Theo-Political Militarism, and the Crisis of US Hegemony', *American Journal of Cultural Sociology*, 5, 3, pp. 373–91.
Hellyer, H. A. (2007), *Muslims of Europe: The 'Other' Europeans*, Edinburgh: Edinburgh University Press.
Herbert, J. (2015), *Testosterone: Sex, Power, and the Will to Win*, Oxford: Oxford University Press.

BIBLIOGRAPHY

Herding, M. (2013), *Inventing the Muslim Cool: Islamic Youth Culture in Western Europe*. Bielefeld: Transcript.

Hickman, M. J., Thomas, L., Nickels, H. C. and Silvestri, S. (2012) 'Social Cohesion and the Notion of "Suspect Communities": A Study of the Experiences and Impacts of Being "Suspect" for Irish Communities and Muslim Communities in Britain', *Critical Studies on Terrorism*, 5, 1, pp. 89–106.

Hiro, D. (2003), *Iraq: A Report from the Inside*, London: Granta.

Hirsch, A. (2018), *On Race, Identity and Belonging*, London: Jonathan Cape.

Hitchens, C. (2007), *God Is Not Great: How Religion Poisons Everything*, New York: Atlantic Books.

Hobolt, S. B. (2016), 'The Brexit Vote: A Divided Nation, a Divided Continent', *Journal of European Public Policy*, 23, 9, pp. 1259–77.

Holmes, C. (2016), *Anti-Semitism in British Society, 1876–1939*, London: Routledge.

Home Office (2002), 'Community Cohesion: Report of the Independent Review Team', London: Home Office.

Hopkins, P. E. (2006), 'Youthful Muslim Masculinities: Gender and Generational Relations', *Transactions of the Institute of British Geographers*, 31, 3, pp. 337–52.

———. (2007), 'Young People, Masculinities, Religion and Race: New Social Geographies', *Progress in Human Geography*, 31, 2, pp. 163–77.

Hoque, A. (2018), 'Third-Generation British-Bangladeshis from East London: Complex Identities and a Culturally Responsive Pedagogy', *British Journal of Sociology of Education*, 39, 2, pp. 182–96.

Horgan, J. (2014), *The Psychology of Terrorism*, Abingdon: Routledge.

Huey, L. (2015), 'This Is Not Your Mother's Terrorism: Social Media, Online Radicalization and the Practice of Political Jamming', *Journal of Terrorism Research*, 6, 2. DOI: 10.15664/JTR.1159.

Hulse, K. and Stone, W. (2007), 'Social Cohesion, Social Capital and Social Exclusion', *Policy Studies*, 28, 2, pp. 109–12.

Huntington, S. (2002), *The Clash of Civilizations and the Remaking of World Order*, London: Simon & Schuster.

Husband, C. (1984), *'Race' in Britain: Continuity and Change*, London: Hutchinson.

Hutchinson, R. (2004), *Weapons of Mass Destruction: The No-Nonsense Guide to Nuclear, Chemical and Biological Weapons Today*, London: Weidenfeld & Nicolson.

Hyslop, J. (2009) 'Steamship Empire Asian, African and British Sailors in the Merchant Marine c.1880–1945', *Journal of Asian and African Studies*, 44, 1, pp. 49–67.

Ijaz, A. and Abbas, T. (2010), 'The Impact of Intergenerational Change on the Attitudes of Working Class South Asian Muslim Parents on the Education of Their Daughters', *Gender and Education*, 22, 3, pp. 313–26.

Immerwahr, J. (1992), 'Hume's Revised Racism', *Journal of the History of Ideas*, 53, 3, pp. 481–6.

Ingram, H. J. (2015), 'The Strategic Logic of Islamic State Information Operations', *Australian Journal of International Affairs*, 69, 6, pp. 729–52.

Institute of Race Relations (1985), 'How Racism Came to Britain', London: Institute of Race Relations.

Irvin, G. (2008), *Super Rich: The Rise of Inequality in Britain and the United States*, Bristol: Polity Press.

Irwin, R. (2018), *Ibn Khaldun: An Intellectual Biography*, Princeton, NJ: Princeton University Press.

Jacob, K. and Kalter, F. (2013), 'Intergenerational Change in Religious Salience among Immigrant Families in Four European Countries', *International Migration*, 51, 3, pp. 38–56.

Janmohamed, S. (2018), *Generation M: Young Muslims Changing the World*, London: IB Tauris.

Jayaweera, H. and Choudhary, T. (2008), 'Immigration, Faith and Cohesion: Evidence from Local Areas with Significant Muslim Populations', York: Joseph Rowntree Foundation.

Jessop, B. (2017), 'The Organic Crisis of the British State: Putting Brexit in Its Place', *Globalizations*, 14, 1, pp. 133–41.

Jivraj, S. and Simpson, L. (2015), *Ethnic Identity and Inequalities in Britain: The Dynamics of Diversity*, Bristol: Policy Press.

Jones, H. (2014), '"The best borough in the country for cohesion!" Managing Place and Multiculture in Local Government', *Ethnic and Racial Studies*, 37, 4, pp. 605–20.

Jones, O. (2014), *The Establishment: And How They Got Away With It*, London and New York: Allen Lane.

Jones, S. H. (2013), 'New Labour and the Re-Making of British Islam: The Case of the Radical Middle Way and the "Reclamation" of the Classical Islamic Tradition', *Religions*, 4, pp. 550–66.

Jopkke, C. (1996), 'Multiculturalism and Immigration: A Comparison of the United States, Germany, and Great Britain', *Theory and Society*, 25, 4, pp. 449–500.

———. (2014), 'The Retreat Is Real: But What Is the Alternative? Multiculturalism, Muscular Liberalism, and Islam', *Constellations*, 21, 2, pp. 286–95.

Josse, P. (2017), 'Leaderless Resistance and the Loneliness of Lone Wolves: Exploring the Rhetorical Dynamics of Lone Actor Violence', *Terrorism and Political Violence*, 29, 1, pp. 52–78.

Kalra, V. S. (2009), 'Between Emasculation and Hypermasculinity: Theorizing British South Asian Masculinities', *South Asian Popular Culture*, 7, 2, pp. 113–25.

Kalra, V. S. and Kapoor, N. (2009), 'Interrogating Segregation, Integration and the Community Cohesion Agenda', *Journal of Ethnic and Migration Studies*, 35, 9, pp. 1397–415.

Kaplan, J., Lööw, H. and Malkki, L. (2014), 'Introduction to the Special Issue on Lone Wolf and Autonomous Cell Terrorism', *Terrorism and Political Violence*, 26, 1, pp. 1–12.

Karner, C. and Parker, D. (2011), 'Conviviality and Conflict: Pluralism, Resilience and Hope in Inner-City Birmingham', *Journal of Ethnic and Migration Studies*, 37, 3, pp. 355–72.

Kashyap, R. and Lewis, V. A. (2013), 'British Muslim Youth and Religious Fundamentalism: A Quantitative Investigation', *Ethnic and Racial Studies*, 36, 12, pp. 2117–40.

Kenny, K. (2006), 'Violence, Race, and Anti-Irish Sentiment in the Nineteenth Century', in Lee, J. J and Casey, M. (eds), *Making the Irish American: The History and Heritage of the Irish in the United States*, New York: New York University Press, pp. 354–63.

Khalili, L. (2017), 'After Brexit: Reckoning with Britain's Racism and Xenophobia', *Poem: International English Language Quarterly*, 5, 2–3, pp. 253–65.

Khan, J. (2015), *The Raj at War: A People's History of India's Second World War*, London: Bodley Head.

Khattab, N. and Modood, T. (2015), 'Both Ethnic and Religious: Explaining Employment Penalties across 14 Ethno-Religious Groups in the United Kingdom', *Journal for the Scientific Study of Religion*, 54, 3, pp. 501–22.

———. (2018), 'Accounting for British Muslims' Educational Attainment: Gender Differences and the Impact of Expectations', *British Journal of Sociology of Education*, 39, 2, pp. 242–59.

Kimmel, M. (2015), *Angry White Men: American Masculinity at the End of an Era*, New York: Nation Books.

———. (2017), *Manhood in America*, New York: Oxford University Press.

Kirby, A. (2007), 'The London Bombers as "Self-Starters": A Case Study in Indigenous Radicalization and the Emergence of Autonomous Cliques', *Studies in Conflict & Terrorism*, 30, 5, pp. 415–28.

Klausen, J. (2005), *The Islamic Challenge: Politics and Religion in Western Europe*, New York: Oxford University Press.

———. (2009), *The Cartoons That Shook the World*, New Haven: Yale University Press.

———. (2015), 'Tweeting the Jihad: Social Media Networks of Western Foreign Fighters in Syria and Iraq', *Studies in Conflict & Terrorism*, 38, 1, pp. 1–22.

Klug, B. (2013), 'Interrogating "New Anti-Semitism"', *Ethnic and Racial Studies*, 36, 3, pp. 468–82.

———. (2014), 'The Limits of Analogy: Comparing Islamophobia and Antisemitism', *Patterns of Prejudice*, 48, 5, pp. 442–59.

Koehler, D. (2016), 'Right-Wing Extremism and Terrorism in Europe: Current Developments and Issues for the Future', *Prism: A Journal of the Center for Complex Operations*, 4, 2, pp. 84–104.

Kohlman, E. F. (2004), *Al-Qaida's Jihad in Europe: The Afghan–Bosnian Network*, Oxford: Berg.

Koulouris, T. (2018), 'Online Misogyny and the Alternative Right: Debating the Undebatable', *Feminist Media Studies*, 18, 4, pp. 750–61.

Küçükcan, T. (2004), 'The Making of Turkish-Muslim Diaspora in Britain: Religious Collective Identity in a Multicultural Public Sphere', *Journal of Muslim Minority Affairs*, 24, 2, pp. 243–58.

Kuechler, M. (1994), 'Germans and "Others": Racism, Xenophobia, or "Legitimate Conservatism"?', *German Politics*, 3, 1, pp. 47–74

Kumar, D. (2010), 'Framing Islam: The Resurgence of Orientalism during the Bush II Era', *Journal of Communication Inquiry*, 34, 3, pp. 254–77.

———. (2012), *Islamophobia and the Politics of Empire*, New York: Haymarket.

Kundnani, A (2001), 'From Oldham to Bradford: The Violence of the Violated', *The Three Faces of British Racism, Race & Class*, 43, 2, pp. 41–60.

———. (2007), *The End of Tolerance: Racism in 21st-Century Britain*, London and New York: Pluto.

———. (2009), 'Radicalisation: The Journey of a Concept', *Race & Class*, 54, 2, pp. 3–25.

———. (2012), 'Multiculturalism and Its Discontents: Left, Right and Liberal', *European Journal of Cultural Studies*, 15, 2, pp. 155–66.

———. (2014), *The Muslims Are Coming! Islamophobia, Extremism, and the Domestic War on Terror*, London and New York: Verso.

Lambert, R. and Spalek, B. (2008), 'Muslim Communities, Counter-Terrorism and Counter-Radicalisation: A Critically Reflective Approach to Engagement', *International Journal of Law, Crime and Justice*, 36, 4, pp. 257–70.

Layton-Henry, Z. (1984), *The Politics of Immigration: Immigration, 'Race', and 'Race' Relations in Post-War Britain*, Oxford: Blackwell.

Lentin, A. and Titley, G. (2012), 'The Crisis of "Multiculturalism" in Europe: Mediated Minarets, Intolerable Subjects', *European Journal of Cultural Studies*, 15, 2, pp. 123–38.

Lewis, B. (2004), *The Crisis of Islam: Holy War and Unholy Terror*, London: Weidenfeld & Nicolson.

Lorber, J. (2002), 'Heroes, Warriors, and "Burqas": A Feminist Sociologist's Reflections on September 11', *Sociological Forum*, 17, 3, pp. 377–96.

Lynch, M. (2013), *The Arab Uprising: The Unfinished Revolutions of the New Middle East*, New York: PublicAffairs.

Mabon, S. (2016), *Saudi Arabia and Iran: Power and Rivalry in the Middle East*, London: IB Tauris.

Mac an Ghaill, M. and Haywood, C. (2015), 'British-Born Pakistani and Bangladeshi Young Men: Exploring Unstable Concepts of Muslim, Islamophobia and Racialization', *Critical Sociology*, 41, 1, pp. 97–114.

Macpherson Report (1999), 'The Stephen Lawrence Inquiry: Report of an Inquiry by Sir William Macpherson of Cluny', Cm 4262-I, London: Stationery Office.

Maher, S. (2017), *Salafi-Jihadism: The History of an Idea*, London: Penguin.

Mandeville, P. (2009), 'Muslim Transnational Identity and State Responses in Europe and the UK after 9/11: Political Community, Ideology and Authority', *Journal of Ethnic and Migration Studies*, 35, 3, pp. 491–506.

Markley, R. (2010), *The Far East and the English Imagination*, Cambridge: Cambridge University Press.

Marranci, G. (2004), 'Multiculturalism, Islam and the Clash of Civilisations Theory: Rethinking Islamophobia', *Culture and Religion: An Interdisciplinary Journal*, 5, 1, pp. 105–17.

Marwick, A. and Lewis, R. (2017), *Media Manipulation and Disinformation Online*, New York: Data&Society.

Mason, D. (2000), *Race and Ethnicity in Modern Britain*, Oxford: Oxford University Press.

Mason, H. L. (1984), 'Testing Human Bonds within Nations: Jews in the Occupied Netherlands', *Political Science Quarterly*, 99, 2, pp. 315–43.

Massey, D. B. and Meegan, R. A. (1982), *The Anatomy of Job Loss: The How, Why, and Where of Employment Decline*, London: Methuen.

Matar, N. (2009), 'Britons and Muslims in the Early Modern Period: From Prejudice to (a Theory of) Toleration', *Patterns of Prejudice*, 43, 3–4, pp. 213–31.

Mavelli, L. (2012), *Europe's Encounter with Islam: The Secular and the Postsecular*, London: Routledge.

McDowell, L. (2000), 'The Trouble with Men? Young People, Gender Transformations and the Crisis of Masculinity', *International Journal of Urban and Regional Research*, 24, 1, pp. 201–9.

McGee, D. (2008), *The End of Multiculturalism? Terrorism, Integration and Human Rights*, Milton Keynes: Open University Press.

BIBLIOGRAPHY

McNair, B. (2018), 'From Control to Chaos, and Back Again', *Journalism Studies*, 19, 4, pp. 499–511.

Meer, N. (2009), 'Identity Articulations, Mobilization, and Autonomy in the Movement for Muslim Schools in Britain', *Race Ethnicity and Education*, 12, 3, pp. 379–99.

———. (2013), 'Racialization and Religion: Race, Culture and Difference in the Study of Antisemitism and Islamophobia', *Ethnic and Racial Studies*, 36, 3, pp. 385–98.

———. (2014), 'Islamophobia and Postcolonialism: Continuity, Orientalism and Muslim Consciousness', *Patterns of Prejudice*, 48, 5, pp. 500–15.

Meer, N. and Modood, T. (2009), 'The Multicultural State We're In: Muslims, "Multiculture" and the "Civic Re-Balancing" of British Multiculturalism', *Political Studies*, 57, 3, pp. 473–97.

Meer, N., Dwyer, C. and Modood, T. (2010), 'Embodying Nationhood? Conceptions of British National Identity, Citizenship, and Gender in the "Veil Affair"', *The Sociological Review*, 58, 1, pp. 84–111.

Miah, S. (2017), *Muslims, Schooling and Security: Trojan Horse, Prevent and Racial Politics*, Basingstoke: Palgrave Macmillan.

Miller, D. and Mills, T. (2009), 'The Terror Experts and the Mainstream Media: The Expert Nexus and Its Dominance in the News Media', *Critical Studies on Terrorism*, 2, 3, pp. 414–37.

Miller, J. (2013), 'Resilience, Violent Extremism and Religious Education', *British Journal of Religious Education*, 35, 2, pp. 188–200.

Mirza, H. S. (2013), '"A second skin": Embodied Intersectionality, Transnationalism and Narratives of Identity and Belonging among Muslim Women in Britain', *Women's Studies International Forum*, 36, pp. 5–15.

Mirza, H. S. and Meetoo, V. (2018), 'Empowering Muslim Girls? Post-Feminism, Multiculturalism and the Production of the "Model" Muslim Female Student in British Schools', *British Journal of Sociology of Education*, 39, 2, pp. 227–41.

Mishra, P. (2017), *Age of Anger: A History of the Present*, London: Allen Lane.

Modelski, G. and Thompson, W. R. (1999), 'The Long and the Short of Global Politics in the Twenty-First Century: An Evolutionary Approach', *International Studies Review*, 1, 2, pp. 110–40.

Modood, T. (1990), 'British Asian and Muslims and the Rushdie Affair', *The Political Quarterly*, 61, 2, pp. 143–60.

———. (2005), *Multicultural Politics: Racism, Ethnicity, and Muslims in Britain*, Cambridge: Polity.

Moghadam, V. M. (2002), 'Islamic Feminism and Its Discontents: Toward a Resolution of the Debate', *Signs*, 27, 2, pp. 1135–71.

BIBLIOGRAPHY

Mogra, I. (2016), 'The "Trojan Horse" Affair and Radicalisation: An Analysis of Ofsted Reports', *Educational Review*, 68, 4, pp. 444–65.

Mohiuddin, A. (2017), 'Muslims in Europe: Citizenship, Multiculturalism and Integration', *Journal of Muslim Minority Affairs*, 37, 4, pp. 393–412.

Montagu, A. (1951), *Statement on Race*, New York: Schuman.

Morgan, G. and Poynting, S. (2016) (eds), *Global Islamophobia: Muslims and Moral Panic in the West*, London: Routledge.

Morgan, K. (2007), 'The Learning Region: Institutions, Innovation and Regional Renewal', *Regional Studies*, 41, 1, pp. 147–59.

Murji, K. (2017), *Racism, Policy and Politics*, Bristol: Policy Press.

Myers, M. and Bhopal, K. (2018), 'Muslims, Home Education and Risk in British Society', *British Journal of Sociology of Education*, 39, 2, pp. 212–26.

Nayak, A. (2003), 'Last of the "Real Geordies"? White Masculinities and the Subcultural Response to Deindustrialisation', *Environment and Planning D: Society and Space*, 21, 1, pp. 7–25.

———. (2010), 'Race, Affect, and Emotion: Young People, Racism, and Graffiti in the Postcolonial English Suburbs', *Environment and Planning A: Economy and Space*, 42, 10, pp. 2370–92.

Nielsen, J. S. (1987), 'Muslims in Europe', *Renaissance and Modern Studies*, 31, 1, pp. 58–73.

———. (2010), 'Danish Cartoons and Christian–Muslim Relations in Denmark', *Exchange*, 39, 3, pp. 217–35.

Norris, P. and Inglehart, R. F. (2012), 'Muslim Integration into Western Cultures: Between Origins and Destinations', *Political Studies*, 60, 2, pp. 228–51.

O'Hara, K. and Stevens, D. (2015), 'Echo Chambers and Online Radicalism: Assessing the Internet's Complicity in Violent Extremism', *Policy and the Internet*, 7, 4, pp. 401–22.

Obermaier, F. and Obermayer, B. (2017), *The Panama Papers: Breaking the Story of How the Rich and Powerful Hide Their Money*, London: Oneworld.

Oldfield, J. R. (1998), *Popular Politics and British Anti-Slavery: The Mobilisation of Public Opinion against the Slave Trade 1787–1807*, Abingdon: Routledge.

Ooomen, T. K. (1997), *Citizenship and National Identity: From Colonialism to Globalism*, London: Sage.

Ostrand, N. (2015), 'The Syrian Refugee Crisis: A Comparison of Responses by Germany, Sweden, the United Kingdom, and the United States', *Journal on Migration and Human Security*, 3, 3, pp. 255–79.

Ott, B. L. (2017), 'The Age of Twitter: Donald J. Trump and the Politics of Debasement', *Critical Studies in Media Communication*, 34, 1, pp. 59–68.

Otterbeck, J. and Nielsen, J. S. (2015), *Muslims in Western Europe*, Edinburgh: Edinburgh University Press.

BIBLIOGRAPHY

Papadopoulos, L. (2010), 'Sexualisation of Young People: Review', London: Home Office.

Parekh, B. (2000), *The Future of Multi-Ethnic Britain*, London: Profile Books.

———. (2001), 'The Future of Multi-Ethnic Britain: Reporting on a Report', *The Round Table: The Commonwealth Journal of International Affairs*, 90, 362, pp. 691–700.

Patterson, P. (1965), *Dark Strangers*, London: Pelican.

Peace, T. (2013), 'Muslims and Electoral Politics in Britain: The Case of the Respect Party', in Nielsen, J. (ed.), *Muslim Political Participation in Europe*, Edinburgh: Edinburgh University Press, pp. 299–321.

Peach, C. (1994), 'The Meaning of Segregation', *Planning Practice and Research*, 11, 2, pp. 137–50.

———. (2007), 'Sleepwalking into Ghettoization? The British Debate over Segregation', in Schönwälder, K. (ed.), 'Residential Segregation and the Integration of Immigrants: Britain, the Netherlands and Sweden', Discussion Paper, no. SP IV 2007-602, Berlin: Social Science Research Center Berlin, pp. 7–40.

———. (2009) 'Slippery Segregation: Discovering or Manufacturing Ghettos?', *Journal of Ethnic and Migration Studies*, 35, 9, pp. 1381–95.

Peach, C. and Glebe, G. (1995), 'Muslim Minorities in Western Europe', *Ethnic and Racial Studies*, 18, 1, pp. 26–45.

Pew Research Center (2016), 'U.S. Muslims Concerned about Their Place in Society, But Continue to Believe in the American Dream', Washington DC: Pew Research Centre.

Phan, M. B, Banerjee, R., Deacon, L. and Taraky, H. (2015), 'Family Dynamics and the Integration of Professional Immigrants in Canada', *Journal of Ethnic and Migration Studies*, 41, 13, pp. 2061–80.

Phillips, D. (2006), 'Parallel Lives? Challenging Discourses of British Muslim Self-Segregation', *Environment and Planning D: Society and Space*, 24, 1, pp. 25–40.

Phizacklea, A. and Miles, R. (1980), *Labour and Racism*, London: Routledge & Kegan Paul.

Pickel, G. (2018), 'Perceptions of Plurality: The Impact of the Refugee Crisis on the Interpretation of Religious Pluralization in Europe', in Schmiedel, U. and Smith, G. (eds), *Religion in the European Refugee Crisis: Religion and Global Migrations*, London: Palgrave Macmillan, pp. 15–37.

Piketty, T. (2014), *Capital in the Twenty-First Century*, trans. Arthur Goldhammer, Cambridge, MA: Harvard University Press.

Pisoiu, D. (2015), 'Subcultural Theory Applied to Jihadi and Right-Wing Radicalization in Germany', *Terrorism and Political Violence*, 27, 1, pp. 9–28.

Poynting, S. and Mason, V. (2007), 'The Resistible Rise of Islamophobia: Anti-Muslim Racism in the UK and Australia before 11 September 2001', *Journal of Sociology*, 43, 1, pp. 61–86.

Pratt, D. (2015), 'Islamophobia as Reactive Co-Radicalization', *Islam and Christian–Muslim Relations*, 26, 2, pp. 205–18.

Pupcenoks, J. and McCabe, R. (2013), 'The Rise of the Fringe: Right Wing Populists, Islamists and Politics in the UK', *Journal of Muslim Minority Affairs*, 33, 2, pp. 171–84.

Ramadan, T. (2010), *What I Believe*, Oxford and New York: Oxford University Press.

Rattansi, A. (1992), 'Changing the Subject? Racism, Culture and Education', Donald, J. and ―― (1992) (ed.), *Race, Culture and Difference*, London: Sage, pp. 11–48.

――. (2007), *Racism: A Very Short Introduction*, Oxford: Oxford University Press.

Raudvere, C. and Stenberg, L. (2008) (eds), *Sufism Today: Heritage and Tradition in the Global Community*, London: IB Tauris.

Ravndal, J. A. (2013), 'Anders Behring Breivik's Use of the Internet and Social Media', *JEX Journal for Deradicalization and Democratic Culture*, 2, pp. 172–85.

Reeves, F. (2009), *British Racial Discourse: A Study of British Political Discourse about Race and Race-Related Matters*, Cambridge: Cambridge University Press.

Reisgl, M. (2000), *Discourse and Discrimination: Rhetorics of Racism and Antisemitism*, Abingdon: Routledge.

Rich, P. B. (2010), *Race and Empire in British Politics*, Cambridge: Cambridge University Press.

Richardson, R. (2015), 'British Values and British Identity: Muddles, Mixtures, and Ways Ahead', *London Review of Education*, 13, 2, pp. 37–48.

Rodrik, D. (2014), 'The Past, Present, and Future of Economic Growth', *Challenge*, 57, 3, pp. 5–39.

Roy, O. (2004), *The Failure of Political Islam*, Cambridge, MA: Harvard University Press.

――. (2010), *Holy Ignorance: When Religion and Culture Part Ways*, London and New York: Columbia University Press/Hurst.

――. (2018), *Globalized Islam: The Search for a New Ummah*, New edn, New York: Columbia University Press.

Runnymede Trust (1997), 'Islamophobia: A Danger for Us All', London: Runnymede Trust.

――. (2018), 'Integration for All: Why Race Equality Matters', London: Runnymede Trust.

BIBLIOGRAPHY

Saeed, A. (2007), 'Media, Racism and Islamophobia: The Representation of Islam and Muslims in the Media', *Sociology Compass*, 1, 2, pp. 443–62.

Saeed, T. (2016), *Islamophobia and Securitization: Religion, Ethnicity and the Female Voice*, Basingstoke: Palgrave Macmillan.

Said, E. (1978), *Orientalism: Western Conceptions of the Orient*, London: Routledge & Kegan Paul.

———. (1981), *Covering Islam: How the Media and the Experts Determine How We See the Rest of the World*, London: Routledge & Kegan Paul.

Salazar, P. J. (2018), 'The Alt-Right as a Community of Discourse', *Javnost: The Public*, 25, 1–2, pp. 135–43.

Salih, R. (2004), 'The Backward and the New: National, Transnational and Post-National Islam in Europe', *Journal of Ethnic and Migration Studies*, 30, 5, pp. 995–1011.

Salvatore, A. (2004), 'Making Public Space: Opportunities and Limits of Collective Action among Muslims in Europe', *Journal of Ethnic and Migration Studies*, 30, 5, pp. 1013–31.

Samad, Y. (1992), 'Book Burning and Race Relations: Political Mobilisation of Bradford Muslims', *New Community*, 18, 4, pp. 507–19.

Sardar, Z. and Davies, M. W. (2003), *Who Do People Hate America?*, London: Icon.

Sassen, S. (1998), *Globalization and Its Discontents: Essays on the New Mobility of People and Money*, New York: The New Press.

Saull, R. (2015), 'Capitalism, Crisis and the Far-Right in the Neoliberal Era', *Journal of International Relations and Development*, 18, 1, pp. 25–51.

Sayyid, S. (2003), *A Fundamental Fear: Eurocentrism and the Emergence of Islamism*, London and New York: Zed.

Sayyid, S. and Vakil, A. V. (2011) (eds), *Thinking through Islamophobia: Global Perspectives*, London and New York: Hurst and Columbia University Press.

Scarman, L. (1982), *The Scarman Report: The Brixton Disorders, 10–12 April 1981*, London: Penguin.

Schiffer, S. and Wagner, C. (2011), 'Anti-Semitism and Islamophobia: New Enemies, Old Patterns', *Race & Class*, 52, 3, pp. 77–84.

Schmid, A. P. (2013), 'Radicalisation, De-Radicalisation, Counter-Radicalisation: A Conceptual Discussion and Literature Review', The Hague, Netherlands: International Centre for Counterterrorism.

Schumann, C. (2007), 'A Muslim "Diaspora" in the United States?', *The Muslim World*, 97, 1, pp. 11–32.

Sculos, B. W. (2017), 'Who's Afraid of "Toxic Masculinity"?', *Class, Race and Corporate Power*, 5, 3, article 6.

Sedgwick, M. (2010), 'The Concept of Radicalization as a Source of Confusion', *Terrorism and Political Violence*, 4, 4, pp. 479–94.

Semati, M. (2010), 'Islamophobia, Culture and Race in the Age of Empire', *Cultural Studies*, 24, 2, pp. 256–75.

Semati, M. and Szpunar, P. M. (2018), 'ISIS beyond the Spectacle: Communication Media, Networked Publics, Terrorism', *Critical Studies in Media Communication*, 35, 1, pp. 1–7.

Shaffer, G. (2008), *Racial Science and British Society*, Basingstoke: Palgrave Macmillan.

Shah, P. A. (2013), 'In Pursuit of the Pagans: Muslim Law in the English Context', *The Journal of Legal Pluralism and Unofficial Law*, 45, 1, pp. 58–75.

Shah, S. (2006), 'Educational Leadership: An Islamic Perspective', *British Educational Research Journal*, 32, 3, pp. 363–85.

Shah, S. and Shaikh, J. (2010), 'Leadership Progression of Muslim Male Teachers: Interplay of Ethnicity, Faith and Visibility', *School Leadership and Management*, 30, 1, pp. 19–33.

Shain, F. (2013), 'Race, Nation and Education: An Overview of British Attempts to "Manage Diversity" since the 1950s', *Education Inquiry*, 4, 1, pp. 63–85.

Shaw, A. (2000), *Kinship and Continuity: Pakistani Families in Britain*, London: Routledge.

Sheridan, L. P. (2006), 'Islamophobia Pre- and Post-September 11th, 2001', *Journal of Interpersonal Violence*, 21, 3, pp. 317–36.

Sian, K. P. (2015), 'Spies, Surveillance and Stakeouts: Monitoring Muslim Moves in British State Schools', *Race Ethnicity and Education*, 18, 2, pp. 183–201.

Sieckelinck, S., Kaulingfreks, F. and Winter, M. D. (2015), 'Neither Villains Nor Victims: Towards an Educational Perspective on Radicalisation', *British Journal of Educational Studies*, 63, 3, pp. 329–43.

Sikand, Y. (1994), 'Muslims and the Mass Media', *Economic and Political Weekly*, 29, 33, pp. 2134–5.

Silverstein, P. A. (2005), 'Immigrant Racialization and the New Savage Slot: Race, Migration, and Immigration in the New Europe', *Annual Review of Anthropology*, 34, 1, pp. 363–84.

Simpson, L. (2007), 'Ghettos of the Mind: The Empirical Behaviour of Indices of Segregation and Diversity', *Journal of the Royal Statistical Society A*, 107, 2, pp. 405–24.

Singh, G. and Cowden, S. (2011), 'Multiculturalism's New Fault Lines: Religious Fundamentalisms and Public Policy', *Critical Social Policy*, 31, 3, pp. 343–64.

Sinno, A. H. (2012), 'The Politics of Western Muslims', *Review of Middle East Studies*, 46, 2, pp. 216–31.

BIBLIOGRAPHY

Siraj, A. (2010), '"Because I'm the man! I'm the head": British Married Muslims and the Patriarchal Family Structure', *Contemporary Islam*, 4, 2, pp. 195–214.

Smith, A. D. (1992), 'National Identity and the Idea of European Unity', *International Affairs*, 68, 1, pp. 55–76.

Smith, D. J. and Tomlinson, S. (1989), *The School Effect: A Study of Multi-Racial Comprehensives*, London: Policy Studies Institute.

Sneddon, C. (2012), *The Untold Story of the People of Azad Kashmir*, London: Hurst.

Solomos, J. (1988), 'Institutionalised Racism: Policies of Marginalisation in Education and Training', in Cohen, P. and Bains, H. S. (eds), *Multi-Racist Britain: Youth Questions*, London: Palgrave Macmillan, pp. 156–94.

———. (1989), *Race and Racism in Contemporary Britain*, London: Palgrave Macmillan.

———. (2003), *Race and Racism in Britain*, Basingstoke: Palgrave-Macmillan.

Song, M. (2003), *Choosing Ethnic Identity*, Cambridge: Polity.

Sowell, T. (1983), *Ethnic America: A History*, New York: Basic Books.

Suiter, J. (2016), 'Post-Truth Politics', *Political Insight*, 7, 3, pp. 25–7.

Sullivan, A., Parsons, S., Wiggins, R., Heath, A. F. and Green, F. (2014), 'Social Origins, School Type and Higher Education Destinations', *Oxford Review of Education*, 40, 6, pp. 739–63.

Sunstein, C. R. (2017). *#Republic: Divided Democracy in the Age of Social Media*, Princeton, NJ: Princeton University Press.

Sussman, R. W. (2014), *The Myth of Race: The Troubling Persistence of an Unscientific Idea*. Cambridge, MA: Harvard University Press.

Thomas, H. (1999), *The Slave Trade: History of the Atlantic Slave Trade, 1440–1870*, London: Weidenfeld & Nicolson.

Thomas, P. and Sanderson, P. (2011), 'Unwilling Citizens? Muslim Young People and National Identity', *Sociology*, 45, 6, pp. 1028–44.

Tinker, C. and Smart, A. (2012), 'Constructions of Collective Muslim Identity by Advocates of Muslim Schools in Britain', *Ethnic and Racial Studies*, 35, 4, pp. 643–63.

Tomlinson, S. (2008), *Race and Education: Policy and Politics in Britain*, Maidenhead: Open University Press/McGraw-Hill Education.

———. (2015), 'The Empire Disintegrates', *Ethnic and Racial Studies*, 38, 13, pp. 2208–15.

Torres-Soriano, M. R. (2016), 'The Caliphate Is Not a Tweet Away: The Social Media Experience of Al Qaeda in the Islamic Maghreb', *Studies in Conflict & Terrorism*, 39, 11, pp. 968–81.

Troyna, B. (1987), 'Beyond Multiculturalism: Towards the Enactment of Anti-Racist Education in Policy, Provision and Pedagogy', *Oxford Review of Education*, 13, 3, pp. 307–20.

Tyrer, D. and Sayyid, S. (2012), 'Governing Ghosts: Race, Incorporeality and Difference in Post-Political Times', *Current Sociology*, 60, 3, pp. 353–67.

Uhlmann, M. (2008), 'European Converts to Terrorism', *Middle East Quarterly*, 15, 3, pp. 31–7.

Uslaner, E. M and Brown, M. (2005), 'Inequality, Trust, and Civic Engagement', *American Politics Research*, 33, 6, pp. 868–94.

Van Dijk, T. A. (1991), *Racism and the Press*, London and New York: Routledge.

———. (1992), 'Discourse and the Denial of Racism', *Discourse & Society*, 3, 1, pp. 87–118.

———. (1993), *Elite Discourse and Racism*, London: Sage.

Vergeer, M., Hermans, L. and Sams, S. (2013), 'Online Social Networks and Micro-Blogging in Political Campaigning: The Exploration of a New Campaign Tool and a New Campaign Style', *Party Politics*, 19, 3, pp. 477–501.

Vertovec, S. (2001), 'Transnational Challenges to the "New" Multiculturalism', Paper presented to the Association of Social Anthropologists annual conference, 30 March–2 April, University of Sussex, UK.

Vertovec, S. and Peach, C. (1997) (eds), *Islam in Europe: The Politics of Religion and Community*, Basingstoke: Macmillan.

Vieten, U. M. and Poynting, S. (2016), 'Contemporary Far Right Racist Populism in Europe', *Journal of Intercultural Studies*, 37, 6, pp. 533–40.

Virdee, S. and McGeever, B. (2017), 'Racism, Crisis, Brexit', *Ethnic and Racial Studies*, 41, 10, pp. 1802–19.

Visram, R. (1986), *Ayahs, Lascars and Princes: Indians in Britain 1700–1947*, London: Pluto.

Voas, D. and Fleischmann, F (2012), 'Islam Moves West: Religious Change in the First and Second Generations', *Annual Review of Sociology*, 38, 1, pp. 525–45.

Wallerstein, I. (1983), *Historical Capitalism*, New York: Monthly Review Press.

———. (1989), *The Modern World-System III*, New York: Academic Press.

Warner, C. M. and Wenner, M. W. (2006), 'Religion and the Political Organization of Muslims in Europe', *Perspectives on Politics*, 1, 3, pp. 457–79.

Warsi, S. (2017), *The Enemy Within: A Tale of Muslim Britain*, London and New York: Allen Lane.

Weaver, S. (2010), 'Liquid Racism and the Danish Prophet Muhammad Cartoons', *Current Sociology*, 58, 5, pp. 675–92.

Weimann, G. (2015), *Terrorism in Cyberspace: The Next Generation*, New York: Columbia University Press.

Weller, P. (2006), 'Addressing Religious Discrimination and Islamophobia: Muslims and Liberal Democracies; The Case of the United Kingdom', *Journal of Islamic Studies*, 17, 3, pp. 295–25.

———. (2009), *A Mirror for Our Times: 'The Rushdie Affair' and the Future of Multiculturalism*, London: Continuum.

Werbner, P. (2007), 'Intimate Disciples in the Modern World: The Creation of Translocal Amity among South Asian Sufis in Britain', in Van Bruinessen, M. and Howell, J. (eds), *Sufism and the 'Modern' in Islam*, London: IB Tauris, pp. 195–216.

Westerlund, D. and Rosander, E. E. (1997) (eds), *African Islam and Islam in Africa: Encounters between Sufis and Islamists*, London: Hurst.

Wiktorowicz, Q. (2004), *Islamic Activism: A Social Movement Theory Approach*, Bloomington: Indiana University Press.

Wiley, T. G. and Wright, W. E. (2004), 'Against the Undertow: Language-Minority Education Policy and Politics in the "Age of Accountability"', *Educational Policy*, 18, 1, pp. 142–68.

Williamson, M. and Khiabany, G. (2011), 'State, Culture and Anti-Muslim Racism', *Global Media and Communication*, 7, 3, pp. 175–9.

Wilson, C. A. (1996), *Racism: From Slavery to Advanced Capitalism*, London: Sage.

World Policy Institute (2011), 'Anatomy of Islamophobia', *World Policy Journal*, 28, 4, pp. 14–15.

Wray, H. (2006), 'The Aliens Act 1905 and the Immigration Dilemma', *Journal of Law and Society*, 3, 2, pp. 302–23.

Wyler, D. (2017), 'The Swiss Minaret Ban Referendum and Switzerland's International Reputation: A Vote with an Impact', *Journal of Muslim Minority Affairs*, 37, 4, pp. 413–25.

Young, R. (2011), *Colonial Desire: Hybridity in Theory, Culture and Race*, Abingdon: Routledge.

Younge, G. (2011), *Who Are We? And Should It Matter in the 21st Century?*, London: Penguin.

Zebiri, K. (2008), 'The Redeployment of Orientalist Themes in Contemporary Islamophobia', *Studies in Contemporary Islam*, 10, pp. 4–44.

Zelin, A. Y. (2015), 'Picture or It Didn't Happen: A Snapshot of the Islamic State's Official Media Output', *Perspectives on Terrorism*, 9, 4, pp. 85–97.

Zempi, I. and Awan, I. (2019) (eds), *The Routledge International Handbook of Islamophobia*, Abingdon: Routledge.

INDEX

Abdullah, Sheikh, xvii
Afghanistan, xxi–xxiii, xxvii, 74, 80, 90, 150
   Soviet invasion of, 33, 73
African Caribbeans, xix
Age of Discovery, 4
Age of Enlightenment, 11
Age of Reason, 4
Ahmed, Lord Nazir, xxv
Algeria, xxi, 45
Ali, Abbas, xix, xviii
alienation, 11, 74, 77, 82, 92, 100, 105, 107, 124, 126, 169, 172
   cultural, 62
   political, 57
Ali, Zaman, xvi, xviii
Al-Muhajiroun, 101
Al-Qaeda, xix, xxii, 109–111
alt-right, 115–116
American Muslims, 32
Ankar-Bachlakra, xv
anti-discrimination, 7
anti-Islamism, 80
anti-multiculturalism, 124, 147
anti-Muslimism, 130
anti-Muslim sentiment, 98, 123
Anti-Paki League, 15
anti-racism laws, 7
anti-Semitism, 3, 19, 45, 63, 99, 113, 123

Arab Oil Crisis of 1973-4, 33
Arab Spring, xxiii, 33, 76, 109, 150, 157, 168
Aristotle, 2
Asian tiger economies, 156
al-Assad, Bashar, 76
Atlantic slave trade, xv, 18
Australia, 32, 33
authoritarian nationalism, 116
automation, 58
Azad Kashmir, xix, xv, xviii, xx

Bachlakrans, xvi–xviii, xx
al-Baghdadi, Abu Bakr, 117
Balkans, 32
Bangladesh, 80, 150
Barefoot in the Park (film), 159
Barelwi order, 38
Battle of Singapore (1942), xv, xvii
Bernard Shaw, George, 6
Bhatti Rajput Bachlakrans, xx
bigotry, xxiv, xxv, 11, 17, 68, 117, 127, 128, 130, 139, 145, 147, 160
bin Laden, Osama, xix, xxii
biopolitics, 116
biraderi, 41
Birmingham City Council, leadership in charge of schools at, 128–129

237

INDEX

black crime, 50
Blair, Tony, xxi, xxii
Blunkett, David, xxiv
BNP. *See* British National Party (BNP)
Bosnia, xxi, 74
Bosnia-Herzegovina, 90
Bosnian War, 45
Brazil, 156
Breivik, Anders Behring, 25, 97–99
Brewlvis, xxvi
Britain. *See* UK
Britain First, 15, 23, 41, 63, 101
British Council, 53
British Merchant Navy, xix, xvi, xvii
British Muslims, xxiii–xxvi, xxviii, 8, 47, 58, 59, 62, 88, 89, 93, 94, 101, 118, 130, 134, 137, 138
British National Party (BNP), 15, 63–64, 98
Britishness, 21, 26, 30
British Union of Fascists, 15
Buddhism, 13
Bush, George W., xxi
Byzantine Empire, 49

Caffe Reggio, 159
Caliphate of Córdoba, 2
Cambridge Analytica, 25
Cameron, David, 94, 144, 154
Canada, 154
Cantle Report, 93
capitalism, 18, 119, 150
    crisis of, 64
    hyper-capitalism, 122
    industrial, 21
    late, 41
    Western, 163
Central Europe, 31
Channel 4, 55, 145
China, 156

Christianity, 2, 4, 11, 13
Churchill, Winston, 6
Citizen Khan, 54
clash of civilisations, 34
class conflict, 6
Cohen, Leonard, 159
Cold War, xxi, 29, 45, 76, 104, 119, 140
Commonwealth Immigrants Act of 1968, 154
community cohesion, 143
Confucianism, 13
Conquistadors, 3–4
Conservative Party, 68, 127
convert radicalisation, 102
Copeland, David, 25
corruption, 42, 48, 150
counter-extremism, 59, 60, 78, 80
countering violent extremism (CVE) policy, 105
counter-narrative strategies, 109
counterterrorism, 20, 59, 60, 138, 140, 167, 171
Counter-Terrorism and Security Act of 2015, 129, 136
Cox, Helen Joanne, 20, 23–27, 103
cronyism, 42
cultural adaptation, 146
cultural alienation, 62
cultural capital, 143
cultural discrimination, 65
cultural disenfranchisement, 123
cultural ethnocentricism, 120
cultural ethnocentrism, 120
cultural exclusion, 57, 79, 94
cultural identity politics, 93
cultural imperialism, 90
cultural Islamism, 80
culturally responsive pedagogy, 138
cultural marginalisation, 173
cultural pluralism, 90, 91

INDEX

cultural racism, 1, 7, 8, 11, 93
cultural relativism, 169
cumulative extremism, 68, 98, 147
CVE. *See* countering violent extremism (CVE) policy

Dabiq (magazine), 110, 111
Darwin, Charles, 6
deindustrialisation, xxiii, 15, 21, 33, 58, 65, 69, 100, 123, 126, 127, 154
democracy, 110, 121, 143, 157
Democratic Union Party, 76
Denmark, 32
Deobandi order, 38
Deobandis, xxvi, xxvii
Dickens, Charles, 6
digital tribalism, 112, 116, 118
discrimination, xxiii, xxiv, xxv, 2, 3, 7–9, 29, 35, 37, 66, 69, 73, 82, 93, 100, 117, 120, 122, 129, 130, 139, 141, 143, 148, 149, 161, 173
    anti-discrimination, 7
    cultural, 65
    religious, 65, 100, 147
    structural, 63
disenfranchisement, 17, 75, 124, 169
    cultural, 123
    economic, 123
    political, 62, 69, 102, 123
Ditta, Allah, xv–xvi
Duncan, Admiral, 25
Dylan, Bob, 159

Eastern Europe, 31, 159
    collapse of communism in, 48
economic disenfranchisement, 123
economic exclusion, 79
economic marginalisation, 57, 62, 65, 90

economic racism, 1
EDL. *See* English Defence League (EDL)
Edward I, 19
Egypt, 80, 168
11 September 2001 (9/11), xx–xxii, xxvii, 10, 29, 37, 40, 43, 46, 53, 59, 61, 63, 65, 68, 88, 95, 102, 103, 137, 141, 142, 147, 168
elitism, 150
Elizabeth I, 4
Empire State Building, 159
English Defence League (EDL), 15, 63–64, 98, 101
English nationalism, 127, 147
Englishness, 21, 26, 30, 49
English riots of 2011, 126
Enlightenment, 4
equality, 22, 36, 95, 122
Erdoğan, Recep Tayyip, 76, 114
Erie Canal, 159
eschatology, 110
ethnic capital, 143
ethnic conflict, 6
ethnic exclusion, 33
ethnicity, 2, 7, 9, 21, 37, 61, 63, 73, 87, 93, 120, 138, 140, 146, 154, 155, 161
    See also race/racism
ethnic nationalism, 12, 17, 21, 30, 75, 104, 108, 113, 128, 130, 154
ethnocentric norms, 120
ethno-nationalism, 39
ethnonational multiculturalism, 85
EU. *See* European Union (EU)
European Christianity, 121
European Union (EU), 121, 127, 146
    UK exit from, xxvii, 17, 30
Eurozone, 59–60

239

INDEX

exclusion, xxiv, 19, 66, 72–74, 78, 131
   cultural, 57, 79, 94
   economic, 79
   ethnic, 33
   political, 79
   social, 11
   structural, 130
extremism, 10, 25, 38, 42, 54, 57, 66, 77, 82, 85, 94, 129, 136, 145, 150, 151, 170–172
   counter-extremism, 59, 60, 78, 80
   cumulative, 68, 98, 147
   far-right, 20, 24, 27, 67, 97–106
   Islamic, 20, 62, 69, 97–106
   Muslim, 54
   radical right, 20
   violent, 20, 22, 24, 26, 59, 67, 69, 73, 78–80, 97–100, 105, 106, 112, 125, 126, 134, 146, 167, 169

Farage, Nigel, 24
far-right extremism, 20, 24, 27, 67, 97–106
far-right nationalism, 13, 113
fascism, 19, 98
femininity, 35, 102
feminism, 37
Ferdinand II of Aragon, 19
first-generation immigrants, 34–35
France, 9, 32, 33, 91, 92
   immigrant workers, 19
   Islamophobia in, 46
   National Front, 63
freedom, 121, 157
freedom of expression, 51–52
free labour, 17–18
frustration, 124
Fukuyama, Francis, 45

fundamentalism, 42

Galton, Francis, 6
gender equality, 174
Generation M, xxvi
Germany, 9, 32, 33, 97
   Berlin Wall, fall of, 10, 47, 61, 119
   immigrant workers, 18
   Islamophobia in, 46
   Pax Europa Citizen's Movement, 63
   second-generation Muslims, 35
global financial crisis of 2008, 126, 155
globalisation, 9, 12, 26, 33, 42, 54, 87, 95, 98, 100, 102, 105, 121, 123, 128, 137, 138, 150, 154
   cultural, 116
   neoliberal, 27, 69, 70, 83, 117, 173
Global North, 15, 37, 39, 69, 130
Gogh, Theo van, assassination of, xxiv, 52
Gove, Michael, 129, 133
Great Depression, xxvii, 159
Greece, 32
Grenfell Tower incident (2017), 66

Hari Singh, xvii
Henry Jackson Society, 91
hijab, 37, 43, 90
hijra, 110, 125
Honeyford, Roy, 58
Honeyford Affair, 58
Hume, John, 4
Hungary, 32
Hunger Games (film), 111
Huntington, Samuel, 45
Hussain, Saddam, xxii, xxiii
hyper-capitalism, 122

INDEX

hyper-localisation, 173
hyper-masculinity, 102, 104, 174
hyper-sexuality, 102

Iberian Peninsula, 19, 30
identity politics, 89
illiberalism, 11, 54
imagined communities, 12
IMF, 126, 156
imperialism, 66
India, xvii, xviii, 4, 27, 150, 156
Indian Mutiny, 38
individualism, 3, 39
Indonesia, 156
industrial capitalism, 21
inequality, 12, 22, 75, 77, 140, 156
    social, 90
    socioeconomic, 140
    structural, 90
Innocence of Muslims, The (film), 54, 55
Inside Llewyn Davis (film), 159
Inspire (magazine), 109, 110
institutionalised racism, 1, 8, 11, 89
inter-culturalism, 85, 139
International Sociological Association, xxv
intimidation, 66
intolerance, xxii, xxv, 3, 11, 17, 54, 55, 68, 89, 113, 117, 127, 128, 130, 139, 147, 154, 160
Iran, 77
Iranian Revolution of 1979, 33, 47
Iraq, xxii–xxiv, xxvii, 74, 80, 125
Ireland, 159
Isabella I of Castile, 19
ISIS, xxii, 20, 33, 46, 59, 71, 73, 74, 76–79, 101, 103, 108–111, 116, 124, 125, 129, 135, 144, 168
Islam, 124
    political, 77
    irrational fear of, 45
    negative representations of, 49
    and self-empowerment, 88–89
Islam4UK, 101
Islamic extremism, 20, 62, 69, 97–106
Islamic political militancy, 50
Islamic revivalisms, 86–88
Islamification, 63
Islamism
    anti-Islamism, 80
    cultural, 80
    radical, 80–81
    redux, 71–83
    violent, 81
Islamophobia, as new racism, 57–70
    See also individual entries
Italy
    Northern League, 63

Jamaat-e-Islamis, xxvi, xxvii, 72
Jammu, xvii, xviii
Jenkins, Roy, 154
Jerusalem, 162
Jews, 2–3, 18–20, 30
jihadi movement, 80
jihadis, 65, 102
Jinnah, Mohammed Ali, xvii
Judaism, 19
Jyllands-Posten (magazine), 50–51, 52

Kant, Immanuel, 4
Kashmir, xvi–xviii
Kashmiris, xvi
Khaldun, Ibn, 163–164
Khan, Sadiq, 171–172
Khomeini, Ayatollah, 49
Kipling, Rudyard, 6
Knox, Robert, 6

INDEX

Ku Klux Klan, 115
Kurdistan Workers' Party, 76

Labour Party, 122, 154
Lewis, Bernard, 45
liberalism, 3, 146
Libya, 168
'lone actor' terrorism, 112

Macpherson Report (1999), 1, 89
Madrid train bombings (2004), xxiv
Mair, Thomas, 23–25
Malaysia, 156
Mangla Dam, xix
marginalisation, 17, 32, 82, 123, 124, 129, 137, 147, 149, 150, 169
   cultural, 173
   economic, 57, 62, 65, 90
Marx, Karl, 163
masculinity, 101, 102, 117
Maududi, Maulana, 80
May, Theresa, 167
MCB. *See* Muslim Council of Britain (MCB)
media communication, and Islamophobia, 50–51
MENA. *See* Middle East and North Africa (MENA)
mercantilism, 30
metropolitan elites, 113
Middle East and North Africa (MENA), 71, 76, 110, 114, 121, 157, 168
migration theory, 35
militarism, 150
monoculturalism, 90
multiculturalism, 10, 36, 37, 63, 66, 88, 90, 92, 95, 115, 137–139
   anti-multiculturalism, 124
   egalitarian, 39

ethnonational, 85
failures of, 57
imagined, 39
securitisation of, 22
multicultural radicalisms, 85–96
multicultural societies, 151
muscular liberalism, 124, 154
Muslim Brotherhood, 72
Muslim Council of Britain (MCB), xxvi, 142
Muslimness, 30, 79, 85, 124, 149
Muslims
   British, xxiii–xxvi, xxviii, 8, 47, 58, 59, 62, 88, 89, 93, 94, 101, 118, 130, 134, 137, 138
   framing, 45–55
   as fundamentalists, 88
   origins and destinations, 29–43
   as suspect communities, 81, 137, 138
   as terrorists, 88

National Front, 63
national identity, 10, 12, 13, 17, 26, 30, 66, 69, 70, 91, 93, 102, 124, 128, 137
nationalism, 6, 9, 13, 15, 25, 31, 98
   authoritarian, 116
   English, 127, 147
   ethnic, 12, 17, 21, 30, 75, 104, 108, 113, 128, 130, 154
   ethno-nationalism, 39
   far-right, 13, 113
   transnationalism, 29, 87
nationhood, 9, 30, 37, 85
NATO, xxvii, 156
Nazism, 98
Nehru, Jawaharlal, xvii
neoclassical economic theory of the free market, 140

INDEX

neoliberal globalisation, 27, 69, 70, 83, 117, 173
neoliberalism, 20, 22, 33, 42, 77, 99, 103, 104, 114–115, 116, 126, 135, 137, 150
Netherlands, the
   Islamophobia in, 46
   Party for Freedom, 63
   second-generation Muslims, 35
New Labour, xxiii, 135, 142, 154
Niccolò di Bernardo dei Machiavelli, 26
Nigeria, xxi
niqab (face veil), 43, 85, 91
North America, 6, 34, 35, 113
Northern League, 63

Obama, Barack, 157, 168
Occidentalis, 82
Occidentophobia, 57
occupational segregation, 161
Office for Standards in Education (Ofsted), 129, 135, 136
Ofsted. *See* Office for Standards in Education (Ofsted)
Operation Enduring Freedom, xxii
oppression, 16, 33, 142, 149, 150
Oriental culture, 48
Orientalism, 9, 29, 31, 48, 64, 66, 67, 73, 82, 120, 137, 140, 168
Orientalism (Said), 48
Osborne, Darren, 66
Ottoman Empire, 32, 77

Pakistan, xix, xvii, xviii, xxi, 80, 150
Palestine, 74
Palestine–Israel conflict, 42
Palestinian Arabs, 162
Party for Freedom, 63
Pax Europa Citizen's Movement, 63

Phillips, Trevor, 145–147
pillarisation, 154
P&O, xvii
Policy Exchange, 91
political alienation, 57
political disenfranchisement, 62, 69, 102, 123
political exclusion, 79
populism, 25–27, 60, 62, 68, 83, 98, 113, 115
Portugal, 19
post-colonialism, 42
prejudice, xvi, xxiii, 2, 3, 7–9, 11, 55, 130, 139, 141, 147
Prevent policy, 59–61, 105, 136, 138, 170, 191
Prince, The (Machiavelli), 26
progressive liberalism, 169
progressive tax system, 165

Quilliam, 91
Qutb, Sayyid, 80

race/racism
   and imagined community, 1–14
   of radical right, 15–27
   See also ethnicity
Race Relations (Amendment) Act (2000), 89–90
race riots of 2001, 90, 144
racial prejudice, xvi
racism, xix
   cultural, 1, 7, 8, 11, 93
   economic, 1
   institutionalised, 1, 8, 11, 89
   scientific, 6, 9, 16, 17, 31, 67
   situational, 1
   structural, 7, 57, 63, 67, 93
   symbolic, 1
radical black feminism, 139
radical Islamism, 80–81

INDEX

radicalism, 10
radical right extremism, 20
radical right, racism of, 15–27
Rasool, Ghulam, xvi
reactive co-radicalisation, 98
Reaganomics, 15, 155, 160
regionalism, 9
religiosity, 29, 77
religious discrimination, 65, 100, 147
religious diversity, 146
Research Information Communications Unit of the Home Office, 171
residential segregation, 161
RESPECT, 41, 42
reverse engineering, 109
Robinson, Tommy, 64
Rumi, Jalaluddin, 177–178
Runnymede Trust, 45
Rushdie, Salman, 10–11, 49
Rushdie Affair, 10–11, 49, 61, 87, 92
Russia, 76
    military intervention in Chechnya, xxi

sacralisation, 138
Saddam, xxii
Said, Edward, 13, 48
Salafis, 38
Salafism, 38, 79–80
Saleem, Mohammed, 98
Satanic Verses, The (Rushdie), 49, 51–53
Saw (film), 111
Scandinavia, 6
Scarman Report, 93
school effect, 134
scientific racism, 6, 9, 16, 17, 31, 67

Scotland, 4
second-generation immigrants, 35–36
Second World War, xv, xvii, xviii, xxvii, 12, 18, 19, 21, 31, 32, 79, 99, 119, 153
sectarianism, 75
secularisation, 138
secularism, 143
securitisation, 22, 124, 129, 140
self-censorship, 51
self-ghettoising, 39–40
selfishness, 127
Selimiye Cami, 177
Serpico (film), 159
7/7 event, xxvi, xxvii, 53, 59, 63, 145
sharia councils, 39
Shia Islam, 71
situational racism, 1
skin colour, 5–6
slave trade, 5, 18
social capital, 143
social conflict, 148
social Darwinism, 6
social exclusion, 11
social inequality, 90
social justice, 22
social media, 108–109, 111
socioeconomic inequality, 140
Somalia, xxi
Sonboly, Ali David, 97
South Asia, 150
South Asian Muslims, 10
South Asian Sufi Islam, 38
Southern Europe, 159
Soviet Union
    collapse of communism in, 48
Spain, 4, 19
    Islamophobia in, 46
Spencer, Herbert, 6

INDEX

SS *Empire Fowey,* xvii
stereotypes/stereotyping, 8, 9, 47
structural exclusion, 130
structural inequality, 90
structural racism, 7, 57, 63, 67, 93
subjugation, xxviii, 3, 8, 11, 17, 21, 32, 76, 89, 92, 101, 124, 139, 142, 149
Sudan, xxi, 45
Sufism, 38
Sunni Islam, 38
superiority, 11
Sweden
    second-generation Muslims, 35
Switzerland
    banning of minarets in, 155
symbolic racism, 1
Syria, xxii, xxiii, xxvii, 40, 43, 52, 73–76, 74, 79, 124, 125, 168
Syrian refugee crisis, 23, 59

Tabligis, xxvi
takfirism, 81
takfirist perspective, 80
Taliban, xxii
tawhid (oneness), 177
Taymiyyah, Ibn, 80
technological innovation, 4, 15, 123
Tel Aviv Mike's Place bombing (2003), xxv
terrorism, 10, 13, 22–23, 79, 150
    counterterrorism, 20, 59, 60, 138, 140
    lone actor, 112
Thatcher, Margaret, 155
Thatcherism, 15, 58, 160
transatlantic slave trade, 119
transnationalism, 29, 87
tribal identities, 3
tribalisitic radicalisation, 103
tribalism, 15, 16, 54, 103, 150
    digital, 112, 116, 118
'Trojan Horse' affair of 2014, 119, 129, 130, 135
Trump, Donald, 25, 26, 112, 114–116
Turkey, 3, 27, 77, 150
    displacement of Syrians into, 75–76
Turkish Muslims, 36
Twitter, 108–109, 111

UK, xv, xviii, xxii–xxv, 9, 33, 47, 81, 86, 105
    2003 Iraq invasion, xxiii
    Brexit vote, 23–25, 60, 100, 121, 127–128, 155, 168
    Britain First, 15, 23, 41, 63, 101
    Commission for Countering Extremism, 170
    Commonwealth, 153
    counterterrorism, 20
    English Defence League, 15, 63, 98, 101
    ethnic and religious minorities, 88
    EU referendum (2016) in, 126
    foreign policy, 94
    immigrant workers, 19
    inner-city race riots, xxiii
    Islamophobia in, 46
    leave from European Union, xxvii, 17, 30
    Madrid train bombings (2004), xxiv
    National Action, 15
    policy of austerity in public spending, 126
    post-war approach to multiculturalism, 153, 154
    Prevent policy, 59–61, 105, 136, 138, 170, 191

INDEX

race relations, 89
racism in, 57
regional divisions in, 78
second-generation Muslims, 35
7/7 event, xxvi, xxvii, 53, 59, 63, 145
slave trade, 18
Thatcherism, 15, 58, 160
Unity Coalition, 41
UKIP, 64
ummah, 13, 88
UN, 156
underdevelopment, 42, 150
UNESCO, 7
United States (US), 31, 33, 36–37, 41, 65, 76, 115, 116, 149, 150, 156–157, 165
   foreign policy, 157
   Islamophobia in, 46
   migration of Muslim groups, 72
   military-industrial complex, xxvii
   Navy Seals, xxii
   Reaganomics, 15, 155, 160
   slave trade, 18
US. *See* United States (US)
us–them distinction, 8, 11, 39, 53, 69, 141

vilification, xxiv, 100, 120
violence, 22, 66, 78, 104, 165
violent extremism, 20, 22, 24, 26, 59, 67, 69, 73, 78–80, 97–100, 105, 106, 112, 125, 126, 134, 146, 167, 169
violent Islamism, 81
voucher system, xix

al-Wahhab, Abd, 80

Wahhabis, xxvi
Wahhabism, 72
war on terror, xxii, xxvii, 33, 37, 41, 53, 59, 68, 69, 77, 79, 86, 90, 137, 142, 147, 169
Washington, George, 158, 159
weapons of mass destruction (WMDs), xxii
Webb, Beatrice, 6
Webb, Sidney, 6
Wells, H. G., 6
Western capitalism, 163
Western Europe, 6, 7, 10, 27, 33–35, 37, 39, 113, 119, 120, 123, 150, 156, 165, 170
   acts of terrorism in, 62
   anti-Muslimism, 131
   Islamophobia in, 46
   migration of Muslim groups, 72
   Muslim population of, 173
   Muslims in, 86
What British Muslims Really Think, 145
WMDs. *See* weapons of mass destruction (WMDs)
Workshop to Raise Awareness of Prevent (WRAP), 136
World Bank, 156
WRAP. *See* Workshop to Raise Awareness of Prevent (WRAP)

xenophobia, 9, 29, 31, 48, 66, 73, 115, 120, 127

Yemen, 59, 74

Zionism, 161